ILLUSTRATED BY

LU YANGUANG

100 *Chinese* *Scholars*

WRITTEN BY

WU BOHENG

TRANSLATED BY

WANG XUEWEN

&

SUI YUN

ASIAPAC BOOKS • SINGAPORE

Publisher
ASIAPAC BOOKS PTE LTD
996 Bendemeer Road #06-08/09
Kallang Basin Industrial Estate
Singapore 339944
Tel   : 392 8455
Fax   : 392 6455
Email : apacbks@singnet.com.sg

Visit us at our Internet homepage
http://www.asiapacbooks.com

First published December 1998

Designed by Marked Point Design
Body text set in 10 point Times
Printed in Singapore by Chung Printing

PUBLISHER'S NOTE

*A*s a publisher dedicated to the promotion of works of Chinese philosophy, art and literature, we are pleased to present *100 Chinese Scholars*, the fifth title in our 100 Series Art Album.

This volume provides a quick insight into the life stories of 100 celebrated figures in Chinese history. They include patriotic heroes, influential statesmen, outstanding historians, philosophers, writers, poets, and scientists. One thing is common among these scholars — their integrity, selflessness and achievements have significantly contributed to the rich tradition of the Chinese civilization.

Through study and meditation, the artist Lu Yanguang has drawn 100 portraits of Chinese celebrated scholars. His pictures are beautiful and his combinations of points, lines and planes constitute a sense of musical rhythm — black and white make a sharp contrast; Yin and Yang, gentleness and strength accommodate each other.

We feel honoured to have Lu Yanguang's permission to the translation rights for his art album. Our gratitude, too, to Wang Xuewen and Sui Yun for translating this book; to Koh Kok Kiang and Seah Bee Bee for their editorial input; and to Pan Shou for his foreword in calligraphy. Last but not least, we would like to thank the production team for putting in their best effort in the publication of this series.

靈心先生線描繡像中國一子當那文化悠久民族不佳有

此藝富藏林治中西技法於一爐通古含聲氣於百世機神里

之縹緲接靈物花鴻溪尾妝陸離細針密縷一幅當如一支如百圖看

曲風移雜日而抱律多異臺態勢形爭奇競爽辭含人摯音低

潤根縈州韻 林利園女士以方州此藝術奇龍不空盡地方牢目眼

於華文書譽將田共來陸室之空太圖書名限弓同出版英譯未管

華文去家以加之讀者藉廣添待衛素一言圖案不覆愛當濡筆

題之如末 一九九〇年歲次甲戌之春 君之潘子

FOREWORD

*T*he line-drawn portraits in the 100 Series Art Album by Mr Lu Yanguang can only be based on the rich cultural heritage of a race with a long history. The portrayal of these figures has been executed with a subtle combination of oriental and western artistic techniques. These beautiful illustrations have been captured in exquisitely refined details. Each picture is like a tune. One hundred pictures, one hundred tunes. They share the same style but each has a rhythm of its own. One just cannot help being overwhelmed by admiration for the artist's creativity in presenting such a wide repertoire of forms and postures.

Madam Lim Li Kok feels that such a masterpiece of artistic work should not be confined to the Chinese Language reading public. She has arranged for an English version of the book to be published by her company, Asiapac Books, so that a larger circle of non-Chinese Language readers may also enjoy it.

I have been asked to write a message for this book. Instead, I have chosen to write a few words with my brush.

Calligraphy by Pan Shou
(Poet and Scholar)
Spring, 1994

ABOUT THE ILLUSTRATOR

*L*u Yanguang was born in Kaiping, Guangdong Province, in 1948. He is presently director of Guangzhou Art Gallery, vice-chairman of Guangzhou Artists' Association and chief editor of *Guangzhou Art Studies*.

His published works since 1985 include *Lu Yanguang's Album of Illustrations, Album of Lingnan Scenery and Legends, 100 Celebrated Chinese Women, 100 Chinese Emperors, 100 Chinese Gods, 100 Chinese Scholars* and *100 Buddhas in Chinese Buddhism*.

A renowned artist, Lu Yanguang started his career drawing illustrations and cartoons. Instead of the traditional Chinese style of brush painting, each character in this collection is a combination of the old — the dynastic eras of ancient China, and the new — Lu Yanguang's refreshingly artistic technique of *xiuxiang hua* (portraits in decorative style). His illustrations are characterized by a strong sense of speed and rhythm.

ABOUT THE TRANSLATORS

*W*ang Xuewen was born in Hebei Province, China, in 1944. He was Professor of English and Dean of the School of International Studies of the University of International Business & Economics, Beijing. Currently, he is the Deputy Editor-in-Chief of the *International Business Daily*, Beijing.

He has translated many books and short stories, including *Yellow Emperor's Medicine Classic, All Creatures Great and Small, James and the Giant Peach* and *Moby Dick*. In this series, he translated the *100 Chinese Gods* that won silver prize at the First Asian Pacific Publishers Association Awards in 1995, *100 Chinese Emperors* and *100 Chinese Scholars*.

Also an author, he has written several textbooks such as *Business Oral Translation, Practical Written Communication,* and *International Trade English*. As an experienced tutor, he has been a mentor to many MA postgraduates majoring in translation theory and practice.

*S*ui Yun, born in Shenyang in 1960, earned her MA in China before completing her further studies in Singapore and the United States. An associate professor of the University of International Business and Economics, she is co-compiler of two business English textbooks and translator of several articles and stories. She is also a proficient simultaneous interpreter and has done interpretation at many international conferences.

PREFACE

This book, *100 Chinese Scholars,* is the fifth volume of Lu Yanguang's 100 Series Art Album. Each volume comprises 100 portraits; and five volumes, 500 portraits. Each portrait is exquisite, life-like and unique. Only young Lu Yanguang in the prime of his youth is able to make that possible.

Taking pride in calling himself "a wild animal", Lu Yanguang is single-minded. He used to live by the temples as a child, in the atmosphere of gods and Buddha, forming in his mind a supernatural mystery complex. There were a great many predecessors with such a complex, and there will be countless to come. But Lu Yanguang may be the only artist with such a complex in the mid-20th century, if this period could be regarded as a gap for gods and Buddha. The outcome of such a supernatural mystery complex is an extraordinary splendour. With unflagging energy and tenacious will power, Lu Yanguang has been constantly expanding the splendour, showing the vitality of his youth.

Youth is as precious as gold. When Lu began drawing the 100 Series Art Album in 1982, he was only 34: with steady hands, sharp eyes, good ears, and an energetic mind. Lu Yanguang has been successful, as he has grasped his youth and made the best use of it.

"If Heaven has feelings, it too will become aged", let alone man. It took him 10 long years — a passage from youth to middle age — to draw the five volumes. Actually he underwent changes, both physiological and psychologicals in the 10 years, which have brought about the changes in the drawings of the five volumes.

The change in *100 Chinese Scholars* is particularly spectacular, with what was hard and straight becoming soft and cursive; rigid becoming loose; narrative becoming interesting and tasty; true and clear becoming indescribable. The tangled masses and clusters of lines that look neither like rock, nor hemp, nor bark, nor creases of clothes, are there in the drawings with a head put on the top. The horizontal and vertical lines, the circles and dots can hardly be called peach or plum, willow or scholar-tree, rose or chrysanthemum.

In other words, the lines whether dense or loose, appropriate or seemingly not, are all drawn with charm and taste. The reluctance of the artist to follow the written explanation is already quite obvious, since he has got tired of the passive way of making his drawings subject to the explanation.

Is it a retrogression or progress? Does it mean maturity or the lack of it? Neither. But it is a transition from being young, elegant, energetic and ambitious, to graying temples, overtaxed energy, and other signs showing the effect of the years. When one is beyond 40, physical fatigue and mental weariness will make him realise the "pains of sticking to a particular artistic approach" and wish for a change and to find "a direct way to the realm of the Buddha".

Then, where is the "realm of the Buddha"? It is in the heart, in the most harmonious part of the heart. Produce stimulating drawings when you are full of vigour and vitality; quiet drawings when you are in a placid state of mind; free and natural drawings when you are above worldly considerations; worldly drawings when you are motivated by material matters; and anguished drawings when you are disheartened. Sing different songs on different hills; and draw different works in different frames of mind.

One important principle of Confucianism is harmony: harmony between people, and harmony between people and matter. Draw in the way that best suits your mind. Harmony promotes the formation of art itself, allowing people to draw in the way they like. And harmony is to create the optimum environment for art. As the saying goes, "Gentlemen are harmonious but varied". It is harmony that has enabled Lu Yanguang to mount the first summit of his career. Now that he is turning to the second summit, I keep my fingers crossed that harmony will again help him.

Tang Jixiang
Guangdong Art Academy

CONTENTS

CONTENTS

CONTENTS

CONTENTS

Confucius

孔子

One day in the Spring and Autumn period, a group of children were playing under a tree in Quyi in the state of Lu. A boy was instructing other children to line peas on a stone and queue up to pray. They attracted many passers-by to stop and watch in surprise. That boy later became the world-famous sage Confucius (551–479 BC).

Confucius, with Kong Qiu as his name and Zhongni as his courtesy name, was from Quyi of the state of Lu (southeast of the present Qufu County, Shandong Province). His ancestors had been nobles of the state of Song who later took refuge in the state of Lu. Confucius' father Shu Lianghe (also called Zou Shuhe) was once an official in the government of Quyi, but he died soon after Confucius was born. Since then, the fortunes of his family waned.

Growing up in Lu, the state of rites, Confucius had since childhood developed a strong interest in the traditional culture of the Western Zhou Dynasty. He became famous among his peers as a young man who "knew the rites". At that time, he was only a clerk in charge of accounting and animal husbandry in the home of a high-ranking official named Ji. Low as his position was, Confucius did not lose heart, but studied diligently. He made a special trip to consult the Viscount of the State of Yan who knew the ancient systems very well. Later, Duke Zhao of Lu sent him and another official Nan Gongjing to learn rites from the historian of Zhou.

When Confucius was 35 years old, internal strife broke out in Lu as contradictions became intense between the Duke of Lu and the Three Huans (Mengsun, Shusun and Jisun, being the offspring of Duke Huan of Lu, and known as the Three Huans in history). As a result, Duke Zhao of Lu was driven to the state of Qi, and power fell into the hands of Ji Pingzi of the Jisun family.

Finding it impossible to live in Lu any longer, Confucius went to Qi and became a staff member of an official named Gao Zhaozi. Duke Jing of Qi, who had long known that Confucius was very learned, invited him to the palace to discuss politics. Amazed at his political insight, Duke Jing intended to appoint him to a senior position but failed due to objections from other officials. Later, Confucius found out that someone plotted to murder him. Hence he returned to Lu.

When Confucius was 42 years old, Duke Zhao of Lu died abroad and was succeeded by Duke Ding. Five years later, Ji Pingzi died, leaving power in the hands of Ji Huanzi. But Yang Hu, a staff member of Huanzi, usurped power and controlled Huanzi after staging a coup d'etat. As Confucius held the view that an official's staff member controlling the state was worse than an official overruling the king, he would rather teach than be a court official. Many people admired him for his profound learning and moral integrity and came to study under him. He was said to have over 3,000 students during his lifetime.

When Yang Hu fell from power, Confucius was nearly 50 years old. He was appointed Minister of Zhongdu. A year later, he was promoted to Minister of Works, and later Minister of Law. In 500 BC when the rulers of Qi and Lu held a meeting, Confucius was acting premier of Lu, and was entrusted with the ceremony of the meeting. He strictly followed the rules of propriety, which maintained the dignity of Lu and awed the ruler and officials of Qi. As a result, Qi returned to Lu the territory they had occupied.

In 498 BC, when the officials of the Ji family rioted in town, Confucius advocated the elimination of the three towns, demolishing the city walls and disarming the troops of the three Huans. But the internal conflicts in Lu were getting intense and Duke Ding could do nothing about it. When Confucius himself was also driven from power, he left Lu with his disciples and travelled to the other states with a view to realizing his political ideas.

Confucius left the state of Lu at the age of 55 and, for 14 years, went around the states of Wei, Song, Chen, Cai and Chu. He suffered hardship, fatigue, and misery from the fact that the heads of the states did not like his conservative ideas. He returned to Lu in 484 BC.

In his later years, Confucius devoted himself to collecting and editing the classics of the Zhou Dynasty. It was said that he collated the *Book of Songs,* compiled *Shangshu (the Book of History)* and the *Spring and Autumn Annals,* and wrote two chapters *Wenyan* and *Xici* of the *Book of Changes.* He died in 479 BC at the age of 73. The *Analects of Confucius* was a record of the speeches and anecdotes of Confucius compiled by his disciples.

Confucius

Zhong You

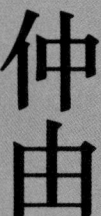

In the Spring and Autumn period, powerful states were fighting for hegemony while officials were fighting for power.

Once, an official in the state of Jin named Zhao Jianzi attacked another official, Fan Zhongxing. A private official of the Fan family, Fo Xi, then the magistrate of Zhongmo county, put up resistance against the Zhao army in Zhongmo and asked Confucius to go there and help him. Confucius was ready to accept the invitation when one of his favourite disciples Zhong You (542– 480 BC) tried to dissuade him from going, "You used to teach us not to get involved with people engaged in bad things. Now, why should you go to Zhongmo when Fo Xi is using it as his base for an uprising?" Hearing these words, Confucius gave up the idea of going. That showed the influence of Zhong You on his master.

Zhong You, with the courtesy name Zi Lu, was from Bian in the state of Lu, (east of the Sishui River of present Shandong) in the late Spring and Autumn period. Before becoming a disciple of Confucius, he had been a very rash but brave and upright young man. Moved by Confucius who treated him with respect, Zi Lu willingly became his disciple after promising to follow the master's instructions.

Zi Lu was very interested in politics and asked Confucius the way to good administration. The sage said, "First of all, you should be very diligent to set a good example for the common people before telling them to work hard." He asked again, "How to be a scholar?" Confucius answered, "Encourage one another and be kind to one another, and you will be a good scholar." Zi Lu then asked how to serve the sovereign, and the master said, "Never cheat him but be frank in remonstrating with him even though you have to offend him."

When travelling between states, Confucius and his students were treated very coldly in the state of Chen. Some of them were even ill from hunger due to lack of food. Zi Lu was very unhappy and asked: "Should gentlemen suffer from poverty and hardship?" Confucius answered: "Gentlemen can endure poverty and hardship, but petty people will commit all kinds of evils in straitened circumstances."

Bearing his master's teachings in mind, Zi Lu wore shabby clothes while waiting upon his teacher. Confucius praised him, "I am afraid only Zhong You can remain at ease wearing shabby clothes among those in fine fur."

After studying with Confucius for some time, Zi Lu was appointed an official of Pudi by the state of Wei, and later, a private official of the Ji family in the state of Lu. He did quite well at his posts.

Despite his official position, Zi Lu respected his teacher just as much. When Confucius was seriously ill, Zi Lu told the fellow disciples to prepare for his funeral in the capacity of his private officials. After Confucius recovered, he criticized Zi Lu for being dishonest as he was no longer an official and was not entitled to have private subordinate officials. And Zi Lu listened to his teacher obediently.

With students around him, Confucius felt very contented. But when he saw the unyielding expression of Zi Lu, he felt a bit worried and said: "I am afraid Zhong You will not come to a good end." Indeed, Zi Lu was killed in the internal conflicts when he was a private official of Kong Kui in the state of Wei. He died at the age of 39, one year earlier than Confucius.

Zhong You

Yan Hui

In the *Analects of Confucius* can be found many instances of Yan Hui (521–490 BC) being praised by his master, of which the most famous is: "Hui, a virtuous man, is contented with simple food and drink and a shabby place to live in. Others cannot put up with the poor conditions, while Yan Hui remains just as happy. What a virtuous man he is."

Indeed, Yan Hui was the favourite disciple of Confucius. Although it was easy for him to obtain an official post with his knowledge and ability, he was willing to pursue further studies with Confucius, unconcerned about poverty and hard work.

Yan Hui, with the courtesy name Zi Yuan, and also known as Yan Yuan, was born in the state of Lu in the late Spring and Autumn period. He was very diligent, learning from his teacher not only his knowledge but also his moral integrity.

Confucius thought highly of Yan Hui's constancy in learning. He said: "Yan Hui always keeps benevolence in mind while other students think of benevolence only from time to time."

Though regarded by Confucius as his best student, Yan Hui was not satisfied. What he wanted was mastery of all of his teacher's ability and knowledge. Once he sighed with feeling: "The more I learn from my teacher, the deeper I find is his knowledge and the more I admire him. His learning seems accessible, yet is so difficult to master. He has been patiently teaching me to read, write, and observe the rites, which make me more eager to learn. Though I have gone all out in learning, I still cannot master the profound knowledge of my teacher."

Confucius took very good care of Yan Hui and answered all the questions he asked. When asked how to run the country, Confucius said: "One should adopt the calendar of the Xia Dynasty, sit in a carriage of the Yin Dynasty, wear the hat of the Zhou Dynasty and play the Shao music (name of music of Emperor Shun) and dance music. The music of Zheng, which is obscene, should be forbidden. Vile characters, who are very dangerous, should be kept at bay."

When they travelled around the states to lobby the dukes, Confucius showed particular care to his favourite student. Once when Yan Hui lagged behind when the master and disciples were besieged by a group of people in Kuang, Confucius became very worried and said to Yan Hui when he caught up, "I did worry a lot about your safety." Yan Hui said, "How can I die when my teacher still needs my service?" Confucius sighed: "I am afraid even Yan Hui can't help me much since he never raises any objection to whatever I say."

As a result of prolonged poverty and hard work, Yan Hui died before his master at the age of 32. Confucius was deeply grieved at his death and said, "Heaven is taking away my life." Someone said, "Master, you should not be so sad." Confucius answered, "If I do not grieve over the loss of Yan Hui, whom shall I grieve over?" All the fellow disciples were very sad at the loss of such a good friend and held a very elaborate funeral for him. Yan Hui was also held in high regard by the later generations and was called "The Duplicate Sage".

顔回

Yan Hui

Duanmu Ci

Confucius liked the *Book of Songs* very much. Once he said to his disciples, "Why don't you study the *Book of Songs*? It can arouse your imagination, improve your observation and make you more sociable".

The most qualified disciple to discuss the *Book of Songs* with Confucius should be Duanmu Ci (520 BC–?). Once he asked his master, "Is it right to say that one should not be obsequious when he is poor, and arrogant when he is rich?" Confucius answered, "Yes, you may say so. But it is better to say that one should be optimistic when he is poor, and courteous when he is rich." Seeing the point of his teacher, Duanmu Ci said, "The line in the *Book of Songs* 'As knife and file make smooth the bone, So jade is wrought by chisel and stone' just means that, doesn't it?" Confucius was very pleased and said, "You may discuss the *Book of Songs* with me now because you can draw inferences."

Duanmu Ci, with the courtesy name Zi Gong, was born in the state of Wei in the late Spring and Autumn period. He became a disciple of Confucius to study his outlook on life, and was regarded highly by his master for his eloquence and administrative ability. Confucius once told an official of the state of Lu that Duanmu Ci had a thorough understanding of society and was qualified for an official post. He compared Duanmu to the precious sacrificial jade vessel in the ancestral temple, meaning that he was a person of high calibre.

Confucius took very great care of Zi Gong and answered every question of his. Once Zi Gong asked, "How can a person be called a worthy scholar?" Confucius answered, "To feel ashamed of his misconduct and be able to fulfil his missions successfully when sent as an envoy by his sovereign." Then, Zi Gong asked again, "What about the scholar of a lower standing?" "Members of his clan praise him for his filial conduct and people of his community praise him for his brotherly affection." Then, Zi Lu asked again, "What about the next grade?" Confucius answered, "Those who insist on keeping their words and seeing their actions through to the end can be called scholars of the next grade even though they stubbornly adhere to their own opinion without questioning whether it is right or wrong." Then Zi Gong asked further, "What about those in power now?" Confucius sighed: "Those narrow-minded people are worth nothing."

Another time Zi Gong asked, "Is there one word that we can uphold for the whole of our life?" Confucius answered, "That should be forbearance. Do not do to others what you do not want others to do to you."

Duanmu Ci had been an official in Wei before holding a post in Lu. He had also been to Qi and Wu to lobby their rulers. He was well-known among the rulers of the various states for his eloquence and readiness to answer their questions about state affairs. Zi Gong was also a good businessman and became very rich trading between Cao and Lu.

Zi Gong never forgot the kindness of his master. When Confucius passed away, Zi Gong, together with Bu Shang (Zi Xia), Zhuansun Shi (Zi Zhang), Yan Yan (Zi You) and other disciples arrayed themselves at the bier and built a very big tomb for him. They lived by the side of the tomb for three years before gathering at Zi Gong's home to recall the teachings and kindness of their master, and bidding farewell to each other in tears.

Duanmu Ci died in Qi.

端木賜

Duanmu Ci

8

Bu Shang

Among Confucius' disciples, Bu Shang (507 BC–?) and Yan Yan (Zi You) were particularly good at literature. Bu Shang had a unique understanding of the *Book of Songs*. Once he asked Confucius, "What does it mean in the *Book of Songs* that charm lies in the smile, beauty lies in the eyes and gorgeousness lies in the plain?" (the third line is not found in the *Book of Songs*, probably it has been lost.) Confucius answered: "Beautiful flowers can be drawn only on white background." Then Bu Shang said, "Does that mean that benevolence came into being before rites and music?" Confucius replied, "Shang, you have indeed enlightened me. Now, I can discuss the *Book of Songs* with you."

Bu Shang, with the courtesy name Zi Xia, was born in Wen of the state of Jin (southwest of the present Wen County, Henan Province) in the late Spring and Autumn period (some people say that he was from Wei).

Confucius was very strict with this close disciple and once said to him, "You should be a virtuous scholar instead of a base scholar."

Bu Shang had a very deep understanding of learning, which covered not only knowledge but also moral integrity. He said, "If a person respects virtuous people, never has lust for women, does his best to look after his parents, serves his monarch whole-heartedly, and remains faithful to his friends, I would regard him as learned though he might never have studied books."

Bu Shang was very determined in learning. He had a good mastery of the *Book of Songs*, a profound understanding of the *Spring and Autumn Annals*, and a deep insight into the *Book of Changes* and the *Book of Rites*. Later he took up the post of County Magistrate in Jufu of the state of Lu. Before leaving for the post, he asked his master about the way of administration, and Confucius said, "Do not make haste whatever you do. Remember: More haste, less speed. Don't covet small advantages, as you will not succeed in important matters if you do." Bu Shang followed his master's advice and brought peace and order to the county.

Bu Shang and the other disciples were very sad over the death of their master, and lived by his tomb for three years. When they noticed that one of the fellow disciples, You Ruo (You Zi) looked very much like Confucius, they decided to treat You Ruo with the respect they had shown to their master. Bu Shang (Zi Xia), Zhuansun Shi (Zi Zhang), and Yan Yan (Zi You) tried to persuade Zeng Shen (Zi Yu) to agree to their idea. But Zeng said: "It won't do. Our master was as pure and clear as washed by the Long River and as bright as the light of the summer sun which no one can be compared to." Thus, Bu Shang and the others gave up the idea of treating You Ruo as the embodiment of Confucius.

Bu Shang advocated the necessity for monarchs to read the *Spring and Autumn Annals* to prevent power from being usurped by influential officials. In his later years, Bu Shang taught Confucian classics such as the *Book of Songs*, the *Spring and Autumn Annals*, the *Book of Changes* and the *Book of Rites* in Xihe (the present Heyang of Shaanxi Province). Many of his students later achieved great success, e.g. Li Kui, who became the premier, and Wu Qi, the military strategist of Marquis Wen of Wei. The Marquis also treated Bu Shang as his teacher and personally consulted him on the way to run the state well. Bu Shang made considerable contributions to the spread of Confucianism.

Bu Shang

Zeng Shen

曾參

Among the disciples of Confucius, few have been regarded by later generations as a "sage", and Zeng Zi (505–420 BC) was honoured as "The Model Sage" for he inherited the Confucianist doctrine.

Zeng Zi, with Shen as his name and Zi Yu as his courtesy name, was born in Wucheng, in the state of Lu (the present Fei County of Shandong Province). His father, Zeng Dian, with the courtesy name Xi, was also a student of Confucius.

Zeng Shen was a filial child. He went to study under the guidance of Confucius together with his father and became one of the best students. To support his family, Zeng Shen willingly did the job of a petty scribe.

Zeng Shen was very strict with himself and very hard working. He paid attention to self-reflection and abided by the principles of loyalty and forbearance. It was written in *Records of the Historian* that he had always adhered to filial piety. The Confucian classic *The Great Learning* was said to be written by him, for which he was also respectfully called "The Narrative Sage".

Zeng Shen attached great importance to the education of his children. There is a story about this in the book *Han Fei Zi*: One day when Zeng Shen's wife was going shopping, his youngest son pleaded in tears to go with her. The wife tried to appease the boy by saying, "You just stay at home. When I come back, I will kill the pig to cook you a delicious dinner." When the wife returned, she saw that Zeng Shen was about to kill a pig. She hurried to stop him, "Why? I was only kidding the child..." Zeng Shen said: "How can you cheat a child? Children would only learn from their parents and do as they are told. Cheating the child means teaching him to cheat others. What is more, if his mother cheats him this time, he will never believe her any more. How can you bring up the child in the proper way?" And Zeng Shen killed the pig for his son. From this we can see his earnestness and strictness. The fact that Zeng Shen became "The Model Sage" was inseparable from this spirit of his.

Zeng Shen lived about 70 years. His self-cultivation method of "three self-reflections a day" and his propositions to "be careful about the end, look far ahead, realize virtue and moral integrity among the people", and "never seek revenge even when offended or wronged" have had great influence on later Confucian scholars.

Zeng Shen

Mencius

When Mencius (c. 372–289 BC) was a small child, his family lived near a public cemetery. Seeing the bereaved families crying over the dead, he imitated them for fun. "This is not a suitable place for my son to live in," said his mother. And they immediately moved to a new place, which was near a fair. When Mencius saw the peddlers boast of their goods for money, he again imitated them. Again, his mother moved the family, and this time to a house near a school. There Mencius learned the etiquette of relations among the people, and he even asked his mother to send him to school. The mother was very pleased and said: "This is the right place for my son." This story of "Mencius' mother moving house three times" was recorded in the *Biographies of Celebrated Women*.

Mencius, named Ke, was from Zou of the Warring States period (the present Zou County of Shandong Province). With the instruction of a strict mother, he was very fond of learning early in his childhood.

The ancestor of Mencius was Meng Sunshi, an aristocrat of Lu, which was the home state of Confucius and the birthplace of Confucianism. Although Mencius lived in a period more than 100 years after Confucius, the influence of Confucianism was very profound, especially with the promotion by Kong Ji (Zi Si), the grandson of Confucius. At that time many people engaged in the study of this school of learning, and Mencius' teacher was Zi Si's student. Holding Confucius and his theory in high esteem, Mencius once said: "My greatest wish is to follow the example of Confucius."

Pondering over the situation at that time on the basis of Confucianism, Mencius developed the Confucian "learning of benevolence" into "benevolent government". He advocated the theory that "the people are more important than the sovereign", and advised the ruling class not to forget the importance of the common people. He upheld that it was justified for the people to overthrow a cruel autocratic ruler, and taught that only those rulers who adopted a benevolent policy and cherished the life of the people could unify the country. He also advocated "learning from the ancient kings", restoring the ancient farming system and reducing punishment and taxation, so that the common people would not suffer from cold and hunger.

In about 320 BC, Mencius visited Wei with his idea of "benevolent government". Although King Hui of Wei treated him with respect, he never accepted the idea of "benevolent government". After the death of King Hui, his successor King Xiang was not interested in "benevolent government" either. So, Mencius went to Qi to sell his theory. Despite the grand welcome with "dozens of carriages and over a hundred people", and acknowledgement of Mencius as a visiting minister, King Xuan of Qi never had any true appreciation of his political ideas. When an internal strife took place in Yan in 314 BC, King Xuan of Qi took the chance to invade the state despite efforts by Mencius to prevent him from sending troops. Therefore, Mencius left Qi for Song, then for Teng. Although Duke Wen of Teng took great interest in Mencius' ideas and often invited him for discussions, he never went beyond the theoretical level. Not long after, Mencius returned to Zou where he offered lectures to a group of students.

In his later years, Mencius engaged himself in book-writing to expound his theory, together with his disciples Wan Zhang and Gongsun Chou. Eleven chapters of *Mencius* were recorded in "Literature and Learning" of the *History of the Former Han Dynasty*, of which only seven chapters have been passed down to the present.

Mencius held that "Man is by nature good", being the first in China to study human nature systematically. He dwelt on the necessity of division of labour in society and pointed out the historical reality that "those who work with their brains rule and those who work with their brawn are ruled." He also raised the theory of "unity of Heaven and man" which combined epistemology and ethics.

Mencius lived to the age of 83. For his rich and profound theory and learning, and his great influence on later generations, he was regarded as the inheritor of Confucius and the idealism of Confucianism, and honoured as "The Lesser Sage" of Confucianism.

孟子

Mencius

Xun Zi

It had been a controversy for more than 2,000 years of Chinese history whether human were good or evil by nature. Mencius held that man's nature was good at birth, whereas Xun Zi (c. 313–238 BC) said, "the human nature is evil, and benevolence is only hypocritical." He also said, "All mortals have things in common: They want to eat when hungry, get warmth when cold, take rest when tired, and they all love advantages and hate disadvantages." In other words, "love of advantage" was inherent in man, which was the origin of "man's evil nature".

Xun Zi, named Kuang, was from the state of Zhao in the Warring States period. He was called Sun Qing by people of the Western Han Dynasty to avoid the name of emperor Xuandi, Liu Xun.

Xun Zi was already very learned early in his youth. At that time, the state of Qi, following the old system of King Xuan, was enrolling famous scholars of the country outside Jin Gate (Jixia) of the capital city, where they were organized to write books and discuss state affairs for salaries similar to those of senior officials.

The number of these scholars once exceeded 10,000 at the time of King Min of Qi. It was in the later years of this king that Xun Zi left Zhao for Jixia. At that time, Qi and Chu were on very bad terms, and the former showed signs of decline. Xun Zi went to see the premier of Qi and advised him to practise benevolent government to rejuvenate the state. Seeing Qi in decline, the Jixia scholars left the state one after another, and Xun Zi also left Qi for Chu. Not long after, King Xiang of Qi ascended the throne and the situation in Qi began to improve rapidly. As King Xiang treated learned men with courtesy and kindness, the number of scholars at Jixia increased again. When Xun Zi returned to Qi, the king held him in high respect.

Being jealous of Xun Zi for the respect he enjoyed, some people slandered him before the king, and Xun Zi had to leave Qi for Chu. Lord Chunshen of Chu, Huang Xie, was very pleased to see Xun Zi and appointed him magistrate of Lanling. But Xun Zi was again slandered, and had to leave Chu for Zhao. King Xiaocheng of Zhao was very delighted to have him and often discussed military affairs with him. But the king never adopted his ideas, and so Xun Zi left for Qin, where he offered his political views to the king and his premier Fan Sui. As his ideas were not adopted, Xun Zi went back to Zhao, before going to Chu at the invitation of Lord Chunshen where he was again appointed magistrate of Lanling. After the death of Lord Chunshen in 238 BC, Xun Zi lost his official position, and stayed at home writing books and teaching disciples, among whom were Han Fei and Li Si who became very famous in later days.

Xun Zi held that Heavens and earth had their own ways, and operated according to the law of nature. Such understanding of nature was different from that of Confucius and Mencius, but was similar to that of Lao Zi. On the other hand, he was of the opinion that human beings should not be awed by nature, but should carry on the struggles against it so that all things in the universe could be controlled and utilized by mankind. The idea that "man can conquer nature" was the quintessence of Xun Zi's thought, which surpassed other schools of thought of the Warring States period.

In politics, Xun Zi advocated administration by combination of rites and law and of benevolence and force, insisting on "getting the name correct", emphasizing the feudal hierarchy against the hereditary system. In economics, he proposed to strengthen production, open up resources and regulate the expenditure, as well as "decrease industrial workers and traders, and increase the number of peasants". He also stressed the importance of fertilizer to farming.

His idea of "getting the name proper" contained rich logic theory. He held that "getting the proper name is to serve the reality", and that the "name" had to be "established through common practice". He wrote *Verses of Chengxiang* on the peace and order as well as chaos of the society, and *Five Rhapsodies*, making considerable contribution to the spreading of the Confucian classics and the thriving of the rhapsody, a new form of literature in the Han Dynasty.

His disciples Han Fei Zi and Li Si, developed his theory, and originated the Legalist school of thought. Xun Zi was buried in Lanling. He represented the realist faction of Confucianism. Among his works, the most important was *Xun Zi*.

荀子

Xun Zi

Lu Jia

Among the sages worshipped in ancient Fanyu (present Guangzhou) were Ren Xiao, the general of the Qin Dynasty who conquered the state of Southern Yue, Zhao Tuo, the king of the state of Southern Yue, and Lu Jia (240–170 BC) who enjoyed the same historical status as Ren and Zhao. Although Lu Jia did not fight in the battlefields, he made a remarkable contribution to the unification of China by his eloquence. Twice he was sent as an envoy to Southern Yue, where he managed to persuade its king, Zhao Tuo, to pay allegiance to the Han Dynasty.

Lu Jia was from the state of Chu. In his early years, he followed Liu Bang, Emperor Gao Zu of the Han Dynasty, as an adviser to fight against the Qin Dynasty and put down rebellions.

In 206 BC when Liu Bang founded the Han Dynasty, Zhao Tuo seized Guilin and Xiangjun and proclaimed himself king of the state of Southern Yue. After the suppression of the rebel forces in various places, some officials of the war faction in the imperial court of Han proposed to conquer the state of Southern Yue to build on the crest of military victories. Lu Jia strongly objected to the proposal. Knowing that Zhao Tuo was able to unite all the forces in his state, Emperor Gao Zu decided to offer amnesty and enlistment to him. In 196 BC, he sent Lu Jia as the envoy to Southern Yue. Lu explained the righteousness of the unification of the country to Zhao Tuo, who then accepted the golden seal granted by Emperor Gao Zu and paid allegiance to the Han Dynasty.

Very pleased to hear that Southern Yue had yielded to Han, Emperor Gao Zu appointed Lu Jia to a senior official post. Lu Jia said to the emperor, "We have seized the country with force, but can we run the country well with force alone?" He proposed administration by advocating Confucianism, practising benevolent government, following the examples of the ancient sages, and absorbing the idea raised by Lao Zi to "govern by non-interference". With the approval of the emperor, his ideas produced positive influence on the politics at the beginning of the Western Han Dynasty. The common people finally got a chance to recuperate and develop production after being relieved from the tyranny of the Qin Dynasty and the years of warfare around the end of the Qin and the beginning of the Han Dynasty.

After the death of Emperor Gao Zu, the despotic Empress Dowager Lu Zhi practised nepotism and put the relatives of her family in important positions. Grieved over the decline of the Han Dynasty, Lu Jia kept close contact with the premier Chen Ping and the supreme military commander Zhou Bo in order to strengthen their unity while waiting for a chance to wipe out the Lu family.

Soon after the death of Empress Dowager Lu in 179 BC, Zhou Bo and Chen Ping got rid of the members of the Lu family clique in a surprise attack, and put Prince Dai (the second son of Emperor Gao Zu) on the throne, who was known in history as Emperor Wendi of Han.

As Empress Dowager Lu had prohibited the export of iron farm tools and female cattle to Southern Yue, and had even detained Yue's envoy, Zhao Tuo proclaimed himself Emperor Wu of Southern Yue in 183 BC and sent troops to attack the fief of Prince Changsha, fighting all the way to Nanjun.

When Emperor Wendi of Han came to the throne, he asked Premier Chen Ping to recommend an envoy to Southern Yue in order to rid the threat from that state. On Chen Ping's recommendation, Lu Jia was nominated envoy by the emperor and went to see Zhao Tuo with only a deputy envoy. He succeeded in persuading Zhao Tuo to give up his imperial title and yield to Han. Again, Lu Jia made meritorious contribution to the reunification of China.

Lu Jia was a political commentator and rhapsody writer in the early period of the Han Dynasty. In philosophy, he held that "heaven can be seen", meaning that nature could be known and the prosperity or decline of a society had nothing to do with heaven. Among his extant works were 12 chapters of *New Comments* advocating adoption of benevolent government and abolition of tyranny. Already lost are his three rhapsodies and his *Spring and Autumn of Chu and Han* which is about the events in the war between Chu and Han. The "Literature and Learning" section of *The History of the Former Han Dynasty* regarded Lu Jia as the head of one of the four schools of rhapsody writers of the Han Dynasty.

陸賈

Lu Jia

Fu Sheng & Fu Sheng Nu

伏胜·伏生女

With Confucianism becoming prominent in the Western Han Dynasty, scholars began to make textual research or expositions of the Confucian classics, forming a particular school of learning.

According to the *Records of the Historian*, Confucius said that six arts were needed in administration: Rites was to regulate people, Music was to create harmony, the *Book of History* was to describe events, the *Book of Songs* was to express ideas, the *Book of Changes* was to change the spirit, and the *Spring and Autumn Annals* was to express ethics and righteousness. What the Confucian scholars studied were mainly these six classics.

Fu Sheng, a scholar of modern-script Confucian classics of the Western Han Dynasty whose date of birth and death is unknown, was from Jinan (west of the present Zhangqiu of Shandong).

He was already an Imperial Academician in the Qin Dynasty with a good mastery of Confucian works. When the first emperor of the Qin Dynasty ordered the burning of books kept by the people, Fu Sheng kept silent, but secretly hid the *Book of History* in the wall of his house. Part of the book was lost in the frequent wars in the period between the Qin and Han dynasties; only 29 chapters remained intact by the founding of the Western Han Dynasty when Fu Sheng took out the book from the wall. Then, he began to teach the *Book of History* in Qi and Lu.

Fu Sheng had a daughter, commonly known as Fu Sheng Nu (daughter of Fu Sheng) and also known as Xi'e. She was very clever as a child. While waiting on her father when he was teaching, she gradually gained a fairly good understanding of the *Book of History*. Fu Sheng was very pleased and often gave her guidance in her studies of the book.

As Fu Sheng gradually became famous for teaching the *Book of History*, even Emperor Wendi of Han sent his official Chao Cuo to study under him. Chao had been a disciple of the Legalist School, and studied the theory of Legalists Shen Buhai and Shang Yang of the Warring States period under the guidance of Zhang Hui. This time he had come to Fu Sheng with the intention to compare the advantages and disadvantages of Confucianism and Legalism. Therefore, he often raised difficult questions unexpectedly. On such occasions, the intelligent daughter of Fu Sheng often helped her father by giving clever and convincing answers.

After completing his studies, Chao Cuo bade farewell to the father and daughter and returned to the capital. He explained the *Book of History* to the emperor with his own comments. Appreciative of his learning, Emperor Wendi promoted Chao Cuo to be attendant of the crown prince, and later, general in charge of the palace gate of the crown prince, and then, Imperial Academician. The promotion of Chao Cuo was the direct result of the meticulous cultivation of Fu Sheng and his daughter.

The news that the emperor had sent his official to study the *Book of History* under Fu Sheng spread very quickly and the number of his students increased greatly. Thus the leading scholars of the Western Han Dynasty were all his disciples. The present version of the 28 chapters of the modern-script *Book of History* was passed down by Fu Sheng. It was said that he also wrote *Explanations on the Book of History*, but later generations suspected that it was written by his students Zhang and Ouyang.

伏勝 一九九二年三月十三日盞于羊石

Fu Sheng &
Fu Sheng Nu

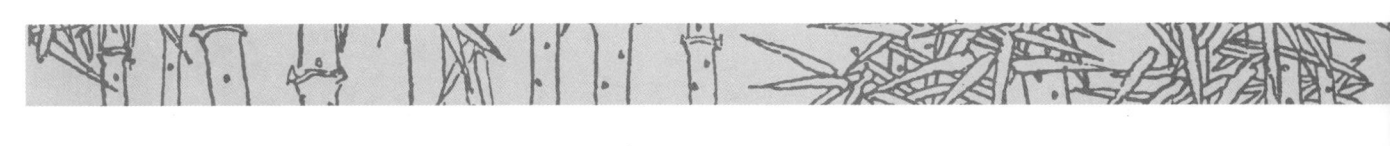

韓嬰

Han Ying

There is a story in the book *Further Study of Han Poems* that when Confucius and his disciples left the state of Lu and travelled to Agu, a place in the state of Chu, they saw a woman washing clothes by the side of a river. Confucius suddenly thought of the lines in the *Book of Songs*: "Women there are in Chu, Courtship they will not respond to." To prove the truthfulness of the lines, he asked his disciple Zi Gong to go and court her. Three times Zi Gong tried but three times he failed, which showed that the lines in the *Book of Songs* were true.

The writer of *Further Study of the Han Poems* was Han Ying.

Han Ying, whose date of birth and death is unknown, was from Yan (present Beijing) in the early years of the Western Han Dynasty. He was the originator of the school of modern-script learning of classical poems known as *The Learning of Han Poems*.

Learned and versatile, Han was selected as an Imperial Academician during the reign of Emperor Wendi of Han, and was made grand tutor of Prince Changshan during the reign of Emperor Jingdi. He was so sharp and eloquent that even the eloquent Dong Zhongshu failed to demolish his argument when they had an argument in the presence of Emperor Wudi.

Han Ying made profound study of the *Book of Songs* and the *Book of Changes*. Making deductions from the *Book of Changes*, he wrote *Studies on the Book of Changes*.

However, his major achievements were in the study of the *Book of Songs*. He wrote 36 volumes of *Han Poems*, 36 volumes of *Theory of Han Poems*, 41 volumes of *Study of Han Poems* and over 10 volumes of *More Study of Han Poems*, and the latter two books alone had several dozen thousand characters. He had different explanations of the *Book of Songs* from *Qi Poems* and *Lu Poems*, and was very outstanding in the study of modern-script learning of poems in the early years of the Western Han Dynasty. Scholars of Yan and Zhao all took his explanations as orthodox in their discussion of the *Book of Songs*. Judging from the only extant 10 volumes of *More Study of Han Poems*, one may find that Han Ying cited ancient stories and quotations to prove the truthfulness of the lines in the *Book of Songs*, just as shown in the story cited at the beginning of this article.

Han Ying's style was elegant and concise, characterized with the tradition of the writing of the Pre-Qin period. But his references were different from those of the pre-Qin scholars, which can be used in our study of the different schools of thoughts of the pre-Qin period.

Han Ying

Jia Yi

賈誼

Li Shangyin, a great poet of the Tang Dynasty, wrote a poem entitled *The Bright Scholar Jia* which reads:

Seeking worthy men the emperor
calledback Jia,
Who had been banished though
with ability peerless.
So eager to consult him at midnight
was his majesty,
A pity it's not about people but about
ghosts and deities.

The poem was about Jia Yi (200–168 BC), a famous political commentator and rhapsody writer of the Western Han Dynasty. Several years after his banishment, he was called back by Emperor Wendi who granted him an interview in the Xuan Palace, and consulted him about the origin of ghosts and deities. The emperor was so absorbed in the detailed reply of the erudite scholar that he even moved his seat nearer to Jia at midnight. While admiring the peerless ability and learning of Jia Yi, the poem also ridiculed the emperor who was more concerned about supernatural beings than about the life of the people.

Jia Yi was from Luoyang of Henan Prefecture (present Luoyang city). Since a boy, he studied very hard and read extensively. He used to study and annotate *Spring and Autumn by Zuo Qiuming* under the guidance of Zhang Cang who had been Xun Zi's student and an Imperial Academician of the Qin Dynasty. Later, he studied the *Book of Songs* and poems written by Qu Yuan as well as Taoist works.

Jia Yi became famous for his literary talent in his home prefecture at the age of only 18. Learning about his talent, the prefect of Henan named Wu (student of Li Si, the premier of the Qin Dynasty) summoned him to be his disciple and often had discussions with him.

In 179 BC, Wu recommended Jia Yi to Emperor Wendi after he was transferred to a senior post in the capital for his successful administration of the prefecture. Thus, the 21-year-old Jia became the youngest Imperial Academician of the time. Because of his ability and literary talent, he got an exceptional promotion one year later.

In 178 BC, Jia Yi submitted to the emperor the well-known memorial *On Hoarding Grain*, advocating "agriculture to restrain mercantilism" in view of the abandonment of farming for business at the time. His proposal was adopted by Emperor Wendi and played a positive role in the restoration and development of agriculture.

Another proposal of his accepted by the emperor was to send the marquises back to their fiefs so as to strengthen the central government. This idea offended influential senior officials like Zhou Bo, as well as the sycophantic courtier Deng Tong. When Emperor Wendi intended to promote Jia Yi, both Zhou Bo and Deng Tong objected. As a result, Jia Yi was banished from the capital in 177 BC to be the mentor of Prince Changsha.

In the remote city of Changsha, Jia Yi wrote a rhapsody *Lamentation over the Death of Qu Yuan* expressing his grief and indignation. In 174 BC, he wrote *The Unlucky Bird* to express his feelings over changes and setbacks in life. Nevertheless, Jia Yi was still very much concerned about state affairs and often submitted memorials to the emperor.

In 173 BC, Emperor Wendi summoned Jia Yi back to the capital Chang'an. However, because of the interference of Deng Tong, Jia was not placed in any important position, but was assigned as the grand teacher of Prince Lianghuai, the youngest and favourite son of the emperor.

In that year, Jia Yi submitted to the emperor a very famous memorial *Policy on Peace and Order.* He advocated that the offspring of the princes should only be allowed to inherit within their original fiefs so as to weaken their power and prevent rebellion, and that measures should be taken to prevent the possible southward invasion of the Huns when they grew stronger. All these suggestions revealed Jia Yi's far-sightedness and deep insight.

Jia's other proposals, such as reducing the princedoms, banning private minting of money and preparing for resistance against the Huns, that were adopted one after another during the reigns of Emperors Jingdi and Wudi, also played an important role in ensuring the long-term stability of the Western Han Dynasty.

Jia Yi died of excessive grief. To commemorate his contribution to the Han Dynasty, Emperor Wudi promoted his two grandsons to be prefects.

賈誼 一九九一年二月

Jia Yi

Gongsun Hong

公孫弘

During the Western Han Dynasty, there was a junior prison scribe who, through his determination and diligence, became an erudite scholar of the Confucian classics. Later, he was appointed by Emperor Wudi as premier in charge of state affairs. This legendary figure was Gongsun Hong (200–121 BC).

Gongsun Hong, with the courtesy name Ji, was from Xue of Zichuan (south of present Shouguang, Shandong Province). When he was young, he was a prison scribe. Prison scribes were regarded by many people as tough, rough and uneducated. But Gongsun Hong was not going to deal with criminals all his life. While working in prison, he made good use of his time for studies. At the age of 40 when he noticed that the emperors of the Western Han Dynasty were interested in Confucianism, he began to study the *Annotations of the Spring and Autumn Annals by Gongyang*.

It was said that the book was written by Gongyang Gao of the Spring and Autumn period recording events between the first year of Duke Yin of Lu (722 BC) and the 14th year of Duke Ai of Lu (481 BC). The events were first passed down orally. Not until the early years of the Western Han Dynasty did Gongyang Shou and Humu Sheng inscribe them on bamboo pieces. The book had been used as a reference in discussing politics as it was a simple and concise record of historical events with emphasis on the cardinal principle of righteousness in the Spring and Autumn period. It showed Gongsun Hong's insight in making exegetical studies of the book.

Indeed news about his studies of the *Annotations of the Spring and Autumn Annals by Gongyang* soon spread far and near, attracting wide attention.

In 140 BC, Emperor Wudi of Han proscribed all non-Confucian schools of thought and espoused Confucianism as the orthodox state ideology based on the proposals raised by officials like Dong Zhongshu and Wei Wan. At that time, Gongsun Hong, who was already a fairly well-known scholar of Confucian classics, submitted a proposal to Emperor Wudi on nominating imperial academicians for the five Confucian classics and enrolling imperial students. In 136 BC, the emperor adopted his proposal and nominated dozens of imperial academicians for the five classics of the *Book of Songs*, *Book of History*, *Book of Changes*, *Book of Rites*, and the *Spring and Autumn Annals*. An imperial college was also established to teach students the Confucian classics. From this time, Gongsun Hong began to earn the appreciation of the emperor.

In 128 BC, Emperor Wudi granted an interview to Gongsun Hong who specialized in *Annotations of the Spring and Autumn Annals by Gongyang*. Finding that Gongsun possessed a good command of learning, law, and administration, the emperor appointed him premier.

Gongsun Hong served as premier for six years till 123 BC. He died at the age of 80.

Gongsun Hong

Mei Cheng

枚乘

During the reign of Emperor Wendi of the Western Han Dynasty, a rhapsody *Seven Fa* inheriting the style of Chuci and pioneering a new style of Han rhapsody was widely read among officials and scholars. Its unique style in description and allegory became so popular that writers and poets vied to imitate it, and there appeared a series of rhapsodies with titles beginning with "Seven". The writer of the *Seven Fa* was Mei Cheng (?–140BC), a scholar under Prince Wu.

Mei Cheng, with Shu as his courtesy name, was from Huaiyin (the present Qingjiang City, Jiangsu Province). His childhood was spent in the peaceful time after the reunification of China by Liu Bang, Emperor Gaozu of the Han Dynasty, and that enabled him to engage himself in studies and rhapsody writing.

After the founding of the Han Dynasty, Liu Bang began to enfeoff the royal family members. Liu Bi, Liu Bang's nephew, was enfeoffed in Pei with the title Prince Wu.

The ambitious Prince Wu made his princedom rich and strong by way of minting money and boiling sea water for salt. He also inducted men of ability and learning, watching for a chance to rise against the central authorities. Mei Cheng was inducted as the prince's honoured guest for his literary talent, and was soon appointed as an official of considerable importance. With the rich southeastern part of the country under his control, Prince Wu often acted in defiance of the court and was reluctant to be a subject.

Seeing through his ambition, Mei Cheng remonstrated with the Prince and tried to persuade him to give up his inordinate ambitions, "What you wish to do is both extremely precarious and impossible to realize. And it would be very easy and completely safe for you to change your mind." Unable to persuade Prince Wu, Mei Cheng left him for the princedom of Liang, and became a distinguished guest of Prince Liang, Liu Wu.

When Emperor Jingdi of Han succeeded to the throne, the nine princes carrying the royal family name were very strong, the total area of their fiefs exceeding that under the court, and they had their own military forces and tax resources; and that aroused the concern of far-sighted officials in court. The imperial prosecutor Chao Cuo submitted to the emperor a proposal to "reduce the princedoms".

The news spread to Prince Wu, who then started a rebellion in collaboration with six other princes such as Zhao and Chu, under the slogan of "Kill Chao Cuo and remove the evil officials by the side of the emperor". Emperor Jingdi had to kill Chao Cuo in the hope of securing the retreat of the troops of the seven princedoms. At that time, Mei Cheng tried to persuade Prince Wu to withdraw his troops to avoid his own destruction. The prince would not listen, and that caused a fatal disaster. After the troops of the seven princedoms were defeated by General Zhou Yafu, Liu Bi escaped to Eastern Yue, where he was caught and killed.

When the revolts of the seven princes were put down, Mei Cheng became well known for his far-sightedness. Emperor Jingdi appointed him to be a prefecture official. Dissatisfied with the position, Mei Cheng resigned on the excuse of poor health, and returned to the princedom of Liang, where all the men of letters held Mei Cheng in high respect. Not long after, Mei Cheng had to return to his hometown in Huaiyin, after the death of his patron Prince Liangxiao.

Highly appreciative of Mei Cheng's ability and learning, Emperor Wudi of Han dispatched a special carriage to bring him to the palace. Old and ill at the time, Mei Cheng died on his way to the capital.

According to the section on "Literature and Learning" of the *History of the Former Han Dynasty*, Mei Cheng left behind two articles, which were recorded in the *History of the Former Han Dynasty* and nine rhapsodies, of which only three, *Seven Fa*, *Rhapsody on Tu Garden*, and *Rhapsody on the Willow* have been passed down to the present. Despite the limited number of extant works, Mei Cheng enjoyed a high status in the history of Chinese literature. Inheriting the past and initiating a new style for later times in artistic form, the *Seven Fa* is still of reference value even today both in artistic quality and ideology.

Mei Cheng

Sima Xiangru

司馬相如

During the Western Han Dynasty, Zhuo Wangsun, a rich man in Linqiong of Sichuan, held a banquet in honour of Sima Xiangru (179–117 BC), a famous rhapsody writer of the time.

Zhuo Wangsun had a beautiful and talented daughter named Zhuo Wenjun, who was newly widowed and staying at her father's home at the time. Being an admirer of Sima Xiangru's rhapsodies, she slipped into the hall to steal a glance at Xiangru from behind the curtain. The young scholar had heard that Zhuo Wangsun had a beautiful daughter. Seeing a figure moving behind the curtain, he began to convey his love for her by means of the music he was playing. Fascinated by the love music and the elegant bearing of the handsome scholar, the young lady eloped with Xiangru to Chengdu that very night. The couple loved each other for many years, until Xiangru wanted to take a beautiful girl from Maoling as a concubine. Wenjun wrote a poem *Song of the White-haired* that made Xiangru give up the idea and the couple loved each other as before.

Sima Xiangru, with the courtesy name Changqing and nickname Quanzi, was from Chengdu of Shu (in present Sichuan). He changed his name to Xiangru out of admiration for Lin Xiangru, the senior minister of the state of Zhao in the Warring States period. He was very bright and fond of reading from childhood. Although he stammered a little, he was able to write beautiful rhapsodies and was good at swordplay and playing musical instruments.

During the reign of Emperor Jingdi of Han, he served as imperial attendant. But Emperor Jingdi was not interested in literature. It happened that Prince Liang, Liu Wu, led a group of literary men such as Zou Yang and Mei Cheng to the capital, and Sima Xiangru had a very good time with them. Then Xiangru resigned his post on the excuse of illness and followed Prince Liang to his fief, where he spent several years and wrote a famous rhapsody titled *Zi Xu* to describe the grand occasion of hunting by the dukes.

After the death of Prince Liang, Xiangru returned to Chengdu. When Emperor Wudi succeeded to the throne after the death of Emperor Jingdi, he happened to read the rhapsody *Zi Xu* and liked it very much. An imperial attendant who was a fellow countryman of Xiangru took the chance to recommend Xiangru to the emperor. Wudi was delighted and summoned him to the palace. Xiangru then wrote another rhapsody *Shang Lin* describing the hunting by the emperor. Much pleased with his rhapsody, the emperor appointed him official of the court.

In order to develop the border areas in the southwest, Emperor Wudi in 135 BC ordered roads leading to Yelang and Bozhong to be built, and recruited over 10,000 labourers from Sichuan for the hard work. The Han generals aroused discontentment from the Sichuan people when they killed the people who disobeyed their orders. The emperor then sent Sima Xiangru to handle the matter. The scholar wrote *Proclamation to Sichuan* which explained the advantages of building the roads and restored order to the area.

Satisfied with Xiangru's success, Emperor Wudi made him a general and sent him to Sichuan again to offer amnesty and enlistment to the rebellious minorities in the southwest. But the local chiefs were not happy with the idea of having relations with the minorities, arguing that it would harm the interests of the local Han people. Again Sima Xiangru wrote a declaration *To Countrymen of Sichuan* explaining the objectives of the imperial decree and asked the local chiefs to give priority to the interests of the whole country. After the successful accomplishment of this mission, Sima Xiangru was rewarded and promoted by Emperor Wudi who was very much satisfied with his work. Not long after that, Xiangru died of illness at the age of 62.

Sima Xiangru was a representative writer of rhapsody of the Han Dynasty. According to the section on "Literature and Learning" of *History of the Former Han Dynasty*, Sima Xiangru wrote 29 rhapsodies, of which six have been passed down to the present. He made considerable contribution with his rhapsodies to the stability and unification of China in fulfilling Emperor Wudi's order to win over the people of Sichuan and pacify the minorities in the southwest.

司馬相如 一九九二年四月

Sima Xiangru

Dong Zhongshu

董仲舒

During the reign of Emperor Jingdi of the Western Han Dynasty, there was a very diligent imperial academician engaged in the study of Confucianism. He lectured on the *Spring and Autumn Annals* and other Confucian classics. He was so attentive in his studies that for three years he did not cast a single glance at the garden, and to be free from distraction, he even drew the curtain so as to shut out the beauty and allurement of the colourful flowers in the garden outside his windows. He was referred to in the *History of the Former Han Dynasty* as "making lectures with drawn curtain" and "casting no glance at the garden for three years". This devoted academician was the erudite scholar Dong Zhongshu (179–104 BC).

Dong Zhongshu was from Guangchuan (present Guangchuan Township, Zaoqiang County of Hebei). He started studying Confucian classics from young, and was particularly good at the *Spring and Autumn Annals*. During the reign of Emperor Jingdi, he became an Imperial Academician.

After Emperor Wudi ascended the throne, he issued an imperial edict to induct learned people with moral integrity. There were altogether more than 100 candidates. Dong Zhongshu who had already been recommended during the reign of Emperor Jingdi offered his strategies to Emperor Wudi, proposing "to take Confucianism as the orthodox while curbing other schools of learning", and advocating "the prohibition of any learning other than the six arts championed by Confucius, i.e. rites, music, archery, charioteering, reading and writing, and arithmetic". Highly appreciative of Dong's proposition, the sovereign rejected those scholars engaged in the study of Shenzi, Shang Yang, Han Fei, Su Qin, and Zhang Yi. That was referred to in history as "proscribing all non-Confucian schools of thought and espousing Confucianism as the orthodox ideology".

In the Spring and Autumn period, Confucianism was but one of the many schools of learning, and during the reign of the first emperor of the Qin Dynasty, Confucianism even suffered a calamity with its books burned and a large number of Confucian scholars buried alive. It remained an ordinary school of learning even at the beginning of the Western Han Dynasty when the orthodox ideology was the Huang-Lao Taoist school of thought. Not until Emperor Wudi accepted Dong Zhongshu's proposition did Confucianism gain the orthodox position which it kept for 2,000 years.

Emperor Wudi then sent Dong Zhongshu to Jiangdu to be the premier of his elder brother Prince Yi, Liu Fei. Dong taught rites to Prince Yi and gradually won the respect of the formerly arrogant prince.

Appreciative of Dong Zhongshu's ability in changing the "hard rock" nature of Prince Yi, Emperor Wudi transferred him to Jiaoxi to be the premier of Prince Yu, Liu Duan, who was even more arrogant and rude than Prince Yi. Performing his duties with great care, Dong Zhongshu finally gained the respect of his new chief. However he resigned his post not long afterwards as he was afraid that he might offend the prince some day. He returned home concentrating on reading and writing. Though living in retirement, he was often consulted by the court on important matters, which showed the respect Emperor Wudi held for him.

Dong Zhongshu lived to the age of 76. According to the records of the *History of the Former Han Dynasty*, altogether he had 123 works of which only 82 were passed down and collected in *Chunqiu Fanlu*. With "great unity of the country" as his ideal, Dong Zhongshu advocated some reforms as political concession to the peasants. He stressed "the interaction between Heaven and Man" and held that "the monarchical power is awarded by Heaven". That was why his doctrine was held in esteem by rulers of all dynasties. His "three cardinal guides (ruler guides subject, father guides son, and husband guides wife) and five constant virtues (benevolence, righteousness, propriety, wisdom and fidelity)" formed the basis of Chinese feudal ethics.

Dong Zhongshu

Sima Qian

司馬遷

In 99 BC, Li Guangli, senior general of the Western Han Dynasty, led an army on an expedition against the Huns. General Li Ling was ordered to manoeuvre behind the enemy front with 5,000 men, where unfortunately they encountered the main forces of the Huns. After 10 days of fierce fighting in which they wounded and killed more than 10,000 enemies, Li Ling surrendered after arrows and other supplies were exhausted and retreat was blocked.

Court Historian Sima Qian (c. 145–c. 86 BC) pleaded with Emperor Wudi in favour of the general, but enraged the emperor all the more. The latter ordered the historian be put in prison to await execution. According to the laws of the Han Dynasty, a prisoner sentenced to death could be pardoned either by paying a large amount of money or receiving castration as punishment. With a view to completing his great work of history, Sima Qian chose the humiliating punishment of castration.

Sima Qian was from Xiayang (south of present Hancheng of Shaanxi) with the courtesy name Zichang. He left the countryside at 10, following his father, Court Historian Sima Tan, to the capital Chang'an. He studied *Spring and Autumn Annals* under the guidance of Dong Zhongshu, and the *Book of History* under the instruction of Kong Anguo, a descendant of Confucius and famous scholar of ancient-script Confucian classics. At 20, he travelled in the Changjiang River basin, investigating social customs and accumulating legends, before returning to Chang'an to take up the post of secretary. At 28, he followed Emperor Wudi to tour famous mountains and rivers. In 108 BC, he inherited the post of his father as Court Historian. Four years later, he compiled the Taichu Calendar together with Tang Du, Luo Xiahong and others. Well in conformity with astronomical science, the new calendar was suitable for use in farming.

He started compiling *Records of the Historian* in 104 BC. According to the preface written by himself, he had taken up the compilation to fulfil the will of his father. But he was put into prison only a few years later for the sake of Li Ling. About 96 BC, he was promoted to be in charge of documents, and was more determined than ever to compile the great historical work. In a letter to his good friend Ren An, he expressed his mental agony, recounting how he suffered because of Li Ling, and explaining his work of compilation.

Records of the Historian, also known as the *Book of the Grand Historian*, is a brilliant historical and literary masterpiece, being the earliest comprehensive history of China. It consists of 130 chapters, 526,500 Chinese characters, with 12 basic annals recording the sovereigns of the various dynasties; 10 tables listing important historical events; eight books recounting institutions and systems, astronomy and calendar, and economy and water conservancy; 30 hereditary houses describing the history of the various states enfeoffed, and the lives and deeds of the officials and generals who had rendered outstanding service to the Han Dynasty; and 70 biographies telling the life stories of figures of different social strata. It covers a period of 3,000 years from the Yellow Emperor to the Taichu period of the reign of Emperor Wudi (101BC), initiating a form of history written in biography.

The book has been admired as a masterpiece that "has covered all the branches of knowledge and the important changes of past and present". Sima Qian's insight and courage can well be seen from his including Xiang Yu, who contended with the founder of the Han Dynasty for the throne, in the basic annals, and the peasant uprising leader Chen Sheng in the hereditary houses. *Records of the Historian* made great artistic achievement in its description of people and narration of events, which profoundly influenced historical study and literature of later generations. It is justified to be called "the poetic masterpiece of historical works, and Lisao (the greatest poetic piece by Qu Yuan) without rhyme." (comment by Lu Xun, the great modern Chinese novelist.)

Sima Qian lived to be about 60 years old. Among his other works were eight rhapsodies included in the section on "Literature and Learning" of the *History of the Former Han Dynasty*. However, the only extant piece is *A Sad Scholar Never Realizing His Ambition* which expressed his indignation and determination after suffering castration.

司馬遷 一九九一年六月二十六日

Sima Qian

Dai De & Dai Sheng

During the Western Han Dynasty, a scholar and his nephew studied Confucian classics together and both became masters of the modern-script study of rites. Some of the books compiled by them became part of the classics of Confucianism. The two scholars, the uncle Dai De and the nephew Dai Sheng, were known as "the Senior and Junior Dais".

Dai De, with the courtesy name Yanjun, was known as "Dai the Senior", and Dai Sheng, with the courtesy name Cijun, as "Dai the Junior". They were from Liang (the present Shangqiu of Henan).

They both studied the *Rites of Zhou* under the guidance of Hou Cang, a scholar of Confucian classics of the Western Han Dynasty who was from Tan of Donghai (the present Tancheng of Shandong). Hou Cang was made an Imperial Academician, and served as Director of Palace Affairs during the reign of Emperor Wudi. He was not only a master of the *Rites of Zhou* but also of the *Book of Songs*. The Dais benefited a lot from his instructions and gained a thorough mastery of the essence of the *Rites of Zhou*.

Dai De later initiated the "Senior Dai School" of modern-script study of rites, and was appointed senior adviser to Prince Xindu, Liu Xiao. Collecting various ancient writings on rites, he compiled the 85 chapters of *Rites by Senior Dai* which, however, is incomplete now as quite a bit of it was lost.

The nephew Dai Sheng made even greater achievement, and originated the "Junior Dai School" of modern-script study of rites. He had been prefect of Jiujiang, and during the reign of Emperor Xuandi, he was made an Imperial Academician, and was authorized to attend imperial meetings to discuss Confucian classics and state affairs. He also collected various ancient writings on rites and systems and compiled the *Rites by Junior Dai* which was referred to by later generations as the *Book of Rites*. Up to the Qing Dynasty, it had been on the list of the required classical works for all the Confucian scholars since Liu Chang of the Northern Song Dynasty included it in the *Seven Classics*.

戴德 • 戴聖

Dai De &
Dai Sheng

Jing Fang

京房

During the Western Han Dynasty, there was a Confucian scholar who specialized in the study of the *Book of Changes* and applied the principle of the Eight Trigrams of the book to the study of music. He extended the 12 temperaments into 60 and created 13 string "pitches" to set the temperament. This scholar-musician was Jing Fang (77–37 BC).

His original surname was Li, and he was from Dunqiu of Dongjun (southwest of present Qingfeng of Henan) with the courtesy name Junming. In his youth, he studied the *Book of Changes* under the guidance of Jiao Yanshou, disciple of Meng Xi, who was the originator of the "Meng School of Learning", a branch of the modern-script school of the *Book of Changes* initiated by Meng Xi's master, Tian He from Zichuan (present Zibo of Shandong).

Though a disciple of the "Meng School of Learning", Jing Fang explained the *Book of Changes* by way of "adaptation" and originated the "Jing School of Learning" in the study of modern-script *Book of Changes*. He was also an accomplished scholar of music theory.

In 49 BC Emperor Yuandi of Han succeeded to the throne. An advocate of Confucianism and the policy of benevolence, the new emperor entrusted Confucian scholars with the administration of the state.

Jing Fang was made an imperial academician. He was for associating natural calamities with the political situation and presented quite a few memorials to the emperor commenting on the state policies on the basis of the "enlightenment" by natural disasters. At the time, a senior official Shi Xian and his clique monopolized state power. Jing Fang presented a memorial to impeach him, only to be banished from the capital to be magistrate of Weijun. Later he was being thrown into prison, where he died at the age of only 40.

Among his works passed down to the present day are three volumes of *Divination based on the Book of Changes*. Besides, some of his writings can be found in the *Annotations to the Book of Changes by 21 Scholars of the Han and Wei Dynasties*.

京房 ·九九二年

Jing Fang

40

楊雄

Yang Xiong

During the Western Han Dynasty, there was a man of letters, Yang Xiong (53 BC–AD 18), in Ba Shu (present Sichuan) who was good at imitating master writers, and even gained his official position for his rhapsody *Ganquan* in imitation of the writings of Sima Xiangru. In his old age, he wrote *Fayan* in imitation of *Analects of Confucius*, and *Taixuan* in imitation of *the Book of Changes*. Generally speaking, imitating others meant repeating their way and style and could not achieve much. But Yang Xiong was an exception. In imitating the form and style of the masters, he imbued new meaning in his writings, and became a famous rhapsody writer and philosopher of the Western Han Dynasty.

Yang Xiong was from Chengdu of Shu (present Chengdu of Sichuan) with the courtesy name Ziyun. He was diligent and well read, and often engaged in meditation. He was simple and easy-going by character, and was a man of few words partly because he stammered a little. Not interested in fame and fortune, he took it easy with his very limited property. Appreciative of the writings of Qu Yuan and Sima Xiangru, he enjoyed their works and often imitated their style.

Yang Xiong did not go to the capital until he was over 40 years old, but his rhapsodies written after the style of Sima Xiangru immediately won the appreciation of the scholars there. Senior General Wang Yin recommended him to Emperor Chengdi who then granted him an audience. Yang Xiong wrote four rhapsodies in admiration of the monarch and was made Imperial Attendant.

However, he did not get further promotion throughout the reigns of Emperors Chengdi, Aidi and Pingdi. When Wang Mang usurped the throne, many people got promotions or rewards through presenting "symbols of mandate of heaven" in admiration of Wang Mang's regime. Yang Xiong wrote a eulogy for the new dynasty but did not get any reward or promotion. He was later conferred the senior title of Dafu simply for his years of service.

Some time later, Liu Fen, son of Duke Liu Xin, and Zhen Xun, son of Duke Zhen Feng, presented another "symbol of mandate of heaven". But at that time Wang Mang did not like such symbols any longer, as he had already seized power. He banished Liu Fen and put Zhen Feng and Zhen Xun to death as a warning to others. When people went to arrest Yang Xiong, who had been associated with Liu Fen, Yang was collating books at Tianlu Pavilion; and he jumped down from the pavilion to end his life. He failed in his suicide bid, but was later pardoned by Wang Mang who learned that he was not involved in the case. Yang was removed from office because of illness, but before long, he was again made a senior official.

Thinking that rhapsodies could not do much good to society, Yang Xiong devoted himself to academic writing in his old age. He wrote *Fa Yan* in imitation of *Analects of Confucius*, and *Tai Xuan* in imitation of the *Book of Changes*. He put forward the idea that "Xuan" was the root of all things in the universe, emphasizing the necessity of knowing the natural phenomena as they were, and advocating that human knowledge should take after nature. He held that "any life would have its death, and any beginning would have its end", refuting such superstition about immortals. In social ethics, he criticized Lao-Zhuang's idea of "rejecting benevolence and righteousness" and favoured the doctrine of Confucianism. These ideas of his held an important academic position in the history of philosophy in China. His *Xunzuan*, which was a wordbook, and *Fangyan*, which dealt with linguistics and exegetics, were important works for the study of ancient Chinese language and characters.

Yang Xiong lived to the age of 72. His writings were compiled in the *Collected Works of Yang Ziyun*. The most comprehensive collection of his rhapsodies and articles can be found in four volumes in the *Complete Works of Xia, Shang, Zhou, Qin, Han, Three Kingdoms, and the Six Dynasties* compiled by Yan Kejun during the Qing Dynasty.

Yang Xiong

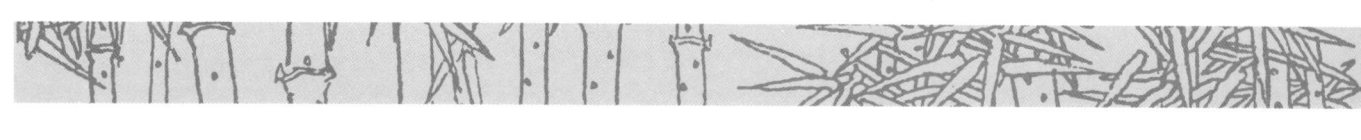

Liu Xin

劉歆

For his mastery of poetry, classics, and writing, Liu Xin (c. 53 BC–AD 23) was appointed imperial attendant in his youth by Emperor Chengdi of the Western Han Dynasty. He got on quite well with another imperial attendant Wang Mang, which 10 years later enabled him to make rapid advances in his official career and become an important figure in Wang Mang's clique that usurped the power of the Western Han.

Liu Xin was from Pei (present Pei County of Jiangsu) with the courtesy name Zijun. He later changed his name to Xiu and his courtesy name to Yingshu. His father, Liu Xiang, was the writer of *Xinxu* and *Shuoyuan*, both being records of historical facts and stories.

A lover of literature since childhood, Liu Xin was ordered to help his father with collating the books in the imperial library, which enabled him to make a profound study of the six Confucian classics, books of various schools of thought, poetry and rhapsodies, mathematics, and medicine.

After the death of his father, he was made Commander of the Northern Army. During the reign of Emperor Aidi, he was promoted by the General Military Director Wang Mang as Imperial Attendant and later further promoted to Brigadier General and Imperial Adviser. He was very much trusted by Emperor Aidi who authorized him to take charge of the collation of books in the imperial library. He discovered among the imperial collection ancient-script *Spring and Autumn Annals*, *Rites of Zhou*, *Spring and Autumn by Zuo Qiuming*, the *Book of Poetry by Mao*, and the *Book of History*, and proposed to the sovereign that these books be included in the subjects to be studied. Emperor Aidi instructed him to discuss the matter with the academicians of the five classics. Being scholars of modern-script classics, the academicians raised objections to his proposal in the discussion. Liu Xin therefore wrote an article

to the academicians, sharply criticizing these scholars. What he did offended the minister in power, and the Confucian scholars all rose against him. Fearing unexpected punishment, he requested for a transfer to a local post. He then served as prefect of Henei, Wuyuan, and finally Zhuojun before resigning his post. Not long after his resignation, he was again appointed general of a vassal state, Anding.

When Wang Mang was at the helm of the state after the death of Emperor Aidi, he was eager to get reliable officials to his help, and called Liu Xin to the capital to take a senior position before further promoting him to be magistrate of the capital and conferring on him the title of Marquis of Honglin, entrusting him with the administration of Confucian scholars, historians and officials in charge of divination. During this period, he compiled the *Santong Calendar* through examining and correcting former calendars.

After Wang Mang usurped the throne and founded the Xin Dynasty in AD 9, Liu Xin was made master of the state with the title Duke of Jiaxin, being a key figure in Wang Mang's regime. In AD 23, the Lulin rebel troops defeated the Xin army at Kunyang and were pressing on towards Chang'an. Bearing a grudge against Wang Mang who had put his third son to death, and harbouring the intention to please the rebel troops for self-protection, Liu Xin plotted with General Wang She to end Wang Mang's life. After their scheme was disclosed, however, Liu committed suicide.

Liu Xin made a lot of academic achievements in his life. In the course of collating the various books, he wrote the *Seven Categories*, the first work of bibliography in China. Though the book is lost, its main contents were included in the section on "Literature and Learning" in *History of the Former Han Dynasty* by Ban Gu. Liu's other writings were compiled in *Collected Works of Liu Zijun*.

刘歆

一九九一年三月盎于越秀山麓三元古宫

Liu Xin

46

Liang Hong

梁鴻

At the beginning of the Eastern Han Dynasty, there was a hermit Liang Hong who was deeply in love with his wife. Each day the wife would serve the meal in a tray which she raised to the level of her brows and respectfully presented to her husband. And Liang Hong would affectionately take the tray before sitting down at the table and enjoying the meal together with his wife. Thus "holding the tray level with the brows" became a Chinese idiom meaning mutual love and respect between husband and wife.

Liang Hong was from Pingling of Fufeng (northwest of Xianyang of Shaanxi) with the courtesy name Boluan. The exact years of his birth and death are not known. It was only recorded that he was born into a very poor family that could not afford even a coffin after the death of his father who was then buried in a roll of mat.

Poor as he was, Liang Hong had lofty aspirations. He read widely in the Imperial College and had a good mastery of the Confucian classics. Nevertheless, he had no interest in an official career. After graduation from the college, he herded pigs in the Imperial Garden, which won him the respect of the local people. Later, he went back to his hometown to do farming. At that time a Meng family in the county had an industrious and good daughter who had declined many offers of marriage, as she detested the lazy and good-for-nothing sons of rich families. Not until she was about 30 years old did she hear that Liang Hong preferred the life of a hermit to being an official. Out of admiration, she hinted to her parents that she would like to marry the young man.

Having heard a lot about the daughter of the Meng family, Liang Hong accepted the marriage proposal. However, for seven days after their wedding, he remained silent to his wife. It turned out that the bride had made up a little and dressed up a bit to please her bridegroom, which caused Liang's misunderstanding. So, removing her ornaments and putting on her coarse-cloth dress, she began to do all kinds of hard work on the eighth day. Very much pleased, Liang said, "Good! That's what I expect of my wife." He named her Guang and they lived in Baling (east of present Chang'an County of Shaanxi) doing farming and weaving.

Once Liang Hong passed by Luoyang on his trip to the east. Indignant at the extravagant life of the officials and nobles, he wrote *Five Alas Song* satirizing the situation:

> *Mounting the northern mound, alas.*
> *I look to the capital city, alas.*
> *Magnificent palaces I see, alas.*
> *People are toiling in the fields, alas.*
> *Their hardships are endless, alas.*

Offended by the song, Emperor Zhangdi issued an order for the capture of Liang Hong, who then had to change his name and escape to Shandong with his wife. They later went to Wu and lived under the porch of a famous local scholar, Gao Botong, husking rice for other people for a living. Each day when Liang Hong came back to their place, his wife would present him the food on a tray which she lifted level with her brows. Amazed, Gao Botong realized Liang Hong was no ordinary person and invited the couple to live in his home, treating them as his guests. Not until then did Liang Hong have time for writing. After writing more than 10 pieces, he died of illness and was buried next to the grave of the gallant ancient assassin Yaoli, whom people referred to as the "Yaoli Martyr".

The life story of Liang Hong was in "Biographies of Hermits" in the *History of the Later Han Dynasty*. Most of his writings were lost. The only extant pieces, *Five Alas Song*, *Song on Coming to Wu*, *Missing a Friend,* are recorded in "Biography of Liang Hong" in the *History of the Later Han Dynasty*.

梁鴻

一九九二年八月二十二日畫于三元古宮野味齋男光題記

Liang Hong

Ban Gu

班固

During the Eastern Han Dynasty, there was a family in which four members, the father, two sons and the daughter, all made distinguished contributions to the country; and Three of them won eternal fame for compiling *History of the Former Han Dynasty*. One after another, the father, the elder son, and the daughter were engaged in this grand project. The elder son Ban Gu (32–92) played the pivotal role.

Ban Gu was from Anling of Fufeng (northeast of present Xianyang of Shaanxi) with the courtesy name Mengjian. He was the son of Ban Biao, a famous historian of the Eastern Han Dynasty. Ban Gu wrote very good articles since the age of nine. When a little older, he became a good rhapsody writer and perused books of various schools of thought as well as books of divination.

Ban Biao was interested in history early in his childhood. At the beginning of the Eastern Han Dynasty, he was recommended as a qualified scholar and appointed magistrate of Xuxian County. He left the official post later because of illness and devoted himself to the study of the history of the Han Dynasty. He often sighed over the fact that the *Records of the Historian* recorded historical events only up to the Taichu period of the reign of Emperor Wudi, and made up his mind to accumulate historical data and write a sequel to the great historical work. However, he only completed 65 chapters by the time he died in AD 54. Out of the love for his father, Ban Gu was determined to complete the great work he had left behind.

The road to success, however, was strewn with obstacles. Someone presented a memorial to Emperor Mingdi accusing Ban Gu of wilfully tampering with the official history, and consequently he was arrested and put in the prison of the capital. Fortunately, his younger brother Ban Chao had been promoted to be Senior General for the illustrious military exploits he had achieved after giving up intellectual pursuits for a military career. Ban Chao presented a memorial to the sovereign, explaining how his elder brother had decided to carry on the will of his father to write a sequel to *Records of the Historian*. The emperor then pardoned Ban Gu before appointing him as Lantai secretary and instructing him to write the biography of Emperor Guangwu, Liu Xiu. Not until Ban Gu fulfilled the assignment was he authorized to start compiling *History of the Former Han Dynasty*.

Ban Gu devoted more than 20 years of painstaking efforts to the compilation of the *History of the Former Han Dynasty*. Being the first dynastic history of China, the book which recorded the rise and fall of the Former Han Dynasty covered a span of 230 years from the uprising of Emperor Gaozu, Liu Bang, to the destruction of Han's usurper, Wang Mang. It followed the stylistic rules and format of *Records of the Historian*, and its records for the period before Emperor Wudi were also based on that great work. Though its literary element was not as strong as that of the *Records of the Historian*, its precise and well-knit narration successfully recorded the history of the Western Han Dynasty, and the two sections on "Literature and Learning" and "Economy" were, in particular, of high documentary value.

In AD 89, Ban Gu was appointed assistant to General Dou Xian on a punitive expedition against the Huns. When the strong army marched through undulating mountains, he wrote the famous piece *Inscription on the Tablet Erected in the Yanran Mountain*. But the expedition ended in defeat, and in a rage Emperor Hedi put Dou Xian and Ban Gu in jail. The historian died of illness in prison at the age of 61, and the unfinished sections on "Astronomy" and "Eight Tables" of his historical work were later completed by his talented younger sister, Ban Zhao.

In addition to the above-mentioned works, Ban Gu wrote 41 pieces among, which were *Rhapsody of the Two Capitals*, *Continuation of the Meritorious Deeds of Yao*.

Ban Gu

Wang Chong

王充

At the beginning of the Eastern Han Dynasty, a young man was often seen in the bookstore in Luoyang, who would take up a book he was interested in and begin reading it page by page. By the time he turned over all the pages of the book, he would have "memorised" all its contents. This young talent with a very retentive memory was Wang Chong (27–c. 100).

Wang Chong was from Shangyu of Kuaiji (in present Zhejiang) with the courtesy name Zhongren. He was born into an impoverished landlord family that was running a small business.

Quite different from other children, Wang Chong was fond of books instead of playing games. He began reading at six, and at eight, he started studying the *Analects of Confucius* and the *Book of History*, being able to recite 1,000 characters each day. Later he entered the imperial college and studied under the guidance of Ban Biao. As his family could not afford to buy books, he often went to the bookstore to read instead of buy. This enabled him to read different kinds of books and to learn the strong points of various schools of thought.

Returning home from the Imperial College, Wang Chong did teaching before serving as an assistant in his prefecture, and later in Yangzhou. He went home after being removed from office in AD 88. His friend Xie Yiwu recommended him to Emperor Zhangdi, saying that he could be compared to Mencius, Yang Xiong, and Sima Qian in ability and learning. When the emperor sent a public carriage to take him to the capital, he failed to make the trip because of illness.

After that he stayed at home devoting himself to writing, not even attending the weddings or funerals of relatives. On the doors and windows were hung writing implements such as pen-brushes and knives so that he could readily record any inspiration he got. After several decades of accumulation and hard work, he completed the masterpiece of philosophy *Lun Heng,* comprising 85 chapters (with one chapter "Zhaozhi" missing) with more than 200,000 words. Being a book advocating atheism, it severely criticized augury and divination prevalent at the time. In Wang's opinion, "the intercourse of the qi of heaven and that of earth gave birth to all things just as the intercourse of the qi of husband and wife gave birth to children"; heaven and earth themselves were also produced by qi, and there never existed a creator with his own will; disaster and calamity were also the result of the changes of qi and had nothing to do with occurrences in human life; and "the death of a man was like the extinction of the fire" and the so-called "soul" was not in existence.

The book *Lun Heng* also dealt with literature, holding that men of letters should write about reality instead of unfounded things.

Wang Chong did not blindly revere Confucius and Mencius, founders of the Confucianist school of learning. He wrote *Interrogation of Confucius*, and *Criticism of Mencius*, pointing out the self-contradictory arguments of the two sages. Wang Chong lived to be over 70, and *Lun Heng* was his only work passed down to the present, all his other writings were lost.

Wang Chong

Xu Shen

許慎

Xu Shen (c. 85–c. 147) was a disciple of the great Confucianist scholar Jia Kui of the Eastern Han Dynasty. Though Jia was a very strict and rigorous master, Xu Shen and other students never made any complaints as Jia himself exercised strict self-discipline.

As a learned scholar and a man of letters, Jia Kui wrote *History of the Former Han Dynasty* together with Ban Gu. And with a good mastery of astronomy, he pointed out that the moon travels at an uneven speed. What inspired Xu Shen and his fellow disciples most was that their tutor had beaten the master of modern-script classics Li Yu in a debate, which had greatly boosted the morale of the school of ancient-script classics. Under the instruction of such a strict master, Xu Shen grew up to be a great scholar.

Xu Shen was from Zhaoling of Runan (present Yancheng of Henan) with the courtesy name Shuzhong. He studied diligently under the guidance of Jia Kui and finally became a learned scholar of Confucian classics, being admired at the time as the "unrivaled master of the five classics".

Xu Shen had been Secretary of the Military Director-General. He had a good command of the classical works, and majored in the study of ancient-script Confucian classics. He wrote the 10-volume *Differences in Meaning between the Ancient and Modern Script Five Classics* which established his position in the field of Confucian classics. Though Zheng Xuan later wrote a refutation to this book, Xu's prestige as the "unrivaled master of the five classics" remained unaffected.

However, Xu's greater achievement was his masterpiece the *Wordbook* comprising 14 volumes, excluding one special volume for introduction and catalogue. Though he was not as talented as his master Jia Kui, he inherited Jia's steadfast spirit in study and research. In the course of studying ancient-script Confucian classics, Xu Shen devoted great efforts to exegetics and completed the *Wordbook* by summing up what he had gained in years of study. He created the way of arranging Chinese characters by radicals, which became the basis for the study of characters and an important method for dictionary compilation, producing great influence on the study of philology.

Xu Shen

Zhang Heng

張
衡

In the third year of the Yonghe period of the Eastern Han Dynasty (138), a bead suddenly came off the mouth of one of the eight dragons on the seismograph and fell into the mouth of the golden toad below it, producing a loud tinkling. Rushing to the instrument upon hearing the sound and seeing the golden dragon on the west side had spat its bead, the attendant hurried into the palace to report it to Emperor Shundi, who then called in the inventor of the seismograph Zhang Heng (78–139) for an explanation. Zhang said that since the bead had come off the mouth of the dragon on the west, it meant that there had been an earthquake in that direction. At that time, there was no trace of any quake at all in the capital Luoyang and nothing happened even after two days. Officials and people began to doubt the reliability of the instrument and some even ridiculed Zhang Heng for his poor technology. Zhang, however, remained perfectly self-possessed. Sure enough, an urgent report about a serious quake came after a few days from Gansu far in the west, asking for relief. The whole capital was then amazed, all admiring Zhang Heng for his miraculous instrument.

Zhang Heng was from Xi'e County, Nanyang Prefecture of Jingzhou (north of present Nanyang of Henan) with the courtesy name Pingzi. In his boyhood, he read extensively in various schools of learning and was particularly interested in astronomy, geography, and mathematics. He was also a good writer and artist and was adept at making novel things. Reluctant to stay idle at home awaiting recommendation, he left for the ancient capital Chang'an at 16. He toured along the Weihe River and the surrounding areas and scaled the summit of Taihua and Zhongnan mountains, visiting all the sites of historical interest in the Guanzhong area, and witnessing the busy life of commerce in towns and farming in the countryside.

A year later, he went to the capital Luoyang, and visited the imperial college to learn from the famous scholars. He thus came to know Ma Rong, Wang Fu, Cui Yuan etc. In a short span of five or six years, he became a learned scholar with a good mastery of the five classics and six arts. Having no interest in an official career and material gains, he declined many recommendations of local officials and appointments of the court. In 107, Zhang Heng wrote the oft-quoted *Rhapsody of the Two Capitals* which won great popularity at the time.

From 108 to 111, Zhang Heng stayed at home, reading and doing research, gradually turning his interest from literature to science and philosophy. Hearing about his many talents, Emperor Andi sent a carriage to take him to Luoyang and put him in charge of palace vehicles, horses and safety, before promoting him to be Court Historian. In 117, he invented the exquisite celestial globe for measuring the heavenly bodies. At the same time, he wrote the famous astronomical works *Lingxian*, and *Illustration of the Celestial Globe*, making great contribution to astronomy and mathematics.

In 121, Zhang Heng was put in charge of the recruitment of scholars and conscription. And in 126, he was again appointed Court Historian. By the time he was 49 years old, he had not got any promotion for 12 years, and people began talking about it. In the circumstances, Zhang Heng wrote an article expressing his lofty ideal: "A man of virtue does not care so much about his position as about his moral character; and is ashamed not so much of low salary but of poor learning." He was against the superstitious means of augury and divination which were taken as a shortcut to promotion at the time, denouncing them as deceptive and demagogic.

Zhang Heng was promoted to be imperial attendant in 133, but was pushed out of the capital three years later to be assistant of Prince Hejian as a result of the jealousy and hostility of the eunuchs. Extravagant and overbearing, Prince Hejian connived at the evil gentry who brought suffering and disaster to the people. Zhang Heng however made efforts to establish law and order by dealing with the evil-doers severely.

In 138, Zhang Heng sent in his request for retirement, but was transferred back to the capital to be a minister. The next year he died in Luoyang. In addition to his distinguished contribution to astronomy and seismology, he was one of the four great rhapsody writers and one of the six great artists of the Han Dynasty. Rich and varied, his works covered both liberal arts and science, part of which can be found in *Collected Works of Zhang Hejian*.

Zhang Heng

Ma Rong

馬融

Ma Rong (79–166) was a well-known scholar of Confucian classics of the Eastern Han Dynasty. Unlike the serious and strict Confucian scholars, he led an unrestrained life, and even gave lectures to his disciples sitting behind a silk curtain while enjoying music played by beautiful women.

Ma Rong was from Maoling of Youfufeng (northwest of present Xingping of Shaanxi) with the courtesy name Jichang. His father Ma Yan was a very strict parent, and entrusted him to a famous Confucian scholar Zhi Xun. As a very intelligent boy, Ma Rong soon read many classics and won the appreciation of his master, who later married his daughter to him.

Impressed by his fame, Commander-in-chief General Deng Zhi invited him to be his senior attendant. Ma Rong declined the offer and travelled in Liangzhou where he witnessed the invasion of the Qiang minority. At the time, the grain prices were exorbitant and the roads were strewn with bodies of people who had starved to death. Seeing the terrible hardship, Ma Rong changed his mind and went to the general. In 110, he took up the post of secretary, and later followed Ban Zhao to study *History of the Former Han Dynasty*.

At that time, Empress Dowager Deng was in power. She caused social turmoil as a result of her adoption of the suggestion of certain mediocre scholars to over-emphasize culture and civil matters to the neglect of military affairs. In view of the situation, Ma Rong presented a memorial elaborating the necessity "to be vigilant of peril and turmoil in times of peace and order". Against his expectations, the memorial offended the Empress Dowager, and as a result he failed to get any promotion for 10 years. He then tried to find an excuse to resign his post and go back home. That further infuriated the Empress Dowager and cost him six years' detention. Not until Emperor Andi took over the reins of government after the death of the Empress Dowager was Ma Rong appointed secretary to Prince Hejian. His *Eulogy of the Eastward Tour,* presented on the imperial tour to Mount Taishan in the east, won the appreciation of Emperor Andi, and Ma was thus made an imperial attaché.

In 133, Emperor Shundi gave him the task of drafting strategies in the capacity of an adviser. Then Commander-in-chief General Liang Shang promoted him to be his senior adviser before transferring him to the post of Wudu prefect. Ma Rong was also good at military strategy. When General Ma Xian and General Hu Chou were sent on a punitive expedition against the revolting Western Qiang minorities, Ma Rong presented a memorial pointing out the disadvantages for the two generals to garrison one city, and volunteered to lead 5,000 troops as the vanguard for the suppression of the rebellion. Later developments of the war were just as he predicted though his suggestions were not adopted. During the reign of Emperor Huandi, Ma Rong served as Nanjun prefect. He was removed from office and banished to Suofang for violating the will of General Liang Ji. Fortunately, there was an amnesty on his way to exile and he was called back to be an adviser. Before long he left the post due to illness and died at the age of 88.

His major achievement was the new height he had reached in the study of ancient-script classics. He annotated such Confucian classics as the *Book of Filial Piety*, *Analects of Confucius*, the *Book of Songs*, the *Book of Changes*, the *Three Rites*, and the *Book of History*, as well as *Biographies of Distinguished Women, Lao Zi*, the *Book by Prince Huainan*, and *Sorrow in Estrangement by Qu Yuan*. His disciples numbered several thousands, among whom were famous scholars like Lu Zhi, Zheng Xuan etc. His unrestrained practice of lecturing in the company of women and music pioneered the way of those scholars of the Wei and Jin Dynasties who tried to break away from the traditional rites and engaged in discussions on lofty and non-mundane matters.

Ma Rong

Zheng Xuan

鄭
玄

Zheng Xuan (127–200) was a disciple of Ma Rong, scholar of Confucian classics of the Eastern Han Dynasty. For three years he did not have any chance to see his master, and only studied under the guidance of advanced fellow disciples. One day Ma Rong gathered his students for a discussion on prophecy and invited Zheng Xuan as he was good at mathematics. This was the first chance for Zheng Xuan to consult his master. After that he bade farewell and went home. Seeing Zheng leaving school, Ma told his disciples, "Zheng's departure will bring my learning to the east." He meant that Zheng Xuan had mastered all his learning and was leaving for the east laden with knowledge.

Zheng Xuan was from Gaomi of Beihai (in present Shandong) with the courtesy name Kangcheng. He was intelligent and fond of learning, and was tall with handsome features and an elegant bearing. In his hometown he served as a junior secretary in charge of lawsuit and tax collection. Leaving the post which he did not like, he went to study at the imperial college, where he gained a good command of the various classics, the Santong Calendar, and Jiuzhang Mathematics. He had been a disciple of Ma Rong before studying as a visiting scholar around Fufeng for 10 years. After returning to his hometown he started a private school in Donglai to support his poor family. Thousands of students came to study in his school out of admiration for his learning.

In 168, with the ban on association, and consequently, on his school, Zheng Xuan devoted himself to writing at home. He was an erudite scholar as he had studied the modern-script *Book of Changes* and *Annotations of Spring and Autumn Annals* by Gongyang in the Imperial College, and the ancient-script *Book of History, Rites of Zhou, Spring and Autumn by Zuo Qiuming* under the guidance of Zhang Gongzu, and finally the ancient-script classics taught by Ma Rong. At that time, the magistrate of Rencheng named He Xiu was the champion of a school of Confucian classics

and had written three important works. Zheng Xuan wrote a comment pointing out the shortcomings and mistakes in each of them. After reading his comment, the author He Xiu sighed, "It seems as if Kangcheng has got into my room and is attacking me with my own spear."

The ban on association was not lifted until the end of the reign of Emperor Lingdi. Hearing Zheng Xuan was very learned, Senior General He Jin invited him to take an official post. Unable to decline the invitation, Zheng Xuan had to go and see the general, but left after staying there for a night. Zheng was already 60 years old at the time. Out of admiration for his moral character and learning, prefect of Beihai Kong Rong ordered the magistrate of Gaomi to establish a "Mr Zheng's Village" where the gate of his home was named "Gate to Moral Integrity".

At the end of the Eastern Han Dynasty, the ruler of Hebei General Yuan Shao once sent for Zheng Xuan, respecting him as an honorable guest, and recommending him to the post of Zhonglang general with the title of learned scholar. Zheng never accepted the recommendation, as he had long lost interest in an official career. He took pleasure in teaching, and annotated the *Book of Changes*, the *Book of Poetry, Analects of Confucius*, the *Book of History*, the *Book of Rites, Ceremonial Rites*, the *Book of Filial Piety, Explanations of the Book of History*, and wrote *Seven Political Treatises, The Meanings of the Rites of Lu, On the Six Arts, Records of Mao Poetry, Refutation of Differences in Meaning between Ancient and Modern-Script Classics by Xu Shen,* etc. In his life of 74 years, he produced various writings of more than a million words.

He was respectfully referred to as "the Later Zheng" (the Former Zheng being Zheng Zhong) for his great achievement in collating and annotating historical documents and ancient books. His annotations to *The Mao Poetry* and *Three Rites* are adopted in the extant version of *Annotations to the Thirteen Classics*.

鄭玄

一九九一年八月十三日畫于鐵嶺秀山麓三元古宮
野味齋蜀龍題記

Zheng Xuan

Cai Yong

蔡邕

During the reign of Emperor Lingdi of the Eastern Han Dynasty, there was erected at gate of the imperial college in the capital a stone tablet on which were engraved the texts of the six Confucian classics in elegant and vigorous strokes. It attracted a lot of visitors who came in an endless stream to see and even to imitate the writing on the tablet widely known as *Classics on the Xiping Stone Tablet* in the history of calligraphy. It was copied by the great calligrapher and man of letters Cai Yong (133–192) of the Eastern Han Dynasty. The tablet was named "Xiping" as it was erected in the fourth year of the Xiping period of the reign of Emperor Lingdi at the request of Cai Yong and another senior official, Yang Ci, to inscribe the texts of the six classics on a stone tablet in standard characters.

Cai Yong was from Yu of Chenliu (south of present Qixian County of Henan) with the courtesy name Bojie. He was already fairly popular in his early teens for his learning and versatility, as a talent good at verse and prose as well as music. Not only well known for his calligraphy but also for his painting, he was one of the four great artists of the Eastern Han Dynasty, the other three being Zhao Qi, Liu Bao, and Zhang Heng. In 170 he served in the staff of the premier Qiao Xuan who showed great respect to him though Cai was only his subordinate. After that he was promoted several times to the position of court adviser.

Taking the occasion of a natural disaster in 178, Cai Yong presented a memorial to Emperor Lingdi criticizing state affairs, which, however, offended the noble and influential. As a result, he was arrested and being banished to Anyang County of Wuyuan.

Cai Yong presented a memorial to Emperor Lingdi stating his intention to complete the supplement to *Records of Later Han* which he had undertaken together with Lu Zhi and Han Yue. The emperor appreciated his talent very much and allowed him to return to his hometown in the amnesty of 179. On his way back, the prefect of Wuyuan, Wang Zhi, who was the elder brother of the eunuch, Wang Pu, gave him a farewell banquet. Having no high opinion of the host, Cai left the banquet in a huff, and thus offended Wang Zhi and the eunuchs in the capital. The prefect then secretly accused Cai of calumniating the court in exile, forcing Cai to flee to Wu and Taishan where he lived in seclusion for 12 years before returning to his hometown.

After the death of Emperor Lingdi in 189, Dong Zhuo became the premier monopolizing state power. He offered Cai Yong an official post as he had heard a lot about his talent. After Cai declined the appointment on the excuse of illness, Dong Zhuo gave a strict order to the local officials to make persistent recommendation of the scholar. Under the despotic power of Dong, Cai Yong had to go to the capital and was appointed Director of the Imperial Academician. A year later he was made Left Zhonglang General and followed Emperor Xiandi of Han to the new capital Chang'an. Whenever Dong Zhuo held a banquet, he would invite Cai to play the musical instrument of qin, admiring Cai's talent in all possible ways. But Dong was a headstrong person, and seldom listened to Cai's ideas in political affairs.

After the execution of Dong Zhuo, Cai Yong could not help sighing over his death. The new premier Wang Yun took it as "being nostalgic of the personal favours received from Dong Zhuo to the negligence of loyalty to the state" and put Cai in prison. Cai Yong finally died in prison and the news caused extensive regrets and sorrow among the scholars and the common people, who put up his statue in Yanzhou and Chenliu in commemoration of this talented scholar.

His daughter Cai Yan (Wenji) had been captured by the Huns in the turmoil and chaos of war and had lived 12 years with the Left Prince of the Huns and bore him two children. After knowing her whereabouts, Cao Cao sent envoys to the Huns and redeemed her with gold and precious jade. That showed the people's regret over Cai's tragic death.

A prolific writer, Cai Yong wrote 104 poems, rhapsodies, tablet inscriptions, and articles according to the record in *History of the Later Han Dynasty*. Extant today are 10 volumes of *Collected Works by Cai Zhonglang*.

Cai Yong

Kong Rong

孔融

The most popular story about Kong Rong (153–208) is how he chose the smallest pear and declined the big ones in favour of his elder brother. When asked why he did that, the four-year-old boy replied, "Being the smallest child, I should eat the smallest pear."

Kong Rong was from Lu (present Qufu of Shandong) with the courtesy name Wenju. He lived in the closing years of the Eastern Han Dynasty and his father Kong Zhou had been the Military Director of Taishan Prefecture. He followed his father to the capital at 10.

At the time, governor of Henan, Li Ying, prided himself on his seniority and importance and would not receive people at home unless they were influential figures or people whose fd amily had friendly ties with his own for generations. Being a descendant of Confucius of the 20th generation, and wishing to see Li Ying out of curiosity, Kong Rong went straight to his home and was let in after telling the gatekeeper that his family had had generations of friendship with the Li family. Seeing a child visiting him, Li Ying asked, "Is it your grandfather who knows me?" Kong replied, "My ancestor Confucius and your ancestor Li Laozi had discussed academic matters and learned from each other, so there existed friendship between our two families many generations ago." All those present were amazed with his wisdom and eloquence.

At 16, Kong Rong and his elder brother were both put into prison for they tried to save his brother's friend. The two brothers then vied with each other to take the blame and punishment, which baffled the local officials. They reported the case to the court which then declared the elder brother guilty of the offence. Kong Rong won fame in this case and was made attaché of a senior official. At his post, he impeached corrupt officials, even the relatives of powerful eunuchs. He was promoted to the post of general in command of imperial guards. When Dong Zhuo monopolized state power, Kong was appointed prefect of Beihai, and suffered quite a few defeats by the peasant uprising army.

After Emperor Xiandi of Han moved the capital to Xuchang, Kong Rong was appointed minister in charge of construction, before being promoted to the post of Shaofu in charge of palace affairs. By this time he had become the authoritative Confucian scholar of the time, which aroused the jealousy and misgivings of Cao Cao, since they held different political views. So Cao found an excuse and removed him from office. Not until a year later was he granted an official position with a sinecure. Kong Rong, however, seemed to be deriving much pleasure from the arrangement, and often held banquets to treat his friends, professing: "I shall be free of worries so long as I often have a large gathering of guests drinking and dining with me." He actually meant that he did not have to worry about the threat of the powerful Cao Cao so long as he had the support of the Confucian scholars both in and out of office. What he did made the impression that he would stand up to Cao Cao as an equal.

At that time, Cao Cao was premier issuing orders to the nobles and local rulers in the name of the emperor who was completely under his control. He ordered a ban on liquor so as to accumulate food supply for his troops that had been battling year after year for the unification of the country. Kong Rong wilfully wrote *A Letter to Cao Cao on the Ban of Liquor* which only aggravated Cao's jealousy and hatred for him. In 208 when the Honorary Inspector-General of the Army Lu Cui impeached Kong Rong for "being engaged in treason and guilty of heresy and deserving severe punishment", Cao Cao took it as an excuse and put to death the 56-year-old Kong Rong and his wife and sons.

Cao Pi commented that Kong Rong's verse and prose were of a "superb and masterly style, excelling many contemporary writers." According to the record in "Biography of Kong Rong" of *History of the Later Han Dynasty* written by Fan Ye, this celebrated writer of "the Seven Scholars of the Jian'an Period" had 25 pieces of poems and articles, most of which have been lost. *Collected Works of Kong Beihai* was compiled by people of later generations.

Kong Rong

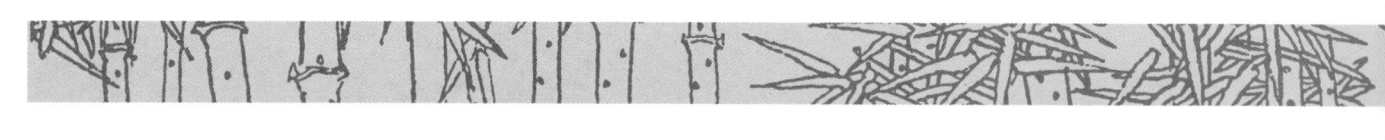

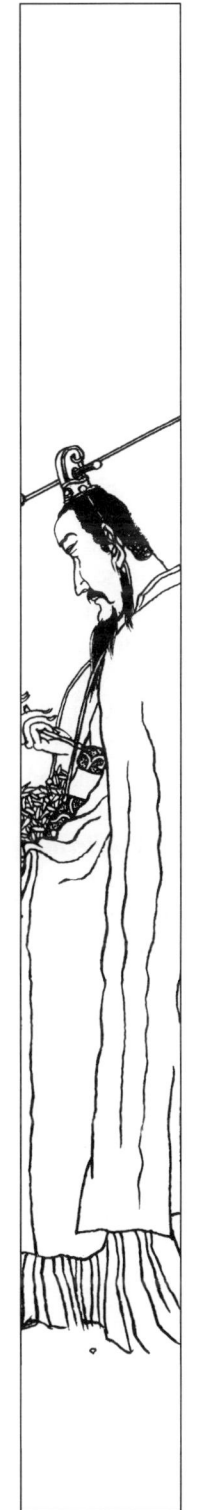

Wang Can

One day, towards the end of the Eastern Han Dynasty, a senior official, Cai Yong, was entertaining guests at home when his attendant announced the arrival of Wang Can. In spite of all the people present, Cai Yong went to the gate personally to meet the young man. Seeing the surprised look of his guests, Cai told them that he would one day give Wang Can all the books he had collected out of respect for his rare talent. Wang's talent and fame could be seen from what Cai Yong did.

Wang Can (177–217) was from Gaoping of Shanyang (southwest of present Zouxian County of Shandong) with the courtesy name Zhongxuan. He had been intelligent with a retentive memory since childhood, and was said to be able to restore the positions of all the pieces of a weiqi game after they were mixed up. Doubting the truth of that, the chess players covered their chess board with a handkerchief, and were amazed to find Wang Can restoring the game exactly on another chessboard. In addition to his wide range of knowledge, photographic memory, and mastery of mathematics, he was particularly good at writing, and was able to write excellent articles at one go without making any corrections.

His talent was already well known when he was only 15. Emperor Xiandi of Han issued a decree to appoint him imperial attendant. Seeing the turmoil in Chang'an, he did not take up the post but went south to Jingzhou to serve Liu Biao. However, Liu failed to see his true worth as he judged people only by appearance; Wang Can was lean and weak and plain looking. Frustrated, he wrote the rhapsody *Mounting the Tower* to express his aspirations. He was with Liu Biao for 15 years. After Liu Biao's death Wang persuaded his son Liu Cong to surrender to Cao Cao.

Cao Cao was very pleased to get Wang Can and appointed him premier attaché with the title of Marquis of Guannei before promoting him Honorary Inspector-General of the army. After Cao was made Duke of Wei by Emperor Xiandi in 213, Wang Can was further promoted to the post of Senior Palace Official. An erudite scholar with a good mastery of rites, he directed the establishment of the family temple of the Caos and the restoration of the various ceremonies. Also a good writer of verse and prose, he wrote three *Poems of Lament* on his way to Jingzhou at the age of 15 which have been popular among readers ever since. The later generations put him at the head of the "Seven Scholars of the Jian'an Period", namely Wang Can, Kong Rong, Chen Lin, Xu Gan, Yuan Yu, Ying Yang, and Liu Zhen. Cao Pi, Cao Zhi and him were close literary friends and often discussed poetry and rhapsodies together.

After his death in a plague, Emperor Wendi of Wei, Cao Pi, attended his funeral in person, after which the emperor said to those present, "Wang Zhongxuan was fond of the braying of the donkey. Let's each imitate a bray to bid him farewell." So everyone did as told. That showed Cao Pi's profound friendship for Wang Can and his deep grief over the death of his literary friend.

Wang Can wrote more than 60 poems and articles, part of which are lost. People of the later generations compiled his writings into *A Collection of Writings by Wang Can* which have been passed down to the present. Liu Xie, writer of the monumental work of literary comment *Carving a Dragon at the Core of Literature*, praised Wang Can in glowing terms in the chapter "Talent and Art": "Quick-witted with great talent, Wang Zhongxuan was ready to produce excellent writings which were almost perfect with barely any shortcoming in diction. And his poems and rhapsodies in particular qualified him to be the first of the 'Seven Scholars of the Jian'an Period'." That was indeed an apt comment.

王粲

王粲

Wang Can

Zhong Changtong

仲長統

Towards the end of the Eastern Han Dynasty, a young man in his early twenties came to Bingzhou. Hearing that he was able to make predictions with miraculous accuracy through careful observation of the changing situation, Bingzhou governor Gao Gan became very curious and invited him to his office to consult him about the situation of the country and the future of Bingzhou. The young man made a detailed reply and said very frankly, "You have great ambition but lack the ability for its realization. You are appreciative of the scholars but are not able to choose the right people to serve you. It is necessary for you to be on guard against these shortcomings." Being a conceited person, Gao Gan failed to heed the advice. Before long he started a revolt against Cao Cao with all the troops in Bingzhou, only to be defeated and killed by Cao's troops. So all the officials and scholars of Bingzhou and Jizhou held the young man in admiration for his miraculous predictions.

His name was Zhong Changtong (180–220), and he was from Gaoping of Shanyang (south of the present Juye of Shandong) with the courtesy name Gongli. He was very diligent and was good at poetry and rhapsody. He read widely in the works of various schools of thought and was particularly interested in history. Taking historical experience as a mirror, he followed the political changes closely and was able to make accurate predictions. In his early twenties, he studied around Qingzhou, Xuzhou, Bingzhou and Jizhou, and was admired for his farsightedness wherever he went. With a free and easy character, he would keep on talking with a steady flow when he was in the right mood, but would not utter a single word when he did not feel like it, no matter what others would say. Frank and straightforward, and careless about trifles, he was called "the unrestrained scholar".

Zhong Changtong had his own ideas about life. In his opinion, all officials wanted to have a fame which, however, could not exist forever. One would be much happier to have an easy and free life in the short span of a few decades. On the excuse of illness, he declined many offers of official posts made by local officials. He wrote an article *My Aspirations* and two poems expressing his preference for the life of a hermit and his disdain of official career. The article said: "Playing refined music and singing a wonderful song, I enjoy living an easy and free life away from the overweening of worldly people and matters, and the criticism of contemporaries. If I can always live like this, my spirit will soar up to heaven and even beyond the universe. What's the point of envying the officials who serve the emperors!" This article could be said to have pioneered the hermit literature of the Wei and Jin dynasties.

Hearing of Zhong Changtong's talent and ability, Xun Yu, adviser to Cao Cao and senior official of Emperor Xiandi of the Eastern Han, recommended him to the court as a secretary. Cao Cao was also appreciative of his wisdom and talent and allowed him to devise military strategies in the premier's office.

Zhong Changtong also made spectacular achievement in philosophy. He was against the traditional theory of destiny and fate, and emphasized the importance of subjective efforts, putting forward the idea that "men's endeavours are the fundamental whereas the heavenly will is the incidental". "It is human efforts instead of the will of heaven that make it possible for one to amaze the world with influence and prestige, bring benefit to the people, achieve meritorious deeds, and enjoy everlasting fame."

His ideas were obviously a criticism of the concept of "interaction between heaven and man" in vogue since the Western Han Dynasty, and the superstition combining divination and mystical Confucianist belief prevalent in the Eastern Han Dynasty.

Zhong Changtong lived only to the age of 41. His *Frank and Appropriate Comments* comprising 34 articles and, more than 100,000 words have been lost. Only three articles, *Administering the Troubled Times*, *Gains and Losses*, and *Law and Commandments*, can still be found in *The History of the Later Han Dynasty*.

仲長統
一九九二年二月

Zhong Changtong

Zhuge Liang

諸葛亮

In the 12th year of the Jian'an period of the Eastern Han Dynasty, Liu Bei together with Guan Yu and Zhang Fei paid three visits to a village called Longzhong, 10 kilometres west of Xiangyang, to see a 27-year-old scholar. But not until the third visit did he finally see the young man whom he consulted respectfully for strategies.

The talented scholar made an earnest analysis of the situation, advising Liu Bei to form an alliance with Sun Quan in the east against Cao Cao in the north, and occupy Jingzhou and Yizhou as the bases before making efforts step by step for the ultimate unification of the country. The analysis impressed Liu Bei very much and he made a cordial request for the young man to assist him in the capacity of an adviser. This young genius was none other than the household name Zhuge Liang (181–234), known as "the Sleeping Dragon", and his analysis was the famous *Dialogue at Longzhong*. Later development of events basically followed his predictions, and thus "Three Visits to Zhuge's Thatched House" by Liu Bei became a favourite topic of conversation generation after generation.

Zhuge Liang was from Yangdu of Langya (present Yinan of Shandong) with the courtesy name Kongming. His father Zhuge Gui, who had been magistrate of Taishan, died early, and he lived with his uncle Zhuge Xuan, first in the place ruled by Yuan Shu and then in Jingzhou under the rule of Liu Biao. Before long his uncle died. Zhuge Liang then lived in Longzhong to do farming and reading. He studied with such famous scholars as Xu Shu and Pang Degong, and together they discussed the situation of the country. He made earnest efforts in studying the theories of Confucianism and other schools of thought as well as military strategies and history, and became the head of the hermit scholars in the Jingzhou area. Indeed the 10 years of hermit life in Jingzhou enabled him to become a celebrated scholar and military strategist.

In 208, the allied forces of Sun and Liu defeated the several hundred thousand troops of Cao Cao at Chibi. After that Liu Bei seized Jingzhou as his base, laying the foundation for the tripartite confrontation of the three kingdoms.

Being a good administrator, he made Shu Han a state with the best order among the three kingdoms. Under his administration, the originally backward Ba and Shu in the remote southwest part of China gained considerable development in economy and culture.

Leading his troops in confrontation against the Wei general, Sima Yi, at Wuzhangyuan south of the Wei River in 234, the premier died of illness at 54. Before his death, he recommended to the emperor the official and general as his successors in charge of civil administration and military affairs, which enabled the Shu Han kingdom to survive 30 more years after his death. Following Zhuge's secret plan for withdrawing the troops to Shu, his general Jiang Wei and Yang Yi kept his death a secret, gradually retreating their troops in due order. Leading his men in pursuit of the retreating Shu army, Sima Yi ran into an ambush and had to stop the pursuit out of apprehension. This event was popularly known as "the dead Zhuge frightening away the living Sima", which had Sima Yi himself sighing in admiration that Zhuge Liang was a rare genius.

Zhuge Liang was buried at Dingjun Mountain and was conferred the posthumous title of Marquis Zhongwu. His writings had been compiled by Chen Shou into 24 chapters of more than 100,000 words. His famous pieces *Dialogue at Longzhong* and *The First Memorial for the Northern Expedition* are included in the extant *Collected Writings of Zhuge Liang*. Today, his *Memorial for the Northern Expedition*, copied by the famous patriotic general Yue Fei of the Song Dynasty, can still be seen in the Temple of Marquis Wu built in his honour in Chengdu, which showed the respect and admiration of later generations for this distinguished statesman and military strategist.

诸葛亮
一九九二年五月二十九日

Zhuge Liang

He Yan

During the period of the Three Kingdoms, there was a famous handsome man with fair complexion, fine features and elegant bearing. Whenever he passed the street in his carriage, ladies vied to see "the handsome Mr He", throwing fresh flowers and fruits to him to attract his attention. This young man was He Yan (?–249), grandson of senior general He Jin of the Eastern Han Dynasty, and adopted son of Cao Cao.

He Yan was from Wanxian County of Nanyang (present Nanyang of Henan) with the courtesy name Pingshu. His grandfather He Jin was a senior general and favourite official of Emperor Lingdi of the Eastern Han Dynasty. After the death of Emperor Lingdi, He Jin put Emperor Shaodi on the throne, and together with Yuan Shao, plotted to kill the eunuchs who tried to arrogate power to themselves. Unfortunately, the general was murdered by the eunuchs after his plot was leaked. He Yan's mother, Madame Yin, was a very beautiful woman who was later married to Cao Cao. Out of his love for her, Cao Cao took He Yan as his adopted son.

He Yan was well known as a handsome and versatile youngster with profound learning. With a good mastery of Confucian classics and a strong interest in the Taoist teachings of Laozi and Zhuangzi, he was very popular in the Cao family, and was married to a princess when he grew up. Instead of taking pride in becoming a relative of the royal family, He Yan devoted his time to discuss Confucianist and Taoist teachings with Xiahou Xuan and Wang Bi. Together with them he advocated metaphysical learning, initiating the practice of "pure conversations", that is, discussions on lofty and non-mundane matters.

When Cao Shuang was at the helm of the state in the first year of the Zhengshi period of Wei, He Yan was appointed senior aide and adviser before being gradually promoted senior minister.

In consideration of the declining influence of the Confucian classics, He Yan, together with Wang Bi and Xiahou Xuan, tried to revitalize Confucianism by enriching it with the Taoist teachings of Laozi and Zhuangzi. Thus they initiated metaphysical learning to replace the classical learning of the Confucian scholars of the Han Dynasty.

Wang Bi was from Shanyang of the kingdom of Wei (present Jiaozuo of Henan) with the courtesy name Fusi. He already enjoyed high prestige in his early teens, and for his talent and eloquence and his interest in and mastery of the teachings of Confucianism and Taoism, he was appointed Senior Secretary. Unfortunately, he had a premature death in the prime of his life at 24.

Belonging to the royal family of Cao, He Yan was regarded as a thorn in the flesh by Sima Yi, who later found a pretext and put him to death when he was about 60 years old.

Introducing Taoism into Confucianism, He Yan regarded "non-action" (understood as no unnatural action rather than complete passivity) as the root of the universe, advocating reigning by non-interference. Being one of the major representative figures of the "non-action school", he made considerable contribution to the development of Confucianism. He was also a good writer of poems, rhapsodies, and prose with his representative works being *On the Virtue of Tao*, *On the Conceptless and Nameless*, *On Non-action*, and *Annotations to Analects of Confucius*, etc.

He Yan

Liu Zhen

劉楨

*T*all and straight on hills stand the pines;
Rustling in the dales is the blowing wind.
Loud and forceful the wind is roaring;
Strong and adamant the pines remain.
Cold and harsh are the ice and frost;
Upright and sturdy the pines remain,
How have they survived the rigours of nature?
The reason lies in their natural quality.

The above is one of the three pieces in *To My Cousin* written by Liu Zhen (?–217), one of the "Seven Scholars of the Jian'an Period". With vivid images and natural application of metaphors that took the pines as the symbol of the lofty sentiment of the poet, this representative piece by Liu Zhen is indeed an excellent poem.

Liu Zhen was born in a family of men of letters in Dongping (in present Shandong) with the courtesy name Gonggan. His father Liu Liang was a talented scholar. Under the influence of his family, Liu Zhen grew up to be a famous poet at the end of the Eastern Han Dynasty.

Appreciative of his talent, Cao Cao made him secretary of the premier's office. Cao's two sons, Cao Pi and Cao Zhi, were both poets, who liked the ingenious diction of Liu's poems and often discussed the art of poetry with him. However, the proud and unbending Liu Zhen never went out of his way to please the powerful and influential. Once, Cao Pi held a banquet in honour of scholars. When the drinking was at its height, the host asked his wife Madame Zhen to express thanks to the scholars for their presence. All the guests stood up and bowed to her except Liu Zhen, who remained sitting on the mattress and looked straight at Madame Zhen. This made the guests worried a lot for him. Just as expected, Cao Cao took this slight as showing contempt for the Cao family and threw Liu Zhen into prison. Liu would have been put to death if the officials and scholars had not persuaded Cao Cao to change the death sentence to imprisonment. Liu Zhen was forced to do hard labour to make up for his offence, and was not set free and given an official post until many years later.

Commenting on poetry, Zhong Rong put Liu Zhen's poems in the top grade and said that Liu was only next to Prince Chensi (the title of Cao Zhi) in his achievement in poetry. Cao Pi was also fond of Liu Zhen's poems which he thought had natural grace. He said Liu's best pentasyllabic poems excelled those of contemporary poets. Cao Pi's favourable comment was an apt appraisal of Liu's achievement in pentasyllabic poetry.

In 217, Liu Zhen died in a plague which took the lives of four of the "Seven Scholars of the Jian'an Period", the other three victims being Chen Lin, Ying Yang, and Xu Gan. Among the several dozen poems and rhapsodies written by Liu Zhen, only 15 poems have been passed down to the present.

Liu Zhen

曹植

Cao Zhi

Beans are being boiled over a beanstalk fire,
Raising a plaintive cry in tears from
the pot:
From the selfsame root we've been produced,
Why should you torment me with fire
so hot?

The above well-known poem was chanted by Cao Zhi (192–232) in tears under the threat of his elder brother, Cao Pi, who forced him to compose a poem describing the relationship between the brothers within seven walking steps. The poem roused the brotherly affection in Cao Pi who then pardoned his younger brother. The extraordinary creativeness and imagination of Cao Zhi and his perilous position can be seen from this masterpiece.

Cao Zhi was from Qiao of Pei (present Boxian County of Anhui) with the courtesy name Zijian, being the third son of Cao Cao and brother of Cao Pi. When he was a little older than 10, he was already able to recite poems and rhapsodies for as many as hundreds of thousands of words.

With a strong memory and wide range of knowledge, he wrote as if guided by spirits. Once after reading one of his articles, Cao Cao did not believe his son could write so well and asked, "I suppose this is written for you by somebody else?" Cao Zhi replied, "What I say makes good argument, and what I write good article. Please give me a test if you don't believe me." The chance for the test came when Cao Zhi was 18 years old. In the 15th year of the Jian'an period of the Eastern Han Dynasty (210) when the Tongque Tower was completed in Yedu, Cao Cao asked all his sons to mount the tower and ordered each of them to write a rhapsody. Taking up the pen-brush, Cao Zhi finished the assignment in one go with beautiful diction and profound meaning. His father was very much satisfied with what he had written and the next year made him Marquis of Pingyuan (later changed to Marquis of Linzi).

With distinguished talent and wisdom and a ready pen as well as the assistance of such famous scholars as Yang Xiu and Ding Yi, Cao Zhi enjoyed the trust of his father who had intended to make him his successor, thinking of him above his other sons in political and literary ability. But Cao Zhi turned out to be the loser in the political competition against his brother Cao Pi, who was finally made the successor as their father later changed his opinion about Cao Zhi, thinking that he was "too wilful, lacking in high aspiration, and taking to drink."

Suspicious and jealous of Cao Zhi, Cao Pi killed the entire family of Ding Yi after ascending the throne in 220 with a view to eliminating the capable assistants of his brother.

In grief and misery after years of confinement, suspicion and jealousy, Cao Zhi wrote quite a number of pieces expressing his grievances such as *To Prince Baima*, *Cao Biao*, *A Song of Lament* etc. However, even in extreme sorrow and suffering, he was also concerned with the hardships of the people and the security of the kingdom, aspiring to perform meritorious deeds for the state. Thus he wrote in his *Seeing off Mr Ying*:

What a bleak sight in the countryside:
No signs of human life wherever I cast my eyes.
Recalling the home where I used to reside,
I cannot speak of worries pent up inside.

Besides, his *White Horses* and *the Liangfu Song at Taishan* are also famous pieces which have been passed down to later generations. And his *Rhapsody of the Fairy of Luo* and *Rhapsody of Moving the Capital* are still very popular even today.

Living under the suspicion, jealousy, and persecution of Cao Pi and his son Cao Rui, Cao Zhi spent the latter part of his life in depression and misery and died at the premature age of 40. A prolific author, he wrote 45 rhapsodies, 42 poems, 55 Yuefu songs, as well as other works. Unfortunately most of the 30 volumes of his complete works have been lost.

Cao Zhi

Du Yu

杜預

At the end of the period of the Three Kingdoms, there was a scholarly general in Western Jin who was both learned and good at military strategy. He was in command of the troops at the border menacing the Wu which was under the reign of the Sun family. Being also a distinguished scholar of Confucian classics, he wrote works which were not only popular at the time but have also been read for over a 1,000 years to the present day.

Du Yu (222–284) was from Duling of Jingzhao (southeast of present Xi'an) with the courtesy name Yuankai. He was diligent and intelligent in childhood, and made rapid progress in Confucian classics. Born in the period of the tripartite confrontation of the three kingdoms of Wei, Shu, and Wu which were engaged in constant fighting, Du Yu developed a strong interest in military strategies and had considerable attainments in his studies of books on the art of war. His talent and ability were soon known in the camps of the Sima family and won the appreciation of Sima Yi, who married his daughter to him. Amidst the favour and honour, Du Yu kept on studying tirelessly and made profound research in economics, politics, military strategies, calendar, law, mathematics, engineering, etc., and in most of which he had written works summarizing his research.

In 265, Sima Yan, grandson of Sima Yi, succeeded his father, Sima Zhao, to be Prince Jin and premier of the kingdom of Wei. Before long, he forced the Wei emperor, Cao Huan, to abdicate in his favour and changed the title of the dynasty to Jin. With Sima Yan becoming the emperor (known in history as Emperor Wudi of Jin), Du Yu was promoted from prefect of Henan to Minister of Finance. He also participated in drawing up "The Law of the Jin Dynasty".

After the death of the deputy premier, Yang Hu, in 278 Du Yu was made Senior General, taking over the command of military affairs in the Jingzhou area left over by Yang. He carried on Yang's policy of making the garrison troops open up and cultivate wasteland, accumulating army provisions, and offering special care to scholars. Meanwhile he kept close watch on the situation in the kingdom of Wu, making preparations for its destruction. In 279, Jin launched a large-scale expedition against Wu. General Wang Jun led strong waterborne troops down the Yangtze River from Ba Shu to Wu's capital Jianye. In 280, the emperor of Wu, Sun Hao, surrendered to Jin, putting an end to his kingdom. Du Yu was conferred the title of Marquis for his contribution in the military action against Wu. He was respectfully referred to at the time as "Du the Military Resource" for his astuteness and resourcefulness.

After the unification of the country by Jin, Du Yu started irrigation projects south of the Yangtze River which benefited over 660,000 hectares of public and private land, making an important contribution to the prosperity of the Taikang period at the beginning of the Jin Dynasty. He lived to be 63 years old and was granted the posthumous title of South-Pacifying General.

Du Yu wrote 30 volumes of *Annotations to Spring and Autumn by Zuo Qiuming* which were included in *Annotations to the Thirteen Classics*, being the earliest annotated version of *Spring and Autumn by Zuo Qiuming*. Collections of his other works were unfortunately lost.

Du Yu

Chen Shou

陳壽

The Biography of Emperor Wudi of Wei in the *History of the Three Kingdoms* described Cao Cao as "smart and resourceful in his early youth, but the people did not regard him as an extraordinary talent as he was unconventional and unrestrained, and was not engaged in any particular profession." The author also commented on Cao Cao through the remarks of Qiao Xuan, General Military Director of the Eastern Han Dynasty, in his talk with Cao: "None of the many celebrated people I have seen is like you. Do make efforts and take good care of yourself." and "The country is going to have troubles. Only exceptionally capable people can save it. The responsibility will probably rest on you." It was not easy for the author Chen Shou (233–297) to be true to history in describing Cao Cao as one with distinguished ability, as Chen had been a subject of Cao's enemy state, the kingdom of Shu.

Chen Shou was from Anhan of Baxi (the present Nanchong of Sichuan) with the courtesy name Chengzuo. He was very diligent from childhood, and benefited a lot from the six Confucian classics which he studied under the guidance of a famous scholar of his prefecture, Qiao Zhou. Also an erudite historian, Qiao had written *A Study of Ancient History*. Under his influence, Chen Shou made a lot of efforts in collecting historical data about the kingdom of Shu, and was later appointed State Historian as his teacher Qiao Zhou had been a senior official. Being an upright official, however, Chen Shou would not attach himself to Huang Hao, the trusted eunuch of the emperor, and was demoted because of that.

Some years after Shu was wiped out by Wei in 263, Chen Shou became a subject of the Jin Dynasty. Appreciating his talent and ability, Zhang Hua, the premier of Western Jin, recommended him to be an official. He was later appointed assistant secretary in charge of writing and publication and was sent to be adviser to Marquis Pingyang. He won a good reputation for what he did on the post, and was promoted secretary in charge of book writing. He left his post later following the death of his mother. After several years, he was offered the post of aide to the crown prince, which, however, he did not take.

During the Taikang period of the Western Jin, Chen Shou completed 65 chapters of *History of the Three Kingdoms* on the basis of the data in the *History of Wei*, *An Outline History of Wei*, the *History of Wu* etc. kept among the people and by the government, and the historical material about the kingdom of Shu he had collected. Though he was compiling history by himself without sufficient data, and there were no "Tables" and "Records" in his book, he made a clear, logical and well organized presentation of the confusing historical facts of the tangled conflicts and wars towards the end of the Eastern Han Dynasty and the tripartite confrontation and struggle of the three kingdoms. Admired as a good history book, *History of the Three Kingdoms* and *Records of the Historian* by Sima Qian, *History of the Former Han Dynasty* by Ban Gu, and *History of the Later Han Dynasty* by Fan Ye, have been referred to as "the four history books of Han". Later in the Song Dynasty, Pei Songzhi complemented the book with his *Annotations to History of the Three Kingdoms*, quoting copiously and increasing the historical value of the book.

Chen Shou lived to be 64 years old. Among his other works are 50 chapters *of History of the Ancient States*, 10 chapters *of Biographies of Bygone Figures of Yidu*, and the *Collected Works by Premier Zhuge Liang* compiled by him. These works made comprehensive and reliable records of the history and historical figures of the three kingdoms of Wei, Shu and Wu.

Chen Shou

Lu Ji

陆机

Towards the end of the Three Kingdoms, a 14-year-old lad named Lu Ji (261–303) became a competent general of the last emperor of Wu, Sun Hao, who put him in command of a large army. He was from a distinguished family of the kingdom of Wu. His grandfather, Lu Sun, had been the premier of Wu, and his father Lu Kang had been the General Military Director. He was strongly built and had original views in military strategies and deployment of troops. As a result, he took command of the troops after his father's death. By that time, Emperor Wudi of Jin had already wiped out the kingdom of Shu, and the war between Jin and Wu was inevitable. Just as Lu Ji was training his troops for resistance, the last emperor of Wu surrendered to General Wang Jun of Jin, much to the disappointment of the patriotic young general who had been making painstaking efforts for defending the kingdom.

Lu Ji was from Huating of Wuxian County of Wujun (west of present Songjiang of Shanghai) with the courtesy name Shiheng. He was exceptionally talented in childhood and was adept with both pen and sword. In 274 he became Yamen general of the kingdom of Wu.

After Wu was destroyed by the Western Jin in 280, Lu Ji went back to his hometown, concentrating on his studies for 10 years; during which he wrote two pieces *On the Destruction of Wu* which dwelt on the rise and fall of the kingdom of Wu. In the last year of the Taikang period of the reign of Emperor Wudi of Jin, Lu Ji and his younger brother Lu Yun left their hometown for the Jin capital Luoyang. Seeing them, a senior official of Western Jin, Zhang Hua, said in delight, "Among the major gains from the expedition against Wu are you two talented young men." Zhang Hua recommended the Lu brothers to another senior official, Yang Jun, who appointed Lu as Director of the Imperial College, and later as Senior Aide to the Crown Prince, and Director of Writing and Publication. After Yang Jun was killed by Empress Jia in 291, Lu Ji became one of the "24 friends" of the influential official Jia Mi. When Prince Wu, Sima Yan, took the post of garrison commander of Huainan, Lu Ji was appointed Senior Attaché, and later promoted Senior Secretary, and Palace Secretary.

After Prince Zhao, Sima Lun, killed Empress Jia in 300, Lu Ji was made adviser to the premier with the title of Marquis of Guanzhong for his credit in removing Jia Mi. And when Sima Lun replaced Emperor Hui Di the next year, Lu Ji was made senior secretary. Later, Sima Lun was killed after being defeated by the rebel forces led respectively by Prince Qi, Sima Jiong, Prince Chengdu, Sima Ying, and Prince Hejian, Sima Yong. Lu Ji was arrested as Prince Qi suspected that he had been involved in drafting the proclamation for the usurper of the throne Sima Lun. Thanks to the efforts of Prince Wu and Prince Chengdu, Lu was pardoned from execution and exempted from banishment in an amnesty.

When Prince Chengdu and Prince Hejian rose in an expedition against Prince Changsha, Lu Ji was made Rear General and Commander of Hebei. He led an army of 200,000 in a fierce battle in Luyuan against Prince Changsha. Unfortunately the troops under his subordinate General Meng Chao were annihilated as Meng launched an attack rashly against the order of Lu Ji. As a result, the major forces of Lu Ji also suffered a devastating defeat with the bodies of his dead soldiers piling up and blocking the river. Meng Chao's elder brother, Meng Jiu, was a eunuch and a trusted subordinate of Prince Chengdu, the premier at the time. In collusion with Lu Ji's subordinates, the eunuch falsely accused Lu Ji of harbouring disloyalty. Out of anger, Prince Chengdu put Lu to death. Before the execution, Lu Ji sighed, "Is it possible to hear the cry of cranes at Huating again?" All his soldiers grieved over the tragic death of Lu Ji who was then only 43 years old.

Lu Ji was good at both the pen and the sword. In respect of achievement in poetry and prose, he was juxtaposed in fame with his brother Lu Yun as "The Two Lus" and as "Pan-Lu" with Pan Yue. His prose *In Lamentation of Emperor Wei Wu* admired the peerless hero Cao Cao and expressed his regret that his son Cao Pi failed to carry on his cause. His *Preface to Rhapsody of a Gallant Gentleman* was an allegory directed at Prince Qi, Sima Jiong, written in beautiful diction and parallel sentences, pioneering the parallel style of writing. Among his 104 extant poems, there are some good lyrics such as *On the Way to Luoyang*. Combing the experience of past writers and his own writing practice, his *Rhapsody on Writing* was the first systematic analysis of the conceptions of the writers, holding an important position in the theory of classical Chinese literature.

陆机

一九九一年七月二十九日画于野味

Lu Ji

84

Guo Pu

郭璞

From the southwest comes the breeze;
Up swim the fish with sparkling scales.
A fairy turns to me with a smile charming,
Her jade-like teeth fine and gleaming.
What a pity I can't find a match-maker
To be sent to her to convey my admiration.

The above was one of the 14 poems entitled *The Wandering Immortal* written by the Eastern Jin poet Guo Pu (275–324). In extolling the fairies and immortals, he was actually singing praises of a life of seclusion. Unable to change the social reality which he was unhappy with, he could only seek imaginary pleasure and spiritual sustenance in his poems in the company of fairies and immortals.

Guo Pu was from Wenxi of Hedong (in present Shanxi) with the courtesy name Jingchun. He spent his childhood in the relatively prosperous Taikang period. Diligent and bent on learning, he perused the six Confucian classics and was also well read in other schools of thought, calendar, mathematics, and astronomy. He was good at divination as he was particularly fond of the *Book of Changes*. Learned and versatile, he was a master of verse and prose, and interested in classics and ancient-script writing and characters. The Jin imperial family and senior officials all thought highly of him.

In 291, with Empress Jia arrogating power to herself and the outbreak of the revolt of eight princes, the Huns and the Jie minority seized the chance to rise against the Western Jin, throwing the central part of the country into chaos. In 307, Emperor Huaidi of Western Jin sent Prince Langya, Sima Rui, to Jianye (later called Jiankang) as East Pacifying General in charge of the area around Yangzhou and south of the Yangtze River. Some Han scholar families and common people in central China followed Prince Langya across the Yangtze River to seek refuge from war and upheaval. Guo Pu went south of the river at this time and served as military adviser of Xuancheng prefect Yin Hu. When the prefect was later promoted commander of Shitou, Guo Pu followed him to the new place.

At that time Wang Dao, chief of the general staff of the East Pacifying General, was recruiting talented scholars from the north in his efforts to help Prince Langya with plans and strategies for stabilizing the south. Appreciating Guo's ability, he appointed him as Adviser.

In 316, Liu Cong of the kingdom of Han put an end to the Western Jin after capturing Luoyang. The next year, Wang Dao and the other officials made Sima Rui King of Jin, founding the Eastern Jin Dynasty, and in 318, the king proclaimed himself emperor, known in history as Emperor Yuandi of Jin.

Guo presented a memorial advising the emperor to make efforts to win the trust and confidence of the people, and before long he was promoted senior imperial assistant. In 322, he presented another memorial for amnesty across the state, which was adopted by the emperor. Later, Guo Pu left his post following the death of his mother. He was in mourning for less than a year before General Wang Dun appointed him Adviser and Secretary.

Bearing a grudge against Emperor Yuandi who trusted Liu Huai and Diao Xie in discrimination against the Wangs, Wang Dun, who was cousin of Wang Dao, led his troops into Jiankang in 322 and killed Diao Xie. He then moved his headquarters from Wuchang to Gushu, posing a threat to the imperial court. Guo Pu was killed by Wang Dun at the age of 49 for his frankness in warning the latter that defeat would be inevitable should he start a rebellion. Just as Guo expected, Wang died of illness when his troops were routed by the strong army sent by Emperor Mingdi of Jin.

Guo Pu was a prolific writer. In addition to his works on divination *Cave Woods*, *New Woods*, and the *Rhyme of Divination*, he wrote several hundred thousand words as annotations to *Meanings of Words*, *Three Books of Words*, *Words and Exegetics*, the *Book of Mountains and Seas*, *Biography of King Mu*, *Songs of Chu*, *Rhapsody of Zixu*, and *Rhapsody of Shanglin*. Among the several ten thousand words of poems, rhapsodies, and funeral eulogies written by him, only 22 pieces have been passed down to the present. Other extant works by Guo Pu are two volumes of *Collected Works of Guo Hongnong* (his posthumous title), and annotations to *Meanings of Words* and *the Book of Mountains and Seas*.

Guo Pu

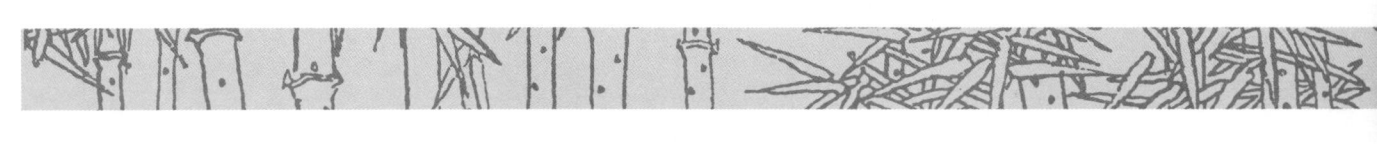

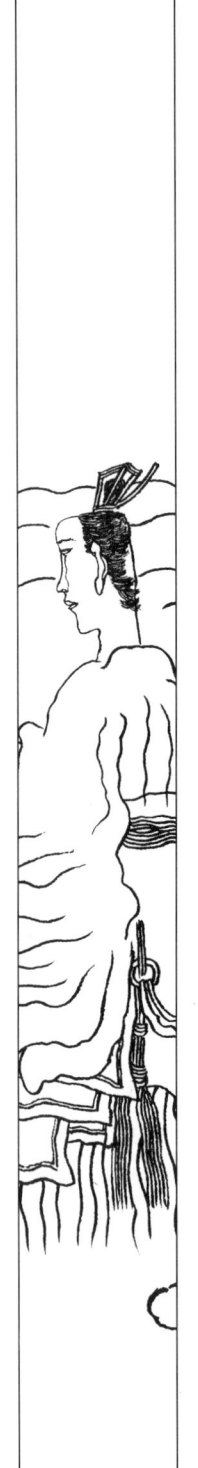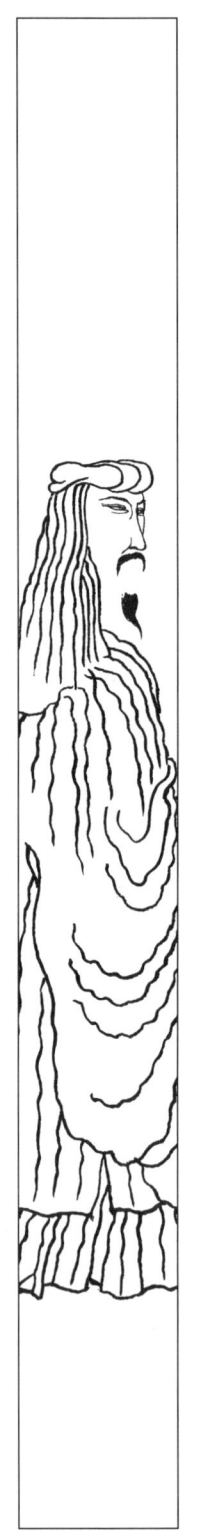

Lady Xuanwen

宣文君

During the Northern and Southern dynasties, the premier of Former Qin, Wang Meng, issued a decree espousing Confucianism as the orthodox learning and banning other schools of thought as heresies. A woman scholar known as Lady Xuanwen (283–?) was invited to the imperial college to lecture on Confucian classics.

Her family name was Song but her personal name and hometown were not known. Born under the reign of Emperor Wudi (Sima Yan) of the Jin Dynasty when the country had just been unified, she spent her carefree childhood in peace and prosperity. The Songs were a family of generations of Confucian academicians engaged in the study of Zhouguan Learning, that is, rites and systems of Zhou, about which she was able to make coherent and cogent arguments in her childhood, thanks to her intelligence and family influence. Her father was so impressed that he taught her all his knowledge.

It was said that the learning of Confucian classics started with Zixia and Xunzi, and became the orthodox ideology of the Han Dynasty after Emperor Wudi proscribed all non-Confucian schools of thought and espoused Confucianism as the orthodox state ideology. Dong Zhongshu originated the school of modern-script Confucian classics by explaining the *Spring and Autumn by Gongyang* in terms of yin and yang and the five elements. With the discovery of ancient-script Confucian classics towards the end of the Western Han Dynasty (for instance the classics found in the walls of the home of Confucius), there arose disputes between the two schools of the ancient-script and modern-script Confucian classics. The modern-script school lost its dominant position during the Eastern Han Dynasty after Zheng Xuan combined the two schools. In the period of the Three Kingdoms and the Jin Dynasty, the school represented by Wang Su waged a struggle against Zheng Xuan's school but it ended in failure.

The Zhouguan Learning which was fairly uncommon specialized in the study of the *Rites of Zhou* which was one of the *Three Rites* (the other two being the *Book of Rites*, and *Ceremonial Rites*). The *Three Rites* and *Spring and Autumn* by *Zuo Qiuming*, *Spring and Autumn by Gongyang*, *Spring and Autumn by Huliang,* the *Book of Changes*, the *Book of History*, the *Book of Songs* were together known as the "Nine Classics".

When Emperor Wudi of Jin died in the first year of the Taiyang period (290), the revolt by the eight princes broke out and it was followed by the turmoil of the 16 kingdoms. The Former Qin was founded in 351, and in 355 its founder died. His son, Fu Sheng, who succeeded to the throne, was a bloodthirsty emperor and was killed and replaced by his cousin, Fu Jian. Thus in more than 60 years the central and northern part of China suffered from wars of various ethnic groups.

How Lady Xuanwen survived the wars was not clear, but she carried on the study of Zhouguan Learning after she was married to a Mr Wei. She did very well in assisting her husband and teaching her children. Her son, Wei Cheng, later became Minister of Rites.

Though of Di nationality, the new sovereign Fu Jian knew very well that he needed the support of the Han people and the scholar-officials for stability in the country. So he espoused Confucianism and established an imperial college. He recruited learned academicians to lecture on Confucian classics in the imperial college, which he would visit once a month to examine the students in person. When he learned that there was no academician of Zhouguan Learning in the college, he sent people across the country and finally found Lady Xuanwen, whom he invited to lecture at the college. Though already above 70 at the time, the lady was still quite healthy, and accepted the royal invitation without hesitation. In great delight, Fu Jian ordered Minister of Rites Wei Cheng to accompany his mother to the college to lecture to more than 120 students. Thus Zhouguan Learning was passed down. That won wide approbation in the Former Qin, and Mrs Wei was admired as Lady Xuanwen generation after generation.

Lady Xuanwen

王羲之

Wang Xizhi

There are many interesting legends about the "Calligraphy Sage" Wang Xizhi (321–379). It was said that he was once in his study practising calligraphy when his page boy brought in his favourite mashed garlic and steamed dumpling. As he did not even cast a glance at the food, the boy had to go to Wang's wife for help. Coming into the study, she found her husband munching away at his dumpling dipped in black ink. Seeing his wife, he began to admire her for the delicious mashed garlic she had prepared. This story about Wang Xizhi "eating ink" showed how he was so absorbed in practising calligraphy as to mistake ink for mashed garlic.

Wang Xizhi was from Linyi of Langya (in present Shandong) with the courtesy name Yishao. He was slow of speech in his childhood, and showed no sign of having any talent. But instead of feeling discouraged, Wang made steady effort in his studies, particularly in calligraphy. Contrary to the expectations of many people, he grew up an eloquent young man without any traces of slow speech.

Honest and upright by nature, he was not particular about ceremony and formality. One day, the General Military Director, Xi Jian, sent his disciple to the home of Wang Xizhi's uncle, Wang Dao, intending to choose a good husband for his daughter from the young men of the Wang family. Wang Dao then told the visitor to take a look at his sons and nephews and make his own choice. Returning from Wang's home, the disciple reported to his master, "The young lords of the Wang family all behaved well and proper except one who kept eating in the eastern bed with bared chest as if he did not know I was there." Xi Jian said, "This young man will make an ideal son-in-law for me." Thus Wang Xizhi became the son-in-law of the Xi family.

Wang Xizhi was a master of calligraphy, especially of the running-script and the cursive-script. He learned from Zhong You's calligraphy, creating a new style of writing in smooth roundish strokes after changing the writing technique prevalent since the Han and Wei dynasties. His *On Yue Yi* and *Huangting Scripture* written in small character regular-script, *Preface to Poems Written at Orchid Pavilion* in running-script, and the well-known 17 cursive-scripts were modelled after by later generations who practised calligraphy.

Wang Xizhi started his official career in his youth as a court secretary. He then served as the Military Attaché and Secretary to General Yu Liang before being promoted to be Ningyuan general and Jiangzhou prefect. Appreciating his talent, the court appointed him to the posts of Senior Imperial Adviser, Minister of Civil Official Administration, etc. But he declined all the offers. It was only under the persuasion of friends that he later took the post of Huguo General. Finally he served as the General of the Right Flank Army, and Minister of Civil Affairs in charge of Kuaiji.

He was fond of quiet life and was reluctant to take official posts in the capital. He had been to Kuaiji and loved the green hills and clear rivers of the place. Together with some good friends, he held a party at the Orchid Pavilion of the Kuaiji Hill where he wrote the famous *Preface to Poems Written at the Orchid Pavilion*. So he was very delighted when he was being transferred to the place, and took great pleasure in exchanging poems and calligraphic works with friends there. Being one of the landscape poets of the Eastern Jin Dynasty, he was also quite good at poetic composition.

Wang Xizhi died at 58. His 10 volumes of collected works have been lost, whereas the calligraphic works he left behind have become national treasures.

Wang Xizhi

Wang Meng

王猛

In 383, Fu Jian, Emperor of the Former Qin, led an army of 900,000 against the Eastern Jin, only to suffer a crushing defeat by the Feishui River. With over 800,000 troops annihilated, the Former Qin was never able to recover after this defeat. Fu Jian was filled with remorse for his failure to follow the deathbed exhortation of Marquis Wu that he should not try to wipe out the Jin Dynasty. The farsighted Marquis Wu was none other than his late premier Wang Meng (325–375).

Wang Meng was from Ju County, Beihai Prefecture of Qingzhou (southeast of present Shouguang of Shandong) with the courtesy name Jingluo. By the time of his birth, Qingzhou had been under the rule of Later Zhao founded by Shi Le, after whose death his son Shi Hong was deprived of power by his nephew Shi Hu. Unable to endure the cruel rule of Shi Hu, his family moved to Weijun Prefecture after drifting from place to place. When only a child, Wang Meng had to sell wicker scoops for a living.

Wang Meng was well-read in Confucian classics and military strategies, and when he was older, he visited the Zhao capital Yecheng. Realizing he was a rare talent, a senior official, Xu Tong, intended to make him his assistant. Wang Meng, however, fled to Huashan Mountain where he stayed in expectation of changes in the political situation. Sure enough, a rebellion broke out after the death of Shi Hu. A senior general, Ran Min, overthrew the Later Zhao and founded the state of Wei which was then wiped out by the state of Yan in less than two years. In 351, the Former Qin was founded in the Guanzhong area and gradually grew strong.

After the death of the first emperor of the Former Qin, the succeeding sovereign Fu Sheng was so cruel as to take pleasure in killing people, and Fu Jian, nephew of the first emperor, was determined to get rid him. Thus he sent for Wang Meng and the two of them were like old friends at their first meeting. With the help of Wang, Fu Jian proclaimed himself Heavenly King of Great Qin after killing Fu Sheng, and appointed Wang Meng vice-minister and magistrate of Shiping.

Once in office, Wang had a treacherous county clerk flogged to death in public, and for that he was framed and escorted to Chang'an. Fu Jian criticized him for being too severe, but Wang argued that strict laws and severe punishment were a must in troubled times. His argument convinced Fu who then said to his officials in appreciation, "Wang Jingluo is indeed the Guan Zhong and Zi Chan of the present day." Before long Wang Meng was promoted to be left minister. The emperor banished or even put to death some of the powerful ministers and court officials who tried to frame Wang and finally succeeded in checking their arrogance and calumniation. In 359, Wang Meng was made premier and magistrate of the capital. He eliminated over 20 corrupt royal relatives and treacherous ministers and established law and order, bringing about security and prosperity to the Former Qin. He enrolled honest and bright people, demoted or removed mediocre officials, and put capable and upright officials like Fu Rong and Liang Chen in important positions.

Under his administration, a new situation appeared in which officials were equal to their posts and the ability of the talents were used to the best advantage. With a view to cultivating more qualified people, he started an imperial college and various local schools to teach Confucian classics. As a result, the advanced culture of the Han nationality was revitalized in the Former Qin. He also did a lot in starting irrigation projects, encouraging farming and sericulture, and promoting the assimilation of different ethnic groups.

From 366 to 376, Wang Meng led the troops fighting across the country and practically unified the north, west, and southwest of the county. But Wang Meng himself fell ill due to overwork, and before his death at the age of 51, he said to Fu Jian, "After my death, remember not to try to wipe out the Jin Dynasty. The nobles of Xianbi and Xiqiang who have surrendered to us are not resigned to their defeat. These enemies of ours who will sooner or later make trouble should be gradually eliminated."

His last words, though brief, had a lot to do with the destiny of the Former Qin. As a result of the failure to follow Wang's last words, Fu Jian not only suffered a devastating defeat by the Feishui River, but was in the end murdered by the treacherous nobles of the Xianbi and Xiqiang nationalities headed by Murong Chui and Yao Chang whom he had put in important positions. Fu Jian's tragedy proved the outstanding foresight of Wang Meng.

王猛
一九九二年二月第二稿

Wang Meng

Tao Yuanming

The scenes described in *The Land of Peach Blossoms* by the great poet Tao Yuanming (365–427) of the Eastern Jin Dynasty have been dwelled upon with great relish for over a thousand years as an ideal haven of peace and happiness away from all worldly troubles. The ideal society described in Tao's article, though Utopian, was of progressive significance at the time.

Tao Yuanming, also known by another name Tao Qian and by his courtesy name Yuanling, was from Chaisang of Xunyang (southwest of present Jiujiang of Jiangxi). His great grandfather Tao Kan had been a senior general of the Jin Dynasty, and his grandfather and father had both been local officials such as magistrate and prefect. But the family's wealth declined by the time of Tao Yuanming, who lived a simple life.

From childhood, Tao worked hard at the classics of Confucianism and Taoism, and had a strong interest in literature and history. Intelligent and learned, all the people in the neighborhood believed he would go far. His ambition could be seen from the following two lines of his:

My soaring ambition goes beyond the seas.
Flapping my wings, I will fly far and high.

At 29, he was made School Inspector of Jiangzhou, but he resigned the post after a short period out of detestation of the corruption of officialdom. When he was 35, he served as a staff member of Jingzhou prefect Huan Xuan for some time before resigning the post again. After that he was appointed Junior Military Adviser but did not stay long either. At 41, he became the magistrate of Pengze. One day an inspector was sent to his county by the prefect and he was unequivocally told to dress up and pay tribute to his superior. Unable to put up with the humiliation, he wrote *The Song for Returning Home* and resigned his post, saying, "How can I bow my dignified head for a few bushels of rice!" Actually Tao Yuanming had taken official posts just to make a living and support his family.

Most of his poems were written after his retirement when he secluded himself for the quiet farm life described in the following lines:
I plant beans at the foot of the Southern Hill,
The weeds are thick and the crops are sparse.
Rising at daybreak, weeding the fields I go,
With the moon shining, I return with my hoe.

The pastoral poems of Tao Yuanming revitalized the circle of poets with their lucidity in expressing true feelings. Actually Tao was not exactly resigned to being in a state of seclusion. Instead, he had the political ambition to "benefit the people" as could be seen from his lines: "A fine man has the country in his mind; My ambition ne'er will get old."

The following lines described his leisurely pastoral life away from the decadent officialdom:
Plucking chrysanthemums at the eastern hedge,
I see the southern hills charming and placid.
The air in the hills is at its best at dusk;
In pairs the flying birds are returning home.

Just before his death at 63, Tao Yuanming wrote three pieces of dirge and a piece of prose called *Self-lamentation*.

After his death, people referred to him as "Mr Jingjie". His writings were compiled in *Collected Works of Tao Yuanming*. He wrote in terse yet elegant language, forming a unique style of his own. His artistic achievement produced considerable influence on poets of later generations such as Li Bai, Du Fu, Gao Shi, Bai Juyi, Wang Wei, Liu Zongyuan, Su Dongpo, and even Huang Zunxian late in the Qing Dynasty.

陶淵明

Tao Yuanming

Fan Ye

In his book *History of the Later Han Dynasty*, Fan Ye (398–445) of Song in the Southern dynasties created some new types of biographies not included in *Records of the Historian* and *History of the Former Han Dynasty*. The most praise-worthy was the creation of *Biographies of Distinguished Women* recording the life-story of various celebrated women including Cai Wenji. Fan Ye thought it was wrong not to include the deeds of eminent women in history books, and his efforts enabled women to occupy some chapters in the annals of history. However, later feudal historians bore a grudge against Fan for including Cai Wenji in his book, simply because Cai had married twice and thus violated the feudal ethics of "serving one husband in the whole life". That showed how far Fan's thinking exceeded that of common scholar-officials.

Fan Ye was from Shunyang (present Xichuan of Henan) with the courtesy name Weizong and another polite name Zhuan. He was the youngest son of Fan Tai, a Senior General of the Jin Dynasty, but was adopted by an uncle, Fan Hongzhi, inheriting the title of fifth-grade Marquis.

Fan Ye was very diligent as a child. He read widely in Confucian classics and history, and was able to write very good articles. Talented and versatile, he was good at official script calligraphy, well versed in music, and proficient in playing the pipa musical instrument.

With a penetrating judgment of the political situation at the end of the Jin Dynasty, he declined to take up the post of chief secretary of his prefecture when it was offered to him. Not until 420, when Liu Yu replaced Emperor Gongdi of Jin and founded the kingdom of Song, did he take up the post of Secretary to the Premier and Senior Assistant before being promoted Chief of the Secretariat. In the midst of a smooth official career,

he lost his father and had to leave his post to observe the mourning period. Later he was appointed in succession Xincai prefect, senior secretary in charge of civil administration, and prefect of Xuancheng, where he accepted many disciples and collected books in relation to the history of the Later Han Dynasty. Modelled on *Records of the Historian* and *History of the Former Han Dynasty*, he began to write *History of the Later Han Dynasty*. Emperor Wendi appreciated the talent and ability of Fan very much and trusted him completely.

Being an enterprising sovereign, Emperor Wendi was good at judging officials before putting them in the right positions. The policies and measures he adopted for economic development ushered in prosperity in the Yuanjia period. Incited by a treacherous official, Kong Xixian, Fan Ye got involved in the conspiracy against Emperor Wendi for putting Prince Pengcheng, Liu Yikang, on the throne. When the rebellious scheme was revealed, Fan Ye was put to death at the age of 47.

The *History of the Later Han Dynasty* written by Fan Ye recorded a period of nearly 200 years from Emperor Guangwu, Liu Xiu, to Emperor Xiandi, Liu Xie. With superb talent, he made a concise but comprehensive record of historical events. Since Fan Ye had only finished *Biographies of Sovereigns* and *Biographies of Distinguished Figures* by the time he was executed, more than 500 years later scholars of the Northern Song Dynasty incorporated the part on *Records* of *Sequel to the History of Han* written by Sima Biao of the Western Jin Dynasty into Fan Ye's book, forming the present version of *History of the Later Han Dynasty* which comprised 120 chapters in 130 volumes including 10 chapters of *Biographies of Sovereigns*, 80 chapters of *Biographies of Distinguished Figures*, and 30 chapters of *Records*.

范
曄

Fan Ye

Bao Zhao

鮑照

The great Song poet Bao Zhao(414–466) during the period of the Southern dynasties has been said to be "endowed with transcendent talent and superb style". In one piece, *The Thorny Way*, he wrote:

I present to you precious wine in golden cups,
A Qin stringed instrument in a painted jade case,
A bed net with colourful feathers and flowers,
And a silk quilt of gorgeous flowery embroidery.
The days of youth are ending with the closing year;
Old age will set in with the coming season bleak.
Pray, refrain from grief and troubled thoughts,
And listen to me singing "the Thorny Way".
Who can still hear music clear and resounding
Of bygone times played on palace pavilions?

Bao Zhao was from Donghai (north of present Lianshui County of Jiangsu) with the courtesy name Mingyuan. Being from a humble family, he made a more determined effort to study hard, and had a good mastery of the Confucian classics and history. He was also able to write excellent poems to express his heartfelt emotions. However, living in the Southern dynasties when influential families held power, it was very difficult for people from humble families to have a successful career. For many years he lived a poor life in strange places with his talent and ability unrecognized by those in power.

Later, Prince Linchuan, Liu Yiqing, read the poems presented by Bao Zhao, and he appreciated them so much that he made Bao Palace Aide, and later promoted him to be Moling Magistrate. During the Yuanjia period of the reign of Emperor Wendi of Song, the Yellow River and the Jishui River were said to have become clear, which was regarded as an extraordinary auspicious sign at the time. Bao Zhao composed the *Eulogy to the Clear Rivers* which was so well written that it became popular among the readers. Emperor Wendi, who loved prose, might have read Bao's *Eulogy*, and promoted him to Senior Assistant in the premier's office. When Prince Linhai, Liu Zixu, was the Garrison Commander in Jingzhou, he appointed Bao Zhao canjun (adviser) and concurrently secretary, hence Bao Zhao was also known as Bao Canjun.

Having lived in poverty and having suffered setbacks, Bao Zhao had a deep understanding of society, and his writings reflected reality far more deeply than that of his contemporaries. Among his excellent poems, the *East Gate Song* reflected the social chaos and the life of refugees; *Song of the Poor and Distressed*, and *Modelled after the Ancients* described the miserable life of the people; his frontier poems *Going Out of Jibei Gate* admired the patriotic spirit of the soldiers who "sacrificed their lives for the country"; *Dongwu Song* described the grief and indignation of the soldiers who "left home young and strong, and got back old and poor". His other famous pieces were *Rhapsody of Wucheng* expressing his emotions, and *A Letter to My Sister* describing the charming landscape. (His sister Bao Linghui was a poetess.)

His poems were of very high artistic value with vivid description, beautiful diction, and elegant and flowing style. His romanticism had a profound influence on the great Tang Dynasty poet Li Bai. Bao was bold in initiating new poetic forms, and wrote a lot of septasyllabic and pentasyllabic quatrains or pentasyllabic poems mixed with septasyllabic lines, making a great contribution to the formation of the modern-style pentasyllabic and septasyllabic poetry of the Tang dynasty.

Misfortune and bad luck seemed to dog him. In 466, Prince Linhai, ended his own life under an imperial edict for getting involved in a conspiracy against the sovereign. Jingzhou was thus thrown into chaos during which Bao Zhao was killed by mutinous soldiers. His writings were included in *A Collection of Bao Canjun*.

Bao Zhao

Zu Chongzhi

As early as the fifth century, a great mathematician, Zu Chongzhi (429–500) of Song during the Southern dynasties, calculated the ratio of the circumference of a circle to its diameter to seven decimal places. That was indeed an extraordinary achievement since only the simplest counting instruments were available at that time. In Europe, the ratio of similar precision was not calculated until the 16th century by a German mathematician and a Dutch mathematician.

Zu Chongzhi, with Wenyuan as his courtesy name, had his ancestral home in Qiu County of Fanyang Prefecture (north of present Laishui County of Hebei). His ancestors were scholar-officials who had moved to the south to get away from wars in the north. Zu Chongzhi received very good education from his family early in childhood and had a good command of the Confucian classics, music, and in particular, natural science. When he was older, he served as assistant in southern Xuzhou, Military Attaché, and later, magistrate of Lou County, Changshui Military Director, etc.

He was very fond of mathematics. On the basis of "cyclotomy" created by Liu Hui, a mathematician of Cao Wei of the Three Kingdoms period, he gradually increased the number of the sides of the inscribed regular polygon and divided the perimeter of each polygon with the diameter of the circle. Since the more sides a polygon has, the closer it is to a circle, "the right ratio" Zu Chongzhi arrived at in this way was somewhere between 3.1415927 and 3.1415926. He also used 22 over 7 for the approximate ratio, and 355 over 113 for the precise ratio which is the best convergent of the ratio. This discovery made by Zu Chongzhi over 1,000 years earlier than the Europeans was a distinguished achievement in the mathematical history of the world.

His *Zhuishu* in six volumes made a systematic summing up of mathematics, and more than 100 years after his death, it was adopted as a textbook of mathematics in the Tang Dynasty.

Zu Chongzhi also made great contribution to astronomy. The intercalation of the calendar used at the time was a bit too large. Inspired by the *Yuanshi Calendar* formulated in 412 by Zhao Fei of the Northern Liang which added 221 leap months every 600 years, Zu Chongzhi formulated a *Daming Calendar* which added 144 leap months to 391 years, with a difference of only 50 seconds from the datum determined in modern times. It was the most precise calendar in the world at the time.

In 462, Zu Chongzhi presented to Emperor Xiaowu a *Memorial for Presenting the Daming Calendar* together with the *Daming Calendar*. Among all the court officials, only the crown prince Luben and General Dai Faxing were against it. They felt "the ancient calendar should be followed though there might be some inaccuracies in it", criticizing Zu for "slandering Heaven and betraying the classics". Though only 33, Zu Chongzhi was not afraid of the powerful and influential. He wrote the famous memorial *Refutations*, rebutting all the fallacies of Dai Faxing on the basis of practical astronomical survey.

The *Daming Calendar* introduced the precession of the equinoxes and improved the way of intercalation. However, not until after the Song and Qi dynasties, was the most accurate calendar at the time formally adopted in 501 during the Southern Liang Dynasty. Zu Chongzhi died at 72 before seeing the adoption of his calendar.

Talented and versatile, Zu Chongzhi designed a water-mill that could both husk rice and mill flour, a vehicle with a wooden figure that always pointed to the south, a speed boat, and other ingenious inventions. He also wrote a novel, *A Strange Story*. With a good mastery of both Confucianism and Taoism, he wrote *An Explanation of the Analects of Confucius*, *An Explanation of the Book of Filial Piety*, *The Meanings of the Book of Changes*, *The Meanings of Laozi*, *The Meanings of Zhuangzi* etc. It is a great pity that most of his writings have been lost except for *Daming Calendar*, *Memorial for Presenting the Daming Calendar*, and the memorial *Refutations*.

祖冲之

Zu Chongzhi

102

Fan Zhen

范缜

A firm believer of Buddhism, Xiao Ziliang, premier of Qi of the Southern Dynasties, invited many people to a grand forum on Buddhism in the Jilong Hill of Jiankang. Among the guests present, Fan Zhen (450–515) was the only one arguing against the existence of Buddha as well as samsara and retribution. In reply to the premier's questioning on why some people were noble and rich while others were humble and poor if there were no retribution and samsara, Fan Zhen said: "People are born like the blossoms of a tree being scattered by the wind. Some fall on a green mattress enjoying fortune and position like your highness, while some fall on a dirty toilet suffering from poverty and humiliation like me. It has nothing to do with samsara and retribution though some are rich and noble while others are poor and humble." This argument reduced the premier to silence.

Fan Zhen was from Wuyin of Nanxiang (northwest of present Biyang of Henan) with the courtesy name Zizhen. Born into a humble family, he studied even harder. At 18, he went to Xiang County of Pei Prefecture to study under the guidance of Liu Xian, and in a few years became a well-known scholar with a good mastery of Confucian classics especially *The Three Rites* (i.e. the *Rites of Zhou*, the *Rites of Ceremony*, and the *Book of Rites*). Nevertheless, he did not get any official post at the time because of his bluntness in expressing extraordinary ideas in defiance of the powerful and influential, and because of the rigid system of Song during the Southern dynasties of choosing officials according to family status. Not until after the replacement of Song by Qi founded by Xiao Daocheng in 479 was Fan Zhen appointed chief secretary of Ningman County. Later he was promoted to Senior Court Assistant. For his erudition and eloquence, he was sent as envoy to Northern Wei in the Yongming period of the reign of Emperor Wudi of Qi.

After reading many books on atheism written since the Wei and Jin dynasties, he did further studies. To contradict the teachings of Buddhism that the soul would never perish, he wrote an article *On the Extinction of the Soul* which caused excitement among scholars and shocked the Buddhists. In 489, Premier Xiao Ziliang called eminent monks and scholars to his place in Jiankang to criticize heresies. Fan refuted all their arguments, pointing out that "extinction of the soul" meant the perishing of the soul with the death of the body. Dumbfounded, the premier then tried to induce Fan to give up his theory with the promise of the position of a senior secretary in court. Fan Zhen said laughing, "If I had intended to earn an official position at the cost of my belief, I should have long been made a senior minister instead of the position you just offered."

Fan Zhen was against Buddhism not only in theory but in practice. When he was Yidu magistrate beginning from 494, he issued an order to dismantle Buddhist temples and ban Buddhism in the area under his administration.

After the Marquis of Donghun, Xiao Baojuan, ascended the throne in 499, civil strife broke out in the country as a result of the cruelty of the new emperor. At the time, Fan Zhen had resigned his post and was observing the mourning period at home following the death of his mother. He followed the Yongzhou prefect, Xiao Yan, in his eastern expedition when the latter rose against Qi in 501. The next year Xiao Yan claimed the throne and founded the Liang Dynasty. Fan Zhen was appointed Jin'an prefect, and two years later, was promoted to be Vice-Minister. Not long after, however, he offended the emperor and was banished to Guangzhou.

He was called back in 507 as senior secretary of the court. By that time, Emperor Wudi of Liang had declared Buddhism to be the state religion. He issued an imperial edict, *In reply to On the Extinction of the Soul,* in a bid to force Fan Zhen into giving up his theory. Fan gave tit for tat and rewrote his paper in the form of questions and answers. He argued that the relationship between the spirit and the physical body was like that between the sharpness and the edge of a sword. The sharpness could not exist without the edge, neither could the spirit exist after the death of the physical body.

With a view to overwhelming Fan Zhen, Emperor Wudi of Liang gathered more than 60 princes, noblemen, senior officials, and eminent monks to refute his *On the Extinction of the Soul*. Though already old, Fan was as adamant and awe-inspiring as ever. He had a heated debate with all the monks and others. He wrote another article *In Reply to the Criticism of On the Extinction of the Soul*, to further elaborate his theory.

In 513, Fan Zhen was transferred to be Academician of the Imperial College, and two years later he died.

Fan Zhen

Xie Tiao

謝朓

*F*resh lotus blooms sway for fish swimming;
Lingering blossoms fall for birds
scattering.
Sunset clouds like coloured brocade
are glowing;
A river clear and calm like white silk
is flowing.

These lines written by Xie Tiao (464–499), a great poet of Qi of the Southern dynasties, still overwhelm the reader with their vivid and refreshing style. No wonder Emperor Wudi of Liang, Xiao Yan, said, "I feel my mouth stinking if I spend three days without reading Xie Tiao's poems."

Xie Tiao was from a noble family in Yangxia of Chen Prefecture (present Taikang of Henan) with the courtesy name Xuanhui. His grandfather, Xie Shu, had been prefect of Wuxing, his father had been senior imperial attaché, and his mother was Princess Changcheng of Song of the Southern dynasties.

An erudite and versatile young man, Xie Tiao was good at writing verse and prose as well as cursive-script and official-script calligraphy. He became an official at only 19, serving as assistant to Prince Jingling, Xiao Ziliang, and Prince Sui, Xiao Zilong. In the Yongming period of the reign of Emperor Wudi of Qi, he was Military Attaché of Prince Yuzhang, then Senior Aide to the Crown Prince, Literary Scholar of Prince Sui, Secretary to Prince Xin'an, Senior Member of the Cabinet.

Prince Jingling, a lover of literature, often invited Xie Tiao, Shen Yue, Wang Rong, Ren Fang, Lu Chui, Fan Yun, Xiao Chen, and Xiao Yan to his place, exchanging poems over wine. They were referred to as "Eight Friends of Prince Jingling" of whom Ren and Lu were good at prose and the other six were poets headed by Xie Tiao.

On the basis of the characteristics of the four tones of ancient Chinese pronunciation (the level tone, the rising tone, the falling tone and the entering tone), Shen Yue put forward the theory that "eight faults" were to be guarded against in poem composition. The poems written by Xie Tiao according to this theory were praised as "The Yongming Style". The works of Xie Tiao and Shen Yue led to the development of the regulated form, which finally became a new distinctive genre in the Tang Dynasty (otherwise known as "the modern style"). Xie Tiao was also referred to as Xie the Junior as he was kin to an earlier poet, Xie Lingyun of Song in the Southern dynasties who was known as Xie the Senior.

Xie Tiao served as Xiao Luan's adviser and secretary when the latter was a marshal. After Xiao ascended the throne, Xie was made Assistant Minister, Prefect of Xuancheng, and Prefect of Nanhai. In 497, Xie Tiao was promoted to be Vice-Minister of Civil Administration for his merit in informing against his father-in-law's rebellious scheme. But when Marquis Donghun took the throne, Xie Tiao was put to death at only 36 on a false charge by Prince Shi'an for his refusal to follow the prince in his conspiracy against the sovereign.

The two greatest Tang Dynasty poets, Li Bai and Du Fu, both thought highly of his poems. Du Fu once said, "Every poem by Xie Tiao is worth chanting and savouring." And Li Bai wrote in a poem to another man of letters, "Your verse and prose are contrived like those of the Jian'an period; And mine is after the style of Xie the Junior, clear and spirited." And once on top of the Luoyan peak of Jiuhua Mountain, Li Bai even said, "On such a high mountain the air must have come from heaven. How I wish to have brought a poem of Xie Tiao to discuss with the blue heaven." These suffice to show the high appreciation by Li Bai and Du Fu of Xie Tiao's poems.

Most of the 12 volumes of Xie's writings were lost. Passed down to the present were five volumes of *Collected writings of Xie Xuancheng* compiled in the Ming Dynasty.

Xie Tiao

106

Li Daoyuan

麗道元

During the reign of Emperor Wudi of the Han Dynasty, Kong Anguo, master of ancient-script Confucian classics, taught ancient-script *Book of History*, and his teachings were passed down after several generations to Tu Hui towards the end of the Western Han. Tu in turn taught his disciple Sang Qin who wrote the *Book of Rivers* in which he listed 137 large and small rivers of the country and expanded to a very large extent the chapter "Yugong" in the *Book of History*. This was a great contribution to geography by the master of ancient-script classics. The *Book of Rivers*, however, was oversimplified. And the inadequacy was not made up until the Northern Wei over 400 years later when Li Daoyuan (466–527) wrote *Annotations to the Book of Rivers*, leaving to later generations a great geographical work of ancient China.

Li Daoyuan was from Fanyang of Northern Wei (present Zhuoxian County of Hebei) with the courtesy name Shanchang. His father had been a general and Qingzhou prefect. As a child, he was diligent and eager to learn. The beautiful mountains and rivers and places of historical interest which he visited when he followed his father to Shandong in his early teens aroused his special interest in geography. He was fond of remarkable books, particularly works among the Confucian classics related to geography, and had a good command of the *Book of Mountains and Seas*, the chapter "Yugong" of the *Book of History*, the chapter "Zhifang" of the *Rites of Zhou*, the volume of "Geography" of the *History of the Former Han Dynasty*, the *Book of Rivers* etc.

During the reign of Emperor Xuanwu of Wei, he served at different local posts as assistant prefect of Jizhou, prefect of Luyang, prefect of East Jingzhou, and prefect of Henan, going around large areas in Shanxi, Hebei, Henan and other places. Wherever he was, the first thing he did was to investigate conditions of rivers and the overall geographical environment.

He was well known for his firm and rigorous administration. At the post of supervising censor in the third year of the Xiaochang period of the reign of Emperor Xiaoming (527), Li Daoyuan arrested Prince Runan's subordinate official Qiu Nian for his secret manipulation of the choice of prefect candidates. Prince Runan then went to Empress Dowager Wei pleading for mercy and leniency on behalf of his subordinate. In spite of that, Li Daoyuan not only had the criminal executed but also impeached the prince. His awe-inspiring righteousness towards members of the royal family shocked the imperial court.

In the same year, the rebellious scheme of Yongzhou prefect Xiao Baoyin was revealed. Harbouring the evil intention to have Li killed by the rebels, Prince Chengyang took advantage of the chance and instigated the court to send Li as representative to the Guanyou area for settlement of the rebellion on the grounds that Li had been the advocate of changing the border military districts to prefectures. Fearing that Li Daoyuan would do harm to him, the rebellious general Xiao sent troops and had him surrounded in a post station on a hill. Li Daoyuan and his brother and two sons were killed by the rebels in the end.

When making annotations to the *Book of Rivers*, Li Daoyuan added 1,252 rivers on the basis of the 137 in the original book. The 40-volume *Annotations to the Book of Rivers* comprised about 300,000 characters, 20 times the size of the *Book of Rivers*. With the rivers as the key link, he made detailed descriptions and comments on the customs, places of historical interest, terrain and mineral resources, irrigation projects, the rise and fall of towns and cities, the changes of the names and courses of the rivers, as well as historical figures and events, legends and fairy tales, etc. related to the regions along the courses of the rivers. As a book of high historical and scientific value, the annotations were fairly rich in such data as of hydrology, climate, soil, and vegetation, many of which were first-hand material collected by himself after trudging along rivers and mountains. Written in beautiful diction, the book is not only a collection of travelogues but has also been held in esteem for its high literary value by generations of men of letters.

Li Daoyuan

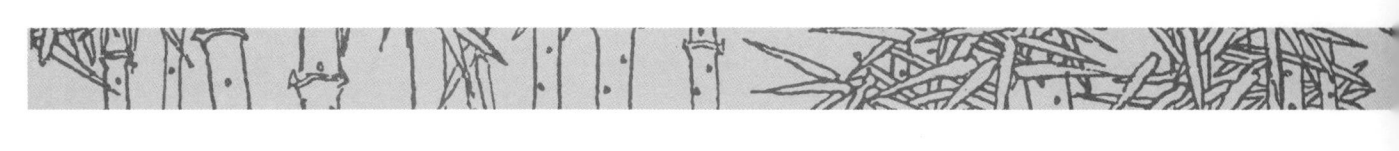

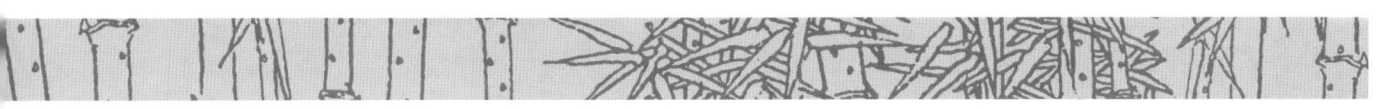

庾信

Yu Xin

The Northern Zhou poet Yu Xin (513–581) died in the first year of the Sui Dynasty. Even Emperor Wendi of Sui who had just ascended the throne expressed heartfelt lamentation over the death of the poet of the preceding dynasty. In addition to confirming Yu's official position in the Northern Zhou Dynasty, the new emperor conferred on him the posthumous titles of Jingzhou prefect and Yongzhou prefect. That was enough to show the prestige Yu Xin enjoyed in the Northern dynasties.

Yu Xin was from Xinye of Nanyang (in present Henan) with the courtesy name Zishan and the pet name Lancheng. His father Yu Jianwu was a well-known court poet. Intelligent and elegant, Yu Xin was well-read in his childhood and was particularly conversant with *Spring and Autumn by Zuo Qiuming*. At 15, he became the reading companion of the Zhaoming crown prince, Xiao Tong, of the Liang Dynasty, and at 19, he was appointed Drafting Scholar.

He had served in the courts of the Liang Dynasty and its successor, the Western Wei.

As a famous scholar from south of the Yangtze River, Yu Xin was held in esteem by Yuwen Tai, the real power holder of the Western Wei who not only returned to Yu all his family members who had been captured, but made him Senior General and Minister. When Northern Zhou replaced Western Wei in 557, Yu Xin was conferred the title of Viscount with a fief of 500 households. In the Northern Zhou of the Yuwen family, he served at various senior posts with repeated promotions up to the position of marshal with the title of Marquis.

Nevertheless, he always cherished the memory of his homeland of the Han nationality south of the Yangtze River. His poetic compositions can be divided into two periods with the year 553 when he was stranded in Chang'an at 41 as the line of demarcation. The poems written in the first period were mostly in the court style, gorgeous but smacking of flashiness and without much significance. The poems of the second period expressed his painful nostalgia and his deep regret and grief over the downfall of his home country. Like a mirror of the times, these poems reflected the historical scenes showing how the Liang Dynasty was destroyed step by step. A good example was *Farewell Again to Minister Zhou* which was gloomy but forceful with profound meaning:

> *The broad road extends far, far away,*
> *But no one is seen back on his way.*
> *Only the geese by the river staying*
> *Will fly southward with autumn coming.*

No wonder the great Tang Dynasty poet Du Fu praised him in the following lines:

Mature were Yu Xin's writings when he was old
With ease and force he wrote in pen-brush bold.
Depressed and gloomy in old age Yu Xin
> *was living,*
But his verse and prose were forceful and
> *touching.*

To some extent, the realistic poetry of Du Fu inherited the style of the poems and rhythmic prose written by Yu Xin in his later years.

Yu Xin resigned his post due to illness before he died at 67. Passed down to the present were 16 volumes of *Collected Works of Yu Zishan*.

Yu Xin

Yan Zhitui

In his rhapsody *My Life*, Yang Zhitui (531–590) regarded himself as one who had suffered from the calamity of national destruction three times. Because of that, he was familiar with the politics, customs, and learning of the Northern and Southern dynasties. Eager to learn and diligent in thinking and study, he had his own particular understanding of various kinds of knowledge. It was on this basis that he wrote the famous *Instructions to the Yan Family* which was read and studied for over 1,000 years.

Yan Zhitui was from Linyi (in present Shandong) with the courtesy name Jie or Jienan. He was born in a family of Confucian scholars engaged in the study of the *Rites of Zhou* and *Spring and Autumn by Zuo Qiuming*. His father Yan Xie had been secretary of Xiao Yi, Prince Xiangdong, of the Southern Liang Dynasty. He read widely and had a good command of classics, history, and practical subjects. Particularly good at writing, he was appointed regular aide to Prince Xiangdong when he was very young, and later promoted to be military attaché. When Xiao Yi sent his son, Xiao Fangzhu, to be garrison commander of Yingzhou, Yan Zhitui was appointed his military attaché and secretary.

In 552, Xiao Yi took the throne himself, and 22-year-old Yan Zhitui was promoted Deputy Imperial Adviser. Only two years later, Jiangling was captured by Western Wei, and Xiao Yi was put to death after surrendering to the invading army. Yan Zhitui was sent to Li Yuan to be secretary by Li's brother, Li Mu, Senior General of Western Wei who thought highly of him. Reluctant to serve the enemy of his country, Yan and his family crossed the rising Yellow River at the risk of their lives and went over to the Northern Qi. The Qi emperor treasured his learning and character very much and immediately made him Senior Imperial Aide. Later he was promoted Military Adviser, Senior Minister, and Imperial Adviser. However, the Northern Qi was destroyed by the Northern Zhou in 577, and for a second time Yan Zhitui experienced the loss of his country. As he was an erudite scholar from the south, Emperor Wudi respected him and made him supervising censor of the Northern Zhou. In a few years, emperor Wendi of Sui overthrew the Northern Zhou in 581, and eight years later Yan Zhitui was recruited by the crown prince, Yang Yong, as imperial scholar. But he felt it was shameful to serve different dynasties. In his rhapsody *My Life* he said that he would not have been put in the awkward position of serving different dynasties if he had been resigned to the position of a common scholar without taking any official post.

Yan Zhitui was learned and conversant with history and capable of writing excellent verse and prose. Particularly praiseworthy were his 20 volumes of *Instructions to the Yan Family* which dealt with moral cultivation and household management. A good example was in the chapter "Cultivation of Children" which described an official of the Northern Qi who once told others: "I have a 17-year-old son who is not only good at writing documents and memorials but also very quick at learning Xianbi language and playing pipa (The imperial rulers of Northern Qi were strong champions of the culture of the Xianbi minority and liked pipa and other musical instruments). I am sure he will win the favour of the nobles and senior officials if he serves them with his talent." Just a few words brought out the servile attitude of the official who was so shamelessly eager to serve a foreign nationality. And some parts in the chapter "Household Management" revealing and criticizing mercenary marriage were also of positive significance.

Yan Zhitui died at about 61. In addition to *Instructions to the Yan Family*, he had 30 volumes of collected works, three volumes of *Wronged Souls*, and 20 volumes of *Records of Spirits*, the last two works being about the mysterious and the supernatural. Simple, easy, and touching, his writings had considerable influence on later generations.

顏之推

Yan Zhitui

Xue Daoheng

薛道衡

The Yuefu poems by Xue Daoheng (540–609), supervisor of officials of the Sui Dynasty, enjoyed high popularity at that time for their freshness and beauty. His typical poem *Night Tune*, describing a young wife feeling the absence of her husband who had been sent on an expedition, was especially touching for its natural blending of feeling and setting. The most famous line "Mud in the swallow's nest fell from the lonely beam" has been very popular among readers.

As such, Xue Daoheng incurred the jealousy and hatred of the despotic emperor Yangdi of Sui who thought highly of his own literary ability. In the fifth year of the Daye period of Sui, Xue was put to death for a political offence against the emperor. Before the execution, Emperor Yangdi went so far as to say, "I'll see whether he can still write 'Mud in the swallow's nest fell from the lonely beam'", fully revealing his ugly jealousy. The tyrant did not survive long; he was hanged by rebel soldiers only nine years later in 618.

Xue Daoheng was from Fenyin of Hedong (present Wanrong of Shanxi) with the courtesy name Xuanqing. His grandfather, Xue Cong, had been Qizhou prefect of the Northern Wei, and his father, Xue Xiaotong, who had been magistrate of Changshan, died when he was only six. The misfortune of the family made him mature earlier. Xue Daoheng became an official in Northern Qi when he was very young, taking the post of Military Attaché of Pengcheng before being promoted to be Chief Secretary of the Military Director-General. After the Northern Qi was replaced by the Northern Zhou, Xue was appointed a supervising censor and later promoted a senior supervisor.

With the destruction of the Northern Zhou by Sui, Xue Daoheng was put in an important position by Emperor Wendi, taking charge of civil official administration in the Huainan area which was then under Prince Jin, Yang Guang. With outstanding insight in political and military affairs, he analyzed the four major reasons that would guarantee the victory of Sui over Chen if the former would launch an expedition against the latter. His analysis even won the admiration of Gao Jiong who was then in control of the state affairs in the Sui court. After the destruction of Chen, Xue Daoheng was appointed Vice-Minister of Civil Official Administration, and later Vice-Premier.

Very satisfied with Xue's writing, Emperor Wendi put him in charge of all important confidential matters and documents. At the time, the crown prince, the other princes, and the court officials were all eager to associate with him. After serving in the central administration for many years, he was transferred to the post of governor of Xiangzhou.

When Yang Guang took power (known in history as Emperor Yangdi of Sui), Xue Daoheng was transferred to be Bozhou prefect. A year later, Xue presented a memorial requesting for retirement. Wishing to keep him in office, the new emperor had intended to appoint him chief secretary in charge of documents and archives, but later changed his mind and made Xue supervisor of officials in the capital as he was unhappy with the article *Eulogy to Emperor Wendi* which Xue wrote on his way back to the capital in praise of the preceding emperor. In 607, Emperor Yangdi had the important official Gao Jiong killed for his criticism of the emperor's life of luxury and dissipation, which grieved Xue Daoheng. In 609 when the court officials were unable to make a decision about a new decree after prolonged discussions, Xue said, "The decree would have long been put into practice if Gao Jiong were still alive." That enraged the emperor, who ordered to put the 70-year-old Xue to death.

As the most outstanding scholar of the Sui Dynasty, Xue Daoheng wrote most of the court documents. His *Longing for Returning Home* was quite close to the pentasyllabic quatrains of the Tang Dynasty in tone and rhyme, showing Xue's contribution to the development of the form of poetry:

> *Seven days only have passed into spring,*
> *But it's my second year away from home.*
> *My return has lagged behind the returning geese,*
> *How I wish to start before flowers blooming.*

Most of his works in 70 volumes were lost.

Xue Daoheng

Kong Yingda

孔穎達

In the Daye period of the Sui Dynasty, Emperor Yangdi called all the scholar officials to Luoyang to discuss Confucian classics. A talented and eloquent scholar in his early thirties surprised all those present with his erudition and argument, and was elected as the best scholar in Confucian classics. A few old scholars who had long established their authority regarded it as a shame to be listed behind such a young man. They even plotted to have him murdered. Kong Yingda (574–648) had a narrow escape, running into the home of Yang Xuangan, Duke of Chu and minister of rites.

Kong Yingda was from Hengshui of Jizhou (in present Hebei) with the courtesy name Chongyuan. He started schooling at eight and after a few years of study, became a well-known scholar with a good mastery of the Confucian classics and the ability to write excellent articles. Not satisfied with his progress, he went on to study under the guidance of Liu Chao, a famous Confucian scholar at that time. Liu was a master of *Mao Poems* and *The Three Rites*, and had written *Explanations of the Five Classics*. Also good at astronomy, he had formulated the *Standard Calendar*. He took great care in teaching young Kong, his favourite student, and made him a celebrated Confucian scholar. After being recommended as Scholar of Classics in 605, Kong was granted the title of Academician of Henei Prefecture and later was made associate lecturer of the imperial college.

To get away from the frequent wars at the end of the Sui Dynasty, Kong Yingda retired to Hulao living as a hermit. Not until the founding of the Tang Dynasty did he become a scholar of the Literary Academy at the invitation of Prince Qin, Li Shimin, being one of Li's "Eighteen Scholars".

When Li Shimin took the throne in 627 (known in history as Emperor Taizong of Tang), Kong Yinda was promoted to be observer of state policies and granted the title of Baron of Qufu. Later he served as Deputy Director of the Imperial College, Right Adviser of the Crown Prince, Director of the Imperial College, etc. Emperor Taizong held this great Confucian scholar in esteem and entrusted him with the compilation of the *History of Sui* together with Wei Zheng. Among the numerous tasks yet to be undertaken at the beginning of the Tang Dynasty, cultivation of qualified personnel was especially imperative.

Acting on the instructions of the Emperor, Kong Yingda presided over the compilation of *Authentic Meanings of the Five Classics*, blazing a new trail and forming a new "Yishu School of Tang" in the study of Confucian classics by combining the ideas and merits of the Northern Classics School, which was profound but jumbled and with references to divination, and the Southern Classics School, which was terse but with a metaphysical approach. Emperor Taizong appreciated the book very much and took it as the criterion for the imperial examinations in the Tang Dynasty. Kong Yingda was later given a higher title of Viscount and his portrait was put among those of the meritorious officials and generals revered in the Lingyan Pavilion

Kong Yingda lived to be 75 years old. His works in 180 volumes on the *Authentic Meanings of the Five Classics* were passed down to the present day.

Kong Yingda

Fang Xuanling

房玄齡

In the 22nd year of the Zhenguan period of the Tang Dynasty, the most outstanding sovereign in Chinese history, Emperor Taizong of Tang, paid a personal visit to his sick premier Fang Xuanling (579–648) and could not help shedding tears before the patient. Sometime later, the emperor paid another visit, bidding farewell to the dying premier. The treatment which Fang received from the emperor showed his extraordinary contributions to the dynasty and the profound friendship between monarch and subject.

Fang Xuanling's name was Fang Qiao, and his ancestral home was in Linzi of Qizhou (east of present Linzi of Shandong). His great grandfather and grandfather had been officials in the Northern Wei and Northern Qi, and his father Fang Yanqian had been a local official in the Northern Qi and later in the Sui Dynasty. Under the influence of his family, he was well read and very knowledgeable, and had a good mastery of Confucian classics. What was more, he had keen political insight and foresaw the downfall of the Sui Dynasty.

In 617, Li Yuan rose against the Sui Dynasty and sent his son, Li Shimin, to attack the Weibei area. Hearing the news, Fang Xuanling who was then magistrate of Xicheng of Sui, resigned his post and walked 400 kilometres to Li Shimin's camp. With the strong recommendation of Wen Yanbo, a well-known man of letters serving in Li's army who had heard a lot about Fang's talent and learning, Li Shimin put him in an important position and let him devise military stratagems. Fang Xuanling then united many officials and generals for the service of Li Shimin. One such example was the military attaché Du Ruhui who was at the time about to be transferred to another unit under Li Yuan. Fang Xuanling advised Li Shimin against the decision, pointing out that Du was a man of extraordinary ability capable of playing an important role in pacifying the country. Li took his advice and Du Ruhui later did become Li Shimin's right-hand man.

When Li Yuan claimed the throne and founded the Tang Dynasty in the fifth month of 618, Li Shimin was conferred the title of Prince Qin, and Fang Xuanling was promoted to be secretary to Prince Qin and granted the title of Marquis of Linzi.

Fang advised Li Shimin to stage a coup on the fourth day of the sixth lunar month of 626. The famous "Coup at the Xuanwu Gate" ended with the killing of the crown prince, Li Tiancheng, and the fourth prince, Li Yuanji. Before long, Li Yuan abdicated in favour of Li Shimin who was known in history as Emperor Taizong of Tang. For his first-class merit, Fang Xuanling was conferred the title of Duke of Xing. After being appointed premier, he worked even harder day and night. Emperor Taizong had full confidence in him, entrusting him with the appointment officials. He and Du Ruhui cooperated very well.

Fang was not only the right-hand man of Emperor Taizong, but also a loyal remonstrator who was bold in making criticisms and proposals. He warned the emperor not to dote on his children too much so as to consolidate the foundation of the dynasty. When Emperor Taizong was planning another expedition against Korea in 648, Fang presented a memorial pleading against the decision in spite of his serious illness, in consideration of the fact that the Tang Empire had suffered heavy losses in the war launched against Korea from 642 to 648 which increased the burden of the people. Deeply moved, the emperor gave up the plan.

Together with the eminent minister Wei Zheng, Fang took charge of the compilation of the histories of the preceding six dynasties. He treated Wei Zheng as his equal, though he was the number one of the 18 renowned scholars of the Tang Dynasty. In a short period of six or seven years up to 636, they completed the *History of Zhou*, the *History of Northern Qi*, the *History of Liang*, the *History of Chen*, and the *History of Sui;* all of which bore the names of Fang Xuanling and Wei Zheng as co-compilers, winning the praise of Emperor Taizong.

Fang Xuanling died of illness in 648 at the age of 70.

Fang Xuanling

Wang Bo

王勃

Among the "Four Talents of the Early Tang", Wang Bo (649–676), Yang Jiong, Luo Binwang, and Lu Zhaolin, the first three were all child prodigies who were able to write good verse and prose before they were 10. At the same time, there were "Three Precious Trees of the Wang family", Wang Mian, Wang Ju, and Wang Bo, all with superb talent and a ready pen. Among the three Wang brothers, the most celebrated was the youngest, Wang Bo, who was the leading poet in the early Tang period.

Wang Bo was from Longmen of Jiangzhou (present Hejin of Shanxi) with the courtesy name Zi'an. His grandfather Wang Tong had been an official in Shu Prefecture in the Sui Dynasty during the reign of Emperor Wendi. Wang Bo's father Wang Fuzhi was an official of the Tang Dynasty.

At six, Wang Bo was already able to write good verse and prose, and at nine, he wrote an article enumerating the mistakes and inaccuracies in the annotations to the *History of the Former Han Dynasty* made by Yan Shigu, a famous scholar at the beginning of the Tang Dynasty. In the first year of the Linde period of the reign of Emperor Gaozong (664), when an important official, Liu Xiangdao, made an inspection tour to the Guannei area, 16-year-old Wang Bo presented a memorial to him. Liu appreciated it very much and recommended him to the emperor. After a court interview, Wang Bo was made a junior official before being transferred to be editor in the staff of Prince Pei. At that time, cockfighting was very popular among the princes, and Wang Bo wrote for Prince Pei a *War Proclamation against the Cock of Prince Ying* just for fun. Emperor Gaozong was very angry at Wang's frivolity in writing such an article and removed him from office.

Wang Bo completed five volumes of *Elaboration of the Book of Changes*. He also wrote a preface to the *Book of Songs* and such works as *On the Analects of Confucius* in his study of Confucian theory.

Later Wang Bo was appointed Military Assistant of Guozhou Prefecture. His colleagues were jealous of him and complained about his airs as a talented scholar. Very unhappy about his own low official position, he made matters worse after committing a capital offence. Though exempted under an amnesty, he was removed from office and even his father was banished to be magistrate of what is part of the present Vietnam. Wang Bo fell into the sea on his way to visit his father by boat. Though rescued at that moment, he died soon of shock at the age of only 28.

In poetic composition, he did his best to get rid of the influence of the style of Qi and Liang dynasties and broadened the subjects of poetry. His special achievement was in the application of tones and rhymes, and he basically succeeded in delineating the orientation for the healthy development of Tang poetry. His poems *Seeing off Vice-Prefect Du* and *In The Mountains*, and his prose work *The Pavilion of Prince Teng* were written in a fresh style with a new horizon. Most popular among generations of readers were the following sentences:

"If you have friends who know your heart,
Distance would never keep you apart."
"A solitary wild duck joins the drifting
sunset cloud;
Autumnal waters merge with the limitless
blue sky."

They are still often quoted even at present. No wonder the "Poetry Sage" Du Fu wrote in his comment on "The Four Talents of the Early Tang" headed by Wang Bo:

The style and approach of the Four Talents
Were laughed at by writers flowery and frivolous.
The names of you mediocre forgotten will be
The Talents will shine as rivers will e'er flow.

Du Fu paid high tribute to Wang Bo and the other three and severely reprimanded those who tried to denounce them. Passed down to the present were 20 volumes of *Collected Writings of Wang Zi'an* compiled by Jiang Qingyi of the Qing Dynasty.

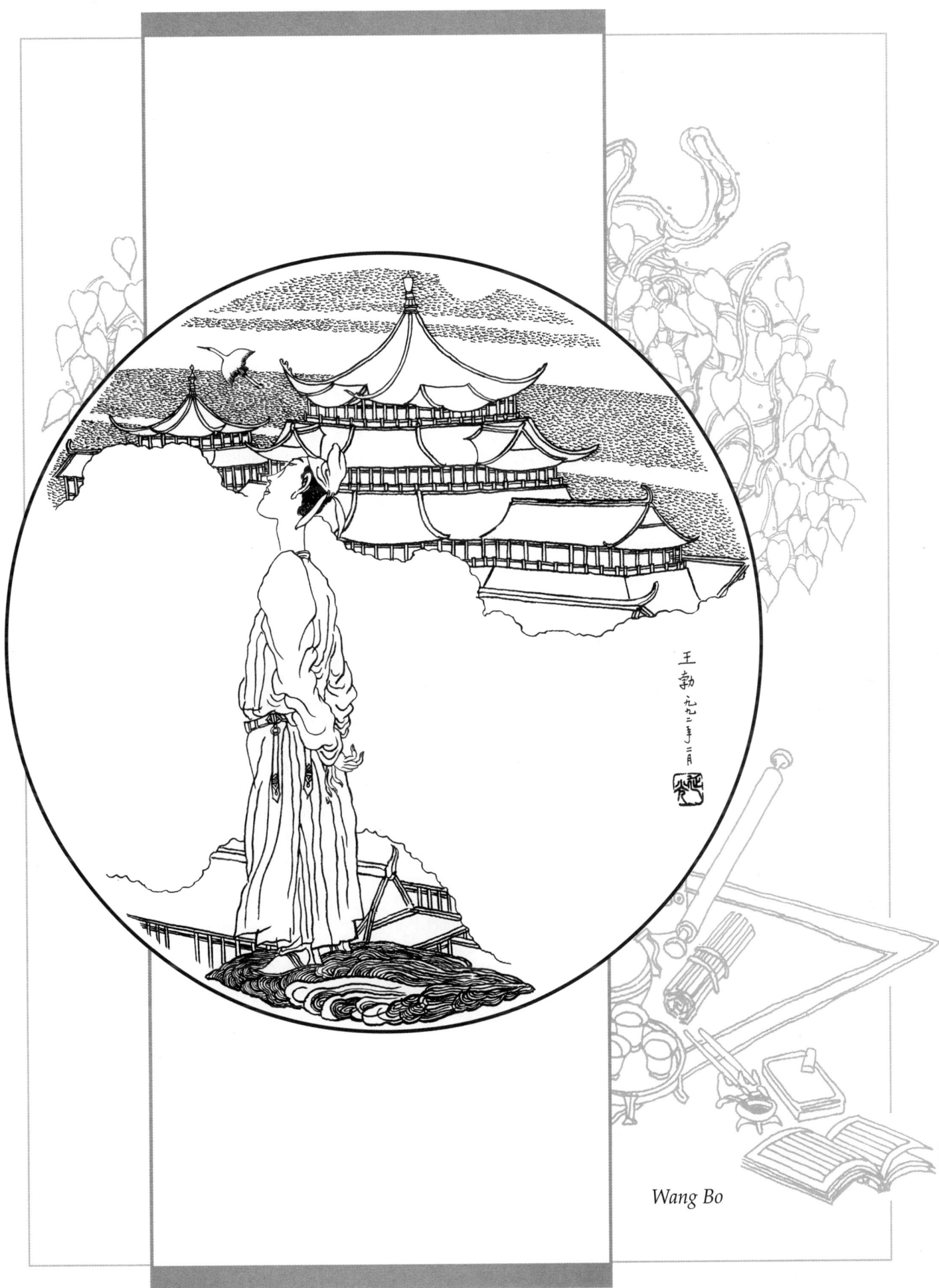

Wang Bo

Chen Zi'ang

陳子昂

*H*eroes of the past I can't see,
Neither those of future years.
Heaven and earth everlasting will be.
O'er my fruitless life alone I shed tears!

With its breadth and pathos, this classic style poem, *Ascending the Youzhou Tower*, written at the beginning of the Tang Dynasty has stirred generations of readers and imprinted on their minds the name of its writer, Chen Zi'ang (661–702).

The poet was from Shehong of Zizhou (in present Sichuan) with the courtesy name Boyu. A gallant lad bent on martial arts, he did not begin to cultivate his moral character and resolve to study hard until he was 18. Three years later he went to Chang'an and entered the imperial college. Despite his failure in the first imperial examination, he did not lose heart but studied even harder, and earned the Jinshi degree at 24 in the first year of the Guangzhai period (684) when Empress Wu Zetian gained power.

The elegant and energetic young scholar presented a memorial *Eulogy to the Inauguration of the Great Zhou* which won the appreciation of Empress Wu, who granted him an audience and appointed him editor of the imperial secretariat. In the second year of the Chuigong period (686), he followed Qiao Zhizhi in the northern expedition against two national minority tribes and was made military attaché after their triumphant return.

Bold and outspoken, he presented memorials on quite a few occasions after being promoted right remonstrator, sharply denouncing the oppressive officials, and admonishing against the abuse of corporal punishment. His straightforward criticism of influential officials and dignitaries incurred enmity, and in the first year of the Yanzai period (694) he was put in prison on a false charge. After being released, he followed Prince Jian'an, Wu Youyi, as military attaché in the northern expedition against the Khitan. An opinionated commander, Wu Youyi brought about setbacks to his army. He not only rejected the military stratagems proposed by Chen Zi'ang, but

treated him unfairly. Full of indignation, Chen wrote the poem quoted at the beginning of this article when he mounted the Jibei Tower in Youzhou. Bearing a grudge against Chen, Wu Youyi demoted him. After returning to the capital, Chen Zi'ang resigned his post in 696 and went back to his hometown. But the ruling clique of the Wus would not let him off even after his retirement. Prince Liang, Wu Sansi, instructed the magistrate of Shehong County to throw him into prison on a fabricated charge, where Chen Zi'ang died at the age of only 42 in grief and indignation.

Upright and outspoken, Chen wrote bold and vigorous poems with profound significance in the style of the Han and Wei dynasties. His 38 pieces of *Observation* and *A View of the Ancient Scene at Jiqiu* expressed his ideals and aspirations, exposing the political evils at the time and sighing over his unrecognized ability. Simple, bold, and vigorous, the style of his poems broke with the decadent way of writing prevalent for about 200 years since the Qi and Liang dynasties and blazed a trail for the healthy development of poetry in the Tang Dynasty. No wonder the great poet Li Bai admired him as "a rare talent", and the "Poetry Sage" Du Fu respected him as "a bold talent" "whose fame would shine as the sun and the moon".

Chen Zi'ang was at his best in pentasyllabic poems and regulated verse. *A View of Chu after Crossing Jingmen*, *Reminiscence of History at Baidi City*, *Reminiscence of History at Xianshan Mountain*, *Arriving at Lexiang County at Sunset* were all excellent regulated poems. He was also good at prose. His articles, whether argumentation or memorials, were simple, refreshing, thorough and forceful. So some people say that the classic prose movement advocated by Han Yu and Liu Zongyuan had its origin in Chen Zi'ang. His writings were compiled into *Collected Writings by Chen Boyu* and included more than 120 poems and 100-odd articles.

Chen Zi'ang

124

Yan Zhenqing

On the cliff by the Wuxi Stream in Lingling of Hunan (known as Yongzhou in the Tang Dynasty), there is a tablet inscription *Eulogy to the Restoration* written by the great calligrapher of the Tang Dynasty, Yan Zhenqing (709–785), which has attracted enthusiastic visitors ever since. Generally known as a great calligrapher, Yan Zhenqing was actually also a distinguished statesman, and *Eulogy to the Restoration* was written by him when he served at his local post in Fuzhou after the suppression of the An-Shi Rebellion, in which he played a positive role.

Yan Zhenqing was from Wannian of Chang'an (in present Xi'an of Shaanxi) with the courtesy name Qingchen. His great-great-grandfather, Yan Zhitui, was a celebrated scholar in the period of the Northern and Southern dynasties. After the death of his father, Yan Weizhen, when he was only three, his mother and the 10 children of the family relied on his maternal grandfather's family for a living. Under the guidance of his mother and cousin, Yan Zhenqing was able to write good articles in excellent script in his early teens.

In 734, 26-year-old Yan Zhenqing passed the Jinshi degree national examination. With excellent records in another examination held by the Ministry of Civil Official Administration two years later, he was appointed editor of the imperial secretariat. Recommended by an important local official, he sat for a special examination in 742 presided over personally by the emperor, and scored the top grades. He was then granted the post of vice-magistrate of Liquan County, which he resigned the next year and went to Luoyang to learn calligraphy from Zhang Xu. In 746, he declined another appointment as vice-magistrate of Chang'an and went on with learning from his calligraphy teacher until he mastered the true essence of the art, forming his own unique style in regular-script and cursive-script.

Yan served the court in various capacities and suffered occasional setbacks.

For his opposition to the manipulation of power by the premier Yuan Zai, Yan was banished in 766 to be assistant prefect of Jizhou before serving as prefect in Fuzhou and Huzhou. Though already 60, he led the local people in reclaiming land and irrigation projects, winning the appreciation and respect of the people for the development of local economy and for the peace and security under his administration.

After the imperious Yuan Zai was put to death in 777 for his manipulation of the court, the succeeding premier Yang Wan called Yan back and appointed him Minister of Punishment, and then Minister of Civil Official Administration. When Emperor Dezong came to the throne, Yang Yan, who had been a member of the Yuan Zai clique, became the premier. Detesting Yan's uprightness, he removed him from the post of Minister of Civil Official Administration and appointed him Junior Adviser to the Crown Prince. The succeeding premier, Lu Qi, who bore a stronger grievance against Yan, tried surreptitiously to lay a trap for him while promoting him to be mentor of the crown prince.

The chance came in 782 when the Huaixi governor, Li Xilie, revolted against Tang and claimed to be king of Jianxing and general marshal of the country. When the rebels fought their way to the outskirts of Luoyang, Lu Qi made a proposal to the emperor to send Yan to the rebel governor to talk him around. Ignorant of the dirty plot, Emperor Dezong decided to send Yan as imperial envoy to Huaixi. All the officials and generals were astonished when the imperial edict was announced. Knowing the mission was fraught with danger, Yan nevertheless mounted a horse and left with only a boy servant despite the objection of the fellow officials, hoping against hope to bring Li Xilie back on the right track.

In face of the threats and inducements of Li Liexi and his accomplices, Yan Zhenqing never budged an inch but condemned the traitorous actions of all the rebels. His righteousness and fortitude even moved two of Li's generals, Zhou Zeng and Wang Bin. They made secret preparations to come over to the side of the central government, but failed as their moves were detected. Seeing no hope to force Yan to submit, Li Xilie had him hanged in Longxing Temple in the eighth lunar month of 785. Yan's coffin was not transported back to Chang'an until 786 when Li Xilie was killed by his generals and the rebellion in Huaixi was put down.

颜真卿

颜真卿 一九九一年四月 [印]

Yan Zhenqing

126

Du Fu

杜甫

The third year of the Tianbao period of the reign of Emperor Xuanzong of the Tang Dynasty was when the 33-year-old Du Fu (712–770) and the 44-year-old Li Bai, who were respectively admired by later generations as "the Poetry Sage" and "the Poetry Immortal", met in Luoyang and became great friends. Framed by those in power, Li Bai, who had been scholar of the imperial academy, was at that time "sent out of the court with valuable gifts". The two great poets toured the places around Henan and discussed the art of poetry while enjoying the beautiful landscape, regretting having not met earlier. Recalling the happy time, Du Fu wrote later in his poems, *Remembering Li Bai in Spring*:

> *Spring trees north of the Wei,*
> *Dusk clouds east of the Jiang,*
> *When shall we sit o'er cups of wine,*
> *Discussing the art of poetry again?*

With the courtesy name Zimei, Du Fu styled himself Shaoling Old Man. His ancestral home was in Xiangyang (in present Hubei), from which his great grandfather moved to Gongxian County (in present Henan). Inheriting the literary tradition of his grandfather Du Shenyan, a famous poet of the early Tang period, he was eager to learn and began to write poems when he was only seven. At 20, he went on a tour around the Huaihe and the lower reaches of the Yangtze River, and at 24 he went to Luoyang to sit for the Jinshi degree national examination. After his failure in the examination, he went on a tour in Hebei and Shandong. And in the Taishan Mountain, he wrote the famous poem *A View of Mount Tai*, the last two lines of which expressed his lofty aspirations and have been on the lips of the people for over 1,000 years since his time:

> *I'll mount its summit at the first chance,*
> *And dwarf the other mountains in a glance.*

He went to Luoyang again at 33, and together with Li Bai toured Henan, Shandong and other places. At 35, he went to Chang'an for the imperial examination, and as a result of the obstacles created by the treacherous premier Li Linfu, not a single candidate passed the examination. After that Du was stranded in the capital for 10 years until he got a junior post at 44 in charge of a military warehouse. He then went to Fengxian County to visit his family only to find

that his youngest son had died of hunger. While he was at home, the An-Shi Rebellion broke out, and on his way to Lingwu in 756 he was captured by the rebels. He did not get away until 757 and after many hardships on the way, he finally reached the headquarters of Emperor Suzong in Fengxiang and was appointed left remonstrator. But not long after that, he was demoted to the post of assistant magistrate of Huazhou, as he offended the emperor in presenting a memorial in an effort to save the Premier Fang Guan.

Du Fu resigned his post and went to Sichuan in 759. With the help of the governor Yan Wu, he had a thatched house built by the Huanhua Stream in Chengdu and settled down there. Here he wrote the famous *Song of the Thatched House Damaged by the Autumn Wind,* the last stanza of which read:

> *How could I get enough houses solid and spacious*
> *To shelter all the poor scholars and give them joy?*
> *And neither wind nor rain will them annoy.*
> *Alas! When these houses overnight stand*
> *before my eye,*
> *I'd be content if my house is broken and*
> *of cold I die.*

Expressing the noble character of the poet in caring for the poor and needy, these lines have enjoyed popular admiration generation after generation.

In 762, Du Fu went to Zizhou and Langzhou to get away from the tangled fighting between warlords in Sichuan. When he got back to Chengdu in 764, the governor Yan Wu recommended him to be adviser of the governor's office and secretary of Gongbu (Ministry of Construction), hence the poet was also known as Du Gongbu. Unfortunately, Yan Wu died the following year, and Du had to leave Chengdu for Kuizhou where he lived for three years. He finally left Sichuan in 768 and went to Hunan via Hubei. The wandering life, coupled with poverty and illness, spoiled the health of the great poet, who died at 59 in a small boat on the Xiangjiang River in Laiyang.

Du Fu was the greatest realist poet in ancient China, and over 1,400 poems and 20-odd articles written by him were passed down to the present.

Du Fu

Han Yu

The great Tang Dynasty poet Han Yu (768–824) was so fond of the plain white plum blossoms that he wrote poems in their admiration as gifts to friends, the most famous being *Present for Zhang Shiyi*. Plum blossoms described in his poems were full of life as if imbued with such human feelings as happiness, anger, grief, and joy. Typical examples were these lines: "Like thousands of piles of snow they look", "Frost petals are gathered on jade twigs", and "So pale are the blossoms that they seem to be in grief"; from which it could be seen how he appreciated the "clean, lustrous" noble quality of plum blossoms.

Han Yu was from Heyang (present Mengxian County of Henan), with the courtesy name Tuizhi. His father, who had been magistrate of Wuchang, died when he was only four years old. It was his elder brother and sister-in-law who brought him up. Later, he went to the capital, and in the eighth year of the Zhenyuan period (792), the talent and ability of the 25-year-old Han Yu won wide recognition and he was recommended to the premier Lu Zhi. He passed the Jinshi degree national examination in the same year.

In the 12th year of the Yuanhe period of the reign of Emperor Xianzong, Han Yu followed the premier Pei Du in an expedition against the rebellious Huaixi military governor Wu Yuanji. They advanced all the way to the enemy headquarters, winning one victory after another, until they captured the arch-criminal. After their triumphant return, Han Yu was promoted Vice-Minister of Punishment.

Two years later, however, the emperor decided to send a eunuch as envoy to escort a piece of the Buddha's bone to the palace, which caused a wild enthusiasm for worshipping the Buddha among officials and people. Ideologically, Han was an advocate of Confucianism in opposition to Buddhism and Taoism, and he presented a memorial *On Buddha's Bone*, earnestly remonstrating against the move. Had it not been for the pleading of the court officials, the enraged emperor would have put him to death. Han Yu was then banished to be prefect of Chaozhou, where he made distinguished achievement.

In the winter of 819, he was transferred to the post of Yuanzhou prefect. Later he was appointed Director of the Imperial College, then Vice-Minister of Military Affairs, Vice-Minister of Civil Official Administration, Magistrate of the Capital and concurrently Chief Supervising Censor, Vice-Minister of Military Affairs, and finally back to the post of Vice-Minister of Civil Official Administration. He died of illness at 57 and was granted the honorary position of Minister of Rites and the posthumous title of Wen, hence he was also known as "Master Han Wen".

Han Yu put emphasis on the tradition of Confucianism that came down in one continuous line from Yao and Shun to Confucius and Mencius, and he held an important position in the development of Confucianism. He maintained the traditional ideology of Confucianism in opposition to Buddhism and Taoism, holding that "noble or humble position, and fortune or misfortune rest with Heaven", and "man's life is decided by fate". He believed in the existence of gods and ghosts, and was of the opinion that history was created by the sages. But he also raised doubts about "what after all is heaven or fate" and put forward the idea that students could surpass their teachers.

His achievement in literature was more spectacular. He was quite creative in poetic composition and was especially good at composing long classic poems.

Even greater was his contribution to prose. Together with Liu Zongyuan, he took the lead in the "classic prose movement" which was against the formalist parallel writing style since the Han and the following six dynasties, and put emphasis on conveying moral and philosophical principles. He also stressed the importance of a writer's moral cultivation and the necessity of getting rid of all stereotyped expressions to achieve fluency and naturalness. Indeed, Han Yu deserves to be the first of the "Eight Prose Masters of the Tang-Song Period". His writings were passed down in *Collected Works by Han Changli*.

Han Yu

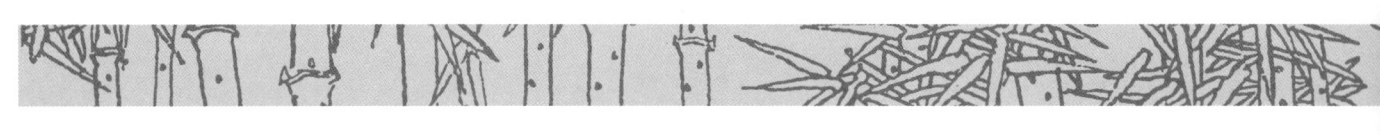

Bai Juyi

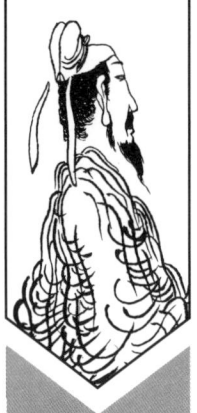

白居易

In the Zhenyuan period of the reign of Emperor Dezong of the Tang Dynasty, a lad about 15 years old came from Fuliang to the capital Chang'an to call on the famous scholar, Gu Kuang, who was then among a great gathering of distinguished guests. Gu did not take the lad seriously until he read the poem *Grass on the Plain* which the latter presented to him:

Luxurious grass covers the plain.
Once a year it'll wax and then wane.
Wildfire is unable to burn it up,
With spring breeze it'll grow again.
It presses on ancient roads far away;
Its verdure reaches the ruined city gate
Off I see my bosom friends again.
The grass will share my sorrow and pain.

"Excellent!" Gu Kuang could not help exclaiming with delight, and personally invited the lad to a seat. Thus Bai Juyi (772–846) became widely known in the capital for his poems.

Bai Juyi's courtesy name was Letian. His ancestors had moved from Taiyuan to Xiagui (present Weinan of Shaanxi), but he was born in Xinzheng (in present Henan). His father died when he was a child, and at 11 he followed his elder brother to Fuliang in the south to seek refuge from war. Experiencing the hardships of life, the child began to learn poetic composition diligently when he was only five or six years old, and was able to write excellent poems in his early teens.

The 29-year-old Bai Juyi passed the Jinshi degree national examination, succeeded in another special examination, and was made imperial editor. In 806, he was appointed military director of Zhouzhi County. The next year he wrote *The Everlasting Sorrow* in which he made a vivid and touching description of the love story between Emperor Xuanzong of the Tang Dynasty and his concubine Yang Yuhuan. The long poem won universal popularity and brought him great fame as a poet. It was most likely that the poem found its way into the palace, as in the same year Bai Juyi was called to the palace for an examination and was made scholar of the imperial academy. The following year, at the age of 37, he was appointed Left Remonstrator.

In the three years as a remonstrator, Bai made many comments and proposals to Emperor Xianzong for the benefit of the country and the people. His straightforward remonstration met with the opposition of the powerful and dignitaries, and he was transferred to the post of left adviser of the crown prince in 814. As a result of his earnest pleading in the following year to punish the murderer of the premier Wu Yuanheng, he incurred hatred from the eunuch clique and was banished to Jiangzhou as assistant prefect. It was here that he wrote another long poem *The Lute Player* which enjoyed everlasting popularity, and *A Letter to Yuan Zhen* in which he summed up the theory of poetic composition.

Later, during the reign of Emperor Wuzong, he retired from the post of minister of punishment and went to live in the Xiangshan Hill in Luoyang where he styled himself Xiangshan Scholar and devoted himself to poetry. He personally made a selection of his poems which he wrote in five collections each containing 3,840 poems. He kept the five copies in five different places, and instructed his descendants to take good care of them generation after generation. Thanks to his extraordinary insight, Bai Juyi succeeded in maintaining his own integrity and in passing down his poems almost completely. He died at 75 and was buried in the Longmen Hill.

An admirer of Du Fu, Bai Juyi wrote poems in popular language, raising his voice for the labouring people. His poems enjoyed great popularity in the country. He classified his own poems into four categories: allegorical, leisurely, sentimental, and miscellaneous. Directed against the malpractice and evils in politics and society, his allegorical poems showed the greatest affinity to the people and could well be taken as a mirror of the time. Inheriting Du Fu's tradition of Confucianism and realism, Bai Juyi wrote 10 pieces *Qinzhong Poems*, 50 pieces *Yuefu Poems*, as well as *the Everlasting Remorse*, *The Lute Player* and other excellent poems. Passed down to the present were 71 volumes of *Selected Poems by Bai Juyi* containing almost 3,000 poems, being the largest number of poems passed down among all the poets of the Tang Dynasty.

Bai Juyi

Liu Yuxi

After his political defeat and demotion to Langzhou, the mid-Tang poet Liu Yuxi (772–842) was determined to create a new form of poetry to transform the local folk rhymes that were not refined enough, following Qu Yuan's example in composing "Jiuge" to transform the god-worshipping songs at his time. So he composed quite a number of new songs based on the traditional folk song tune of "Bamboo Branch" popular in the area of Ba Yu, and wrote many new pieces to the tune of "Willow Branch" sung widely in the Tang Dynasty. He then taught the shamans to sing his songs. As a result, his "Bamboo Branch" and "Willow Branch" songs became popular among the people, and even the national minorities in the Wuling mountains sang the following song to the tune of "Bamboo Branch":

The placid river between willows green
flows along;
My sweetheart in a boat is heard singing a song.
There's sunshine in the east but rain in the west,
His love for me is profound though not fully
professed.

His courtesy name was Mengde, and he was from Luoyang (in present Henan) to which his ancestors had moved from Zhongshan (present Dingxian County of Hebei). Intelligent and apt to learn, he studied poetic composition under two master monks, Jiaoran and Lingche, when he lived in Suzhou. His poems transcended the worldly dimension and won the admiration of the people.

In the ninth year of the Zhenyuan period of the reign of Emperor Dezong (793), Liu Yuxi passed the Jinshi degree national examination and another special examination at the age of 22. After Emperor Shunzong succeeded to the crown in 805, Wang Shuwen was put in an important position. Liu Yuxi and Liu Zongyuan joined Wang's group, and actively participated in the "Yongzhen Reform". Liu Yuxi had a series of rapid promotions to be in charge of land reclamation, revenue, and salt and iron respectively. Unfortunately, the eunuch Ju Wenzhen and his clique staged a palace coup in autumn the same year and forced Emperor Shunzong to abdicate in favour of Emperor Xianzong, which dealt a heavy blow to the reformers.

Liu Yuxi was banished to be Assistant Prefect of Langzhou where he lived for 10 years before being called back to the capital to be Deputy Minister of Rites, Jixian Academy Scholar etc. But before long, he received the order to take the post of Yaozhou prefect as he had been at odds with the premier Wu Yuanheng, and had written a poem satirizing the new dignitaries. Thanks to the pleading of an important official, Pei Du, to the emperor, Liu got a new appointment of Lianzhou prefect. After that he was made Prefect of Kuizhou and then of Hezhou, Secretary of the Ministry of Rites, Prefect of Suzhou, Ruzhou, and Tongzhou.

After 32 years of ups and downs in his official career, he was promoted in 836 to be Taizi Binke (senior adviser of the crown prince) and was called back to take office in the east capital Luoyang. Hence he was also popularly known as Liu Binke. He died at the post of Minister of Rites at the age of 71.

His demotion in 806 marked the beginning of the thriving period of his poem creation. The following famous lines have been extremely popular ever since his time:

Hundreds of sails nimbly pass by the sunken ship;
Thousands of saplings thrive around the
withering tree.
Like flowers in bloom, your love will fade fast;
Like a river ever flowing, my grief will last.
Swallows in grand mansions in bygone days
Are flying now into common people's doorways.
On ruined city-walls the waves beat and
recede in silence.

In his early years, he and Liu Zongyuan were good friends, being referred to as "Liu-Liu". After Liu Zongyuan's death, he often exchanged poems with Bai Juyi and the two of them were known as "Liu-Bai". Also a good writer of prose, he wrote the *Humble Room* which has been widely known among generations of readers. Another field of his achievement was in philosophy. He held that all things in the world had their origin in "qi". The function of nature was to "produce all things" while man was capable of "running all things". Thus he refuted the theory of "retribution" and "interaction between heaven and man". His materialist ideology was embodied in his three articles of *On Heaven*. Passed down to the present day were 40 volumes of *Collected Works of Liu Mengde*.

劉禹錫

Liu Yuxi

Liu Zongyuan

柳宗元

In the movement to restore the classic style of prose writing, Liu Zongyuan (773–819) and Han Yu enjoyed the same fame as protagonists. Liu had a lot of setbacks in his life. After the failure of Wang Shuwen's "Yongzhen Reform" in which he participated, he was banished to the undeveloped areas in the south. Disappointed and pessimistic, he was unsure whether to follow Confucianism or believe in Buddhism. His major achievements in philosophy and literature had been made before he became a follower of Buddhism.

Liu Zongyuan was from Xiexian County of Hedong (southwest of present Yuncheng of Shanxi Province) with the courtesy name Zihou. He was exceptionally intelligent from childhood, and was a well-known talent for the excellent articles he wrote. He passed the Jinshi degree national examination at 21 in the ninth year of the Zhenyuan period (793), and was appointed Imperial Editor before being promoted to be Military Director of Lantian County.

In 803, Liu Zongyuan was back to the capital as a supervising censor. At the time, the crown prince appreciated the ability of his reading mates Wang Shuwen and Wang Pi very much, who were then organizing the core of their political group. Liu Zongyuan and seven other famous scholars became members of the group.

When the crown prince came to the throne in 805 (known in history as Emperor Shunzong of the Tang Dynasty), Wang Shuwen was made Scholar of the Imperial Academy and Liu Zongyuan was promoted Secretary of the Ministry of Rites. In alliance with Liu Zongyuan, Wang Pi, and some other officials, Wang Shuwen initiated a reform historically known as the "Yongzhen Reform" in the middle period of the Tang Dynasty. They removed corrupt officials, eliminated government purchase market, reduced the salt price, and remitted the outstanding liabilities of the people to the government, which soon brought prosperity to the country. They also made preparations to deprive the military power of the eunuchs. It was a great pity that Emperor Shunzong whom they relied on became ill and had to abdicate, assuming the title of super-sovereign, after being on the throne for only a few months. Thus the "Yongzhen Reform" was aborted. Wang Shuwen was demoted and then put to death, and Liu Zongyuan was banished to the south of the country.

His major achievement was in literature, being one of the "eight prose masters of the Tang and Song dynasties". His biographies and articles were based on his experience and observation among the people. *The Snake Catcher* exposed the social reality that tyranny was more rapacious than a tiger through the description of a grandson of a family who went on catching snakes at the risk of his life after his grandfather and father died of snake-bite, as the exorbitant taxes and levies were more fatal than snake poison. *The Story of the Boy Ou Ji* told the story of a boy who carried on struggle with courage and wisdom against the bandits who wanted to sell him. His travelogues represented by *Eight Notes of Yongzhou* were unique with their fresh and lucid style, poetic charm and picturesque beauty. His argumentation articles like *On Enfeoffment* were meticulous and well-knit. Liu Zongyuan also wrote a lot of fables such as *Three Cautionary Tales* and *Brown Bear* which were written with a trenchant pen pregnant with profound meanings between the lines, making fables an independent component in classic Chinese literature.

He was also an excellent poet. His *Farm Life*, *The Caged Eagle*, *Hard is the Way*, etc. either castigated the evils of the rulers or gave expression to his grievances with his demotion. His landscape poems *Fishing in Snow*, *The Old Fisherman*, *The South Ravine* etc. were fresh and neat and beautiful. The following lines were so refined that they seemed to have transcended anything worldly:

O'er all the hills no birds were seen in flight;
On all the paths no footprints remained in sight.
A straw cloaked man in a small boat alone
Was fishing on the river in the falling snow.

Even more touching were his poems *Mounting the Liuzhou City Gate Tower* and *Responding to Mr Cao* which expressed his depression and indignation and his longing for his political allies.

Liu Zongyuan died in office in Liuzhou at the age of 47. His bosom friend Liu Yuxi collected his works into 45 volumes of *Collected Works of Master Hedong* which was passed down to the present day.

柳宗元 一九九二年 七月画

Liu Zongyuan

李賀

Li He

In the Yuanhe period of the Tang Dynasty, a young man was often seen wandering and chanting poems on a lean horse in Henan, indifferent to anything else. Whenever he got any inspiration, he would stop the horse to write it down and put the note into a silk bag. By sunset when he returned home, what was in his bag had been enough for him to write poems. Seeing him so preoccupied with poetry, his mother said, "Alas, the kid is working his heart out!" This young man was none other than the famous Tang Dynasty poet Li He (790–816).

Li He was from Fuchang (west of the present Yiyang of Henan) with the courtesy name Changji. He was born in a distant branch of the Tang royal family, being the descendant of Prince Zheng. By the time of his father's generation, his family had declined.

Li He became well known with his poems even in his childhood and won the appreciation of the great poets Han Yu and Huangfu Shi. He had intended to sit for the imperial examination when he was a bit older. But those who were jealous of his talent spread the rumour that the first character of his father's name Jinsu had the same pronunciation as the first character of the degree Jinshi and that Li He should avoid the taboo on the name of his father and stay from the examination. While Li He was affected by these remarks, the great poet Han Yu paid no heed to the rumour, and specially wrote an article *Analysis of Taboo* to try to persuade Li He to sit for the examination. But Li did not go to the examination. He was very gloomy and depressed after that, since he could only take a very low official post.

The Yuanhe period of the reign of Emperor Xianzong saw political chaos with eunuchs in power in the capital and separatist regimes of military governors in the localities. Seeing the situation, Li He was full of grief and indignation, but was unable to do anything. So he resigned his post and returned to his hometown. He often exchanged poems with his friends Shen Yazhi, Chen Shang, Yang Jingzhi and other poets expressing his indignation over the society by means of poems. His poems embodied his depression and his inability to realize his ambition.

My lost soul I am unable to call back.
The day breaks with the crowing of the cock.
My ambition soars to the sky young as I am.
But, in dimness and cold I can only sit idle.

Some of his poems like *Ode to the Jade Mining Old Man* expressed his sympathy for the labouring people, some like *The Yanmen Magistrate* sang praises of the officers and men at the front, some like *The South Garden* voiced his ambition, some like *General Lu* criticized the muddle-headed court officials, and some like *The Qin Palace* exposed the decadent nobles. As a learned Confucian scholar, he was very unhappy about the emperor's superstition and indulgence in Taoism and immortals, and wrote *Too Short is the Day* and other allegorical poems.

His poems inherited the romantic style of Qu Yuan and Li Bai and followed Han Yu's idea of "making sure to avoid hackneyed words and expressions". His works were original in artistic approach, rich in imagination, eccentrically fascinating in conception, and beautiful in words and expressions. His famous lines "Were Heaven sentient, it too would become aged", "The rocks broke and Heaven shook in the autumn rain", "Hanging over the city-wall, dark clouds were about to destroy it." etc. are still oft-quoted and widely loved even today. Exotic, plaintive, and gorgeous, his poems formed a unique style of his own.

Depression, hardships of poverty and over-taxation by poems took their toll on Li He and he died at 27 in the prime of his life.

Passed down to the present were four volumes of his *Changgu Collection* (also called *Poems by Li Changji*), and one volume of *Additional Collection*. Some of his poems, though fantastic and abstruse, were forerunners of the abstruse poems by later poets represented by Li Shangyin.

一九九二年二月二十日画 于野味斋

李贺

Li He

Du Mu

杜牧

The poets Li Shangyin and Du Mu (803–852) in the late period of the Tang Dynasty were put in parallel as "the Later Li-Du", being the successful continuation of the Li-Du (Li Bai and Du Fu) in the prosperous period of the Tang Dynasty. Du Mu's poetic style was close to that of Li Bai, while Li Shangyin shared the essential spirit of the poems by Du Fu. Du Mu was also fond of discussing military strategies and was a gallant scholar of ability and sagacity. His annotations to the 13 chapters of "the Art of War by Sunzi" were widely read at the time.

Du Mu was from Wannian of Jingzhao (in the present Xi'an of Shaanxi) with the courtesy name Muzhi. He was the grandson of Du You, a well-known premier during the reign of Emperor Dezong. In the second year of the Dahe period of the Tang dynasty (828), he passed the Jinshi degree national examination at the age of 26. Then he passed another special examination and was made Editor of the Hongwen Academy.

Appreciative of the talent and ability of young Du Mu, the civil administrator of Jiangxi, Shen Chuanshi, made him his subordinate official. When Shen was transferred to be civil administrator of Xuanxi, Du Mu followed him to Xuanzhou. Later, Du Mu gained the appreciation of the Huainan governor, Niu Sengru, and became his secretary. Nevertheless, he did not attach himself to the powerful party of Niu Sengru. In Yangzhou, he indulged in drinking and romance, which was perhaps his strategy to conceal his true intentions so as to be free from the power struggle.

In the ninth year of the Dahe period, Du Mu was called to the capital to be a supervisor, and before long, was given the concurrent charge of the eastern capital. Later, he served at the posts of militia administrator of Xuanzhou, left remonstrator, compiler of the history academy, etc.

In 840, Emperor Wenzong died in worry and gloom under the control of the eunuchs. After Emperor Wuzong succeeded to the crown, he put Li Deyu, a man of political competence, in the position of premier. Li suppressed the pro-eunuch officials of Niu Sengru's clique and revitalized the Tang dynasty. Li Deyu thought highly of Du Mu,

but Du did not align himself with his clique to gain high position. Relying on his own ability and family origin, Du took up the post of magistrate of Huangzhou in 842, and later magistrate of Chizhou and Muzhou. In 848, he was back to the capital as a department director and compiler of the history academy, before being promoted to be Zhongshu Sheren in charge of drafting imperial edicts. His ability coupled with his family influence, enabled him to express his ideas without many misgivings.

Du Mu was a prominent prose writer in the late period of the Tang Dynasty. Inheriting the literary tradition of Han Yu, his writings were fresh, fine, and forceful. Du Mu's poems were even more elegant and refreshing, forming a unique school of his own. Quite a number of his poems were about the political situation at the time. Some of his poems embodied his historical views, and his quatrains were so popular that they are still on the lips of the people.

The Red Cliff
*Had the east wind grudged the favour to
General Zhou,
The two fair sisters would have been captives
of the foe.*

Some expressions which seemed at his fingertips had profound meanings. For instance:
*Spring South of the Changjiang River
Four hundred eighty splendid temples
still remain
Of Southern Dynasties in the mist and the rain.*

Mooring on Qinhuai River
*The singsong girls know not the grief of
a nation conquered
And are singing the songs composed by a
sovereign captured.*

A Mountain Trip
*I stop my carriage to admire the maple grove
at nightfall,
Whose frosty leaves are redder than the flowers
of spring.*

Du Mu died at 50. Among his works were *Collected Prose Works by Du Mu* and *Collected Poems by Du Mu* (annotated by Feng Jiwu).

杜牧
一九九三年四月

Du Mu

Li Shangyin

During the Yuanhe period of the reign of Emperor Xianzong, there appeared a child prodigy, Li Shangyin (812–859), in Huaizhou prefecture who was perceptive despite his young age. He was able to write excellent prose in the ancient style instead of drifting with the tide to write in the contemporary parallel style. That was indeed quite extraordinary since the contemporary style was used in the official writings in the Tang Dynasty, and all the scholars who aspired to official positions had to be good at it.

Li Shangyin was from Henei of Huaizhou (present Qinyang of Henan) with the courtesy name Yishan and literary name Yuxisheng. He was diligent and intelligent from childhood, and at 17 he wrote two famous essays, *On the Sage* and *On Talent*, which attracted wide attention from scholars of the country. Appreciative of the talent and learning of this young man, the former premier Linghu Chu, who was then governor of the Taiping Military District, employed him in 829 and made arrangements for him to study together with his own son, Linghu Tao.

Li Shangyin was exceptionally intelligent and soon surpassed Linghu Tao in his studies. Later, Li served in Linghu's staff, specializing in writing memorials and other documents. When Linghu Tao earned his Jinshi degree, he made a point of recommending Li Shangyin in 837, and Li also passed the Jinshi degree national examination. In the same year, Linghu Chu was seriously ill at his post of Xingyuan governor. At his call, Li rushed to his sickbed from the capital the day before his death, and wrote the last memorial to the emperor for Linghu Chu. That showed how the Linghu family trusted and relied on Li Shangyin.

In the late period of the Tang Dynasty, the struggle between the party represented by Niu Sengru and the party headed by Li Deyu became so fierce that they were as incompatible as fire and water. The Linghu family belonged to the Niu faction, and according to the way of power struggle at the time, Li Shangyin should have shared weal and woe with the Niu faction. However, he went to Jingyuan in 838 and became a staff member of Governor Wang Maoyuan, who belonged to the Li faction. Wang was so delighted with the talent and learning of Li Shangyin that he married his daughter to him. As a result, Linghu Tao and other members of the Niu faction detested Li Shangyin and thought he had returned kindness with enmity, forgetting how the Niu fraction had patronized him. From then on, Li Shangyin got inextricably involved in the struggle between the two parties.

Not until Linghu Tao became the premier in 850, did Li Shangyin admit defeat and go out of his way to get in touch with Linghu, who however had always borne a grudge against his former classmate.

Li Shangyin expressed his feeling of oppression over his failure to realize his ambition by means of describing beautiful women. He broadened the realm of love poems, and became a great poet in developing poetry in the late period of the Tang Dynasty. After the death of his wife in 851, he wrote a lot of poems lamenting her death and expressing his deep sincere love for her. In 852, Li Shangyin lost his post as a staff member, and had to turn to Linghu Tao for help. After repeated requests, he was made an academician of the imperial college, an official position of the principal sixth grade. Later he became a staff member of the Dongchuan governor Liu Zhongying, before dying in poverty and depression at the age of only 47.

In the field of love poems, Li Shangyin enjoyed equal fame with Wen Tingyun. However, Wen was a profligate son of rich parents, and his poems were lacking in seriousness and profoundness and were far from the quality of Li's poems. Li's work were rich in material and classical allusions with fine and neat antitheses and unparalleled beauty in form, showing a unique style of his own. Like parables and riddles, his poems were quite difficult to understand. His *Anding City Gate Tower* expressed his political ambition, and two lines of the poem were quite appreciated by Wang Anshi: "Always cherishing the rivers and lakes of the country I retire with hair white; Wishing to return to nature I go by a small boat."

Some of his poems represented by "the Han Yu Memorial Stele" were against the separatist regimes of the military governors; the *Sui Palace*, *Southern Dynasties*, and some other poems used the past to disparage the present; *Bright Scholar Jia* expressed the feeling over unrecognized talent. Among his poems, the following have been popular household lines ever since: "The silkworm till its death keeps spinning silk; The candle till burning into ashes remains shedding tears." Among his writings passed down to the present are *Annotations to poems and prose by Li Yishan*, and three volumes of *Poems by Yuxisheng* in *Literature and Learning* of the *New History of the Tang Dynasty*.

Li Shangyin

Feng Dao

馮道

After the defeat of the uprising led by Huang Chao at the end of the Tang Dynasty, warlords big and small rose one after another to found separatist regimes fighting in an effort to annex each other. In the central part of China, five dynasties appeared in succession: Later Liang, Later Tang, Later Jin, Later Han, and Later Zhou. The power was held by warlords of Han or Shatuo nationalities who put generals in important positions. Their civil officials were greedy and perverted. A typical example was Feng Dao (882–954).

He started his career as a staff officer in Liu Shouguang's army at the end of the Tang Dynasty, and later served 10 emperors as a senior official in four dynasties of the Later Tang, Later Jin, Later Han, and Later Zhou. He even acknowledged allegiance to the ruler of the Khitan nationality, completely forgetting his integrity as a Chinese official. In his life, he was a cabinet member three times, holding the position of premier for over 20 years. Bent on remaining in high position, he was not concerned at all about the death of the sovereign or the fall of the dynasty. He led the officials in greeting one new emperor after another, who all put him in important positions to appease the civil officials.

Feng Dao was from Jingcheng of Yingzhou (northeast of present Xianxian County of Hebei) with the courtesy name Kedao and was self-styled Changlelao (meaning "ever-happy old man"). In the great disorder at the end of the Tang Dynasty, separatist military governors rose against one another, and Feng Dao first served the Governor of Youzhou, Liu Shouguang. After Liu's defeat, he went over to Hedong army supervisor, Zhang Chengye, and was made an inspector. Versed in Confucian classics, he turned the "golden mean" theory in relation to human behaviour into a means and made the most of it.

Lessons of Past Dynasties described Feng Dao in this way: "He was frugal and magnanimous, and people could hardly judge whether he was delighted or angry. Witty and humorous, he was good at pleasing others." and "Equivocal and ambiguous, he seldom made clear-cut decisions."

Regarding Feng as both virtuous and learned, Zhang Chengye recommended him to the Tang Dynasty Prince of Jin, Li Keyong, as secretary of the office of Hedong governor.

After the death of Li Keyong in 908, his son Li Cunxu succeeded him as Prince Jin. In 923, the new prince claimed the throne and founded the Later Tang Dynasty, making Feng Dao Scholar of the Imperial Academy. From this time on, Feng began to have a distinguished position. When Emperor Mingzong of the Later Tang came to the throne in 926, Feng Dao was made Scholar of Duanming Palace. Seeing the new emperor had some sympathy for the misery of the peasants, Feng took the chance to remonstrate with him to show solicitude for the people. Endorsing his suggestion, the emperor appointed him premier. Since this time, Feng Dao had been at the top of the official hierarchy in all the dynasties. Feng Dao also served in the next administrations, the Later Jin and the Later Zhou.

In 951, Guo Wei came to the throne (known as Emperor Taizu of Later Zhou), founding the Later Zhou Dynasty, with Feng Dao remaining at the post of Grand Master. Feng was good at predicting the possibility of victory by comparing strength and weakness. He would not take action until after careful calculation, and was able to greet the strong and desert the weak at the right time when the deserted could not do anything against him, and the greeted were just in need of his support. He was thus able to enjoy fortune and honour without getting into disaster.

However, his strategy failed to work when he tried to persuade Emperor Shizong, the second emperor of the Later Zhou, to give up the plan for northern expedition against the Northern Han Kingdom, as his idea affected the emperor's overall strategy for unification of the country. Holding Feng Dao in contempt, Emperor Shizong sent him in charge of the construction of the mausoleum of Emperor Taizu of Later Zhou. In deep regret for his first miscalculation, Feng Dao ended his life in disgrace. His only credit was the advocacy of the collation of the *Nine Confucian classics* in the third year of the Changxing period of the Later Tang (AD 932). The "nine classics" collated by the imperial college under his proposal were later put into print, which marked the beginning of book printing by government organizations.

Feng Dao

146

Fan Zhongyan

In the fourth year of the Dazhongxiangfu period of the reign of Emperor Zhenzong of the Song Dynasty (1011), a 23-year-old young man left his stepfather's home in Zizhou (present Zouping of Shandong), and came to the prefecture school of Yingtian of Suiyang where he devoted himself to studies. This young man was Fan Zhongyan (989–1052), son of the late secretary of Ningwu Military District, Fan Yong. His mother remarried to a Zhu family after the death of his father and that was how his name was changed to Zhu Yue.

He studied very hard and lived a simple life in the school, having porridge all year round. With a view to tempering his willpower for hard study, he even refused to have any delicacy offered to him by others. In a few years, he had perused Confucian classics like the *Book of Songs*, the *Book of History*, the *Book of Changes*, *Three Rites*, the *Book of Music*, *Spring and Autumn Annals* etc. and was able to write excellent poems. Thus he earned the Jinshi degree the first time he sat for the national examination. He saw Emperor Zhenzong at the imperial interview and was given a banquet by his majesty. He was only 27 years old at the time.

Fan Zhongyan was from Wuxian County of Suzhou (in present Jiangsu) with the courtesy name Xiwen. He was born in Xuzhou but lived in the Changbai Mountain of Zizhou. In his childhood, he studied hard in a mountain temple. After becoming a Jinshi, he was appointed a staff member of Guangde Military District before being transferred to Jiqing Military District. It was at this time that he began to support his mother at his post and restored his family name Fan.

At the age of 35, Fan was transferred to the capital to be assistant judge of the imperial court of justice. In 1026, however, he went back to the southern capital (present Shangqiu of Henan) because of the death of his mother. The magistrate of the southern capital, Yan Chu, invited him to run the prefecture school, as he had long learned that Fan had a good command of Confucian classics especially the *Book of Changes*. Fan Zhongyan lived in the school, supervising the students with their studies, and helping them to make rapid progress. He also sponsored poor students and offered help to a number of talented scholars such as Fu Bi, Hu Yuan, Zhang Zai. Sun Fu, whom he had sponsored, became a great scholar 10 years later.

In 1028, Fan Zhongyan was promoted to be editor of the imperial library with the recommendation of Yan Chu. But before long he was demoted to be deputy magistrate of Hezhong for the remonstration he made against the way by which the birthday ceremony of Empress Dowager Liu was conducted. After the death of the Empress Dowager, Emperor Renzong called Fan back to take charge of remonstration. But he was again demoted to the post of Muzhou magistrate for remonstrating with the emperor against deposing Empress Guo. For his achievement in water control in Suzhou, he was later transferred back to be magistrate of the capital and drafter of imperial edicts, but he was demoted for the third time to be Raozhou magistrate for what he did in revealing the misconduct of the prime minister Lu Yijian who had indiscriminately put his own people in official positions. Thus he got three demotions in 10 years, all because of making straightforward remonstrations. Not until 1038 when the kingdom of West Xia launched a large scale invasion against the country, did Emperor Renzong promote Fan Zhongyan to be deputy high commissioner of Shaanxi at the suggestion of the deputy marshal Han Qi. Meanwhile he was restored to his former title of drafter of imperial edicts and granted a new title of scholar of Longtu Pavilion.

After a personal inspection tour to the front at the age of 52, Fan Zhongyan found a lot of drawbacks in the Song army. He completed the defence of Dashan city so that the Xixia could not invade the Song Dynasty any more. In 1043, as deputy prime minister, Fan put forward a 10-point reform plan. But a year after the implementation of the new policy, the conservatives framed Fu Bi and other reformers, falsely accusing them of conspiring against the state. As a result, Fan Zhongyan and Fu Bi were removed from office and all the reformers were demoted, which meant the end of the new policy.

In 1045, Fan Zhongyan was demoted to be magistrate of Binzhou, then he was transferred to Dengzhou. It was in Dengzhou that he wrote the famous *Yueyang Pavilion*, in which he wrote the well-known sentence "be the first to become concerned with the country's troubles and the last to enjoy its happiness" which has been popular among scholars and the people for generations. In 1052, Fan Zhongyan died of illness at the age of 64 on his way to Yingzhou. The whole country, from officials to the people, grieved deeply. His poems and ci were bold and unrestrained, and his writings were included in *Collected Works of Master Fan Wenzheng*.

范仲淹

Fan Zhongyan

Ouyang Xiu

歐陽修

At the beginning of the Northern Song Dynasty, Yang Yi, Liu Jun and some other poets had special esteem for Li Shangyin, a poet of the late period of the Tang Dynasty. With emphasis on the form to the neglect of content, they were fond of writing poems with classical allusions and unfamiliar words. They were referred to as "the Xikun School of Poets" after the name of their anthology, *Collection of Xikun Poems*.

Ouyang Xiu (1007–1072), leader of the literati of the Northern Song Dynasty, was the first to rise against the Xikun style. He took the lead in composing lucid and elegant poems welling up from the bottom of the heart without following in the footsteps of his predecessors. Such an example was his *Composed in a Dream*:

A flute was heard among the hills on a cool, moonlit night.
The path was darkened with flowers varied and charming.
After chess games, the players knew not the dynasty changed
Mellow with drink, the travellers helpless missed home more.

From this time on, poems of the Song Dynasty gradually followed his style.

Ouyang Xiu was from Luling (present Yongfeng of Jiangxi) with the courtesy name Yongshu, and literary name, Zuiwong. (In his later years he got another literary name, Liuyi Retired Scholar.) His father died when he was only four, and the poverty of his family only made him more diligent and determined in his studies. In the eighth year of the Tiansheng period of the reign of Emperor Renzong (1030), 24-year-old Ouyang Xiu passed the Jinshi degree national examination, and in the next year, was appointed a judge in the Western Capital. In 1034, he took the post of editor of the imperial academy, participating in the compilation of *Chongwen Book Catalogue*.

In the first year of the Jingyou period of the reign of Emperor Renzong, Fan Zhongyan was demoted to be magistrate of Yiling by the prime minister, Lu Yijian. As some people groundlessly accused Ouyang Xiu and Fan Zhongyan of belonging to one clique, Ouyang wrote an article *On the Clique* to refute them. Later he was transferred to the post of magistrate of Qiande County (present Junxian County of Hubei), and in 1040, was called back to the capital to his former editing post for the compilation of the same book.

A supporter of Fan Zhongyan, Ouyang Xiu was demoted to be magistrate of Chuzhou in 1043 and served at local posts for 11 years.

At his post in Henan, Ouyang Xiu exchanged poems and discussed literature with another man of letters, Mei Yaochen. They held that literary works should "convey the Tao" (philosophical and moral principles) and "serve reality". Together with Su Zimei of Suzhou (Su Shunqin), they advocated prose writing in the style prevalent before the Qin Dynasty. Ouyang himself wrote a lot of excellent poems and prose works and became the leader of the literary reform in the Northern Song Dynasty. He was admired by later generations as one of the "eight prose masters of the Tang and Song dynasties" for his elegant and beautiful prose works.

In 1054, Emperor Renzong happened to see the 48-year-old Ouyang Xiu with white hair, and ordered him to go to the capital to be in charge of the selection of officials.

In 1061, Ouyang Xiu was promoted deputy premier. In the fourth year of the Xining period (1071), Ouyang Xiu retired from the position of scholar of Guanwen Palace and junior instructor of the crown prince. He died the next year at the age of 66.

Ouyang Xiu played an important role in the development of prose and poetry of the Song Dynasty. The prose poems pioneered by him paved the way for Su Shi and Huang Tingjian who advocated "composing poems out of poet's own mind and aspiration". He was also an accomplished writer of ci, a new form of poem. And in the field of history, he compiled *A New History of the Tang Dynasty*, *A New History of the Five Dynasties* etc. His writings were included in *Collected Works of Master Ouyang Wenzhong*.

Ouyang Xiu

Sima Guang

司馬光

The 294-volume *History as a Mirror* was a chronicle of ancient Chinese history covering 1,362 years beginning from the 23rd year of the reign of King Weilie of the Zhou dynasty (403 BC) to the sixth year of the Xiande period of the reign of Emperor Shizong of the Later Zhou Dynasty (AD 959). This monumental historical work was unparalleled both in China and the world.

However, its chief compiler, Sima Guang (1019–1086), was neither a child prodigy nor a genius, with neither extraordinary memory nor outstanding comprehension. His knowledge was accumulated bit by bit through life-long diligence and honesty. He began to study history and literature at the age of six under the guidance of his father. He used for pillow a piece of log which he called "alarm pillow", as the log was liable to roll, and he would be awakened at the mere movement of the log and get up to read. There was another thing that he never forgot in his life. In his childhood, he was not able to shell a walnut. But when someone asked him whether the walnut meat he was eating was shelled by himself, he gave the positive answer. After his father Sima Chi got to know this, he criticized the son for having told a lie and taught him to be honest. After that Sima Guang not only took honesty as his motto in life, but put it in practice in reading and learning. That was how he grew up to be a great writer and scholar.

With the courtesy name Junshi, Sima Guang was self-styled Yusou, and was also known as Master Sushui after the name of the little stream in his hometown Xiaxian County of Shanzhou (in present Shanxi). His father, Sima Chi, begot him at his official post in the Prefecture of Guang (the present Guangshan County of Henan) and named his son after the place.

Sima Guang began reading all kinds of books earnestly at six, and at 15 was listed as an official on the strength of the service of his father who had been a fourth grade official. Reluctant to rely on the influence of his father, he sat for the Jinshi degree national examination and succeeded with excellent record. After that, he served at junior posts in Huazhou, Suzhou, etc.

Beginning from 1041, he observed four years of mourning by the grave of his father before taking an official position in Henan. At the recommendation of the premier Pang Ji, he went to the capital and took a post in charge of criminal punishment at the age of 27. Later he was promoted again and again to such posts of assistant imperial lecturer, assistant judge of the imperial court of justice, editor of the imperial academy etc. When Pang Ji was removed from the office of premier, Sima followed him to Yunzhou and Bingzhou as assistant magistrate. In 1057, he was again transferred to the capital as judge of Kaifeng. Four years later, he was promoted as recorder of the emperor's words and deeds, and deputy director of the remonstrance institute which was a post specialized in commenting on and criticizing the state affairs. Disappointed with the emperor's negligence of his ideas, Sima Guang resigned the post five years later to become a scholar of the Longtu Pavilion.

In 1067, Emperor Shenzong came to the throne. Bent on making the country prosperous through reform, this young emperor put Wang Anshi and other reformers in important positions. The emperor also very much appreciated Sima Guang's ability and promoted him to be scholar of the imperial academy and deputy director of the imperial prosecution. But just at this time, differences arose between Sima Guang and his good friend Wang Anshi on how to carry out the reform and what to reform. As a result, Sima Guang was removed from the position of scholar of the imperial academy and was demoted to be a local official in the Yongxing military district in 1070. The next year Sima Guang resigned the position and took up an honorary post in the Western Capital. He lived as long as 15 years in the Dule Garden of Luoyang, devoting himself to the compilation of *History as a Mirror*. With the help of Liu Shu and Liu Ban, Sima Guang completed this monumental historical work in 19 years.

Sima Guang lived to the age of 68, leaving behind a lot of works. In addition to *History as a Mirror*, there were 80 volumes of *Collected Works of Master Sima*, 32 volumes of *Notes by the Sushui River*, 20 volumes of *Records of Ancient History*, and 60 volumes of *Highlights of Lessons of Past Dynasties* etc.

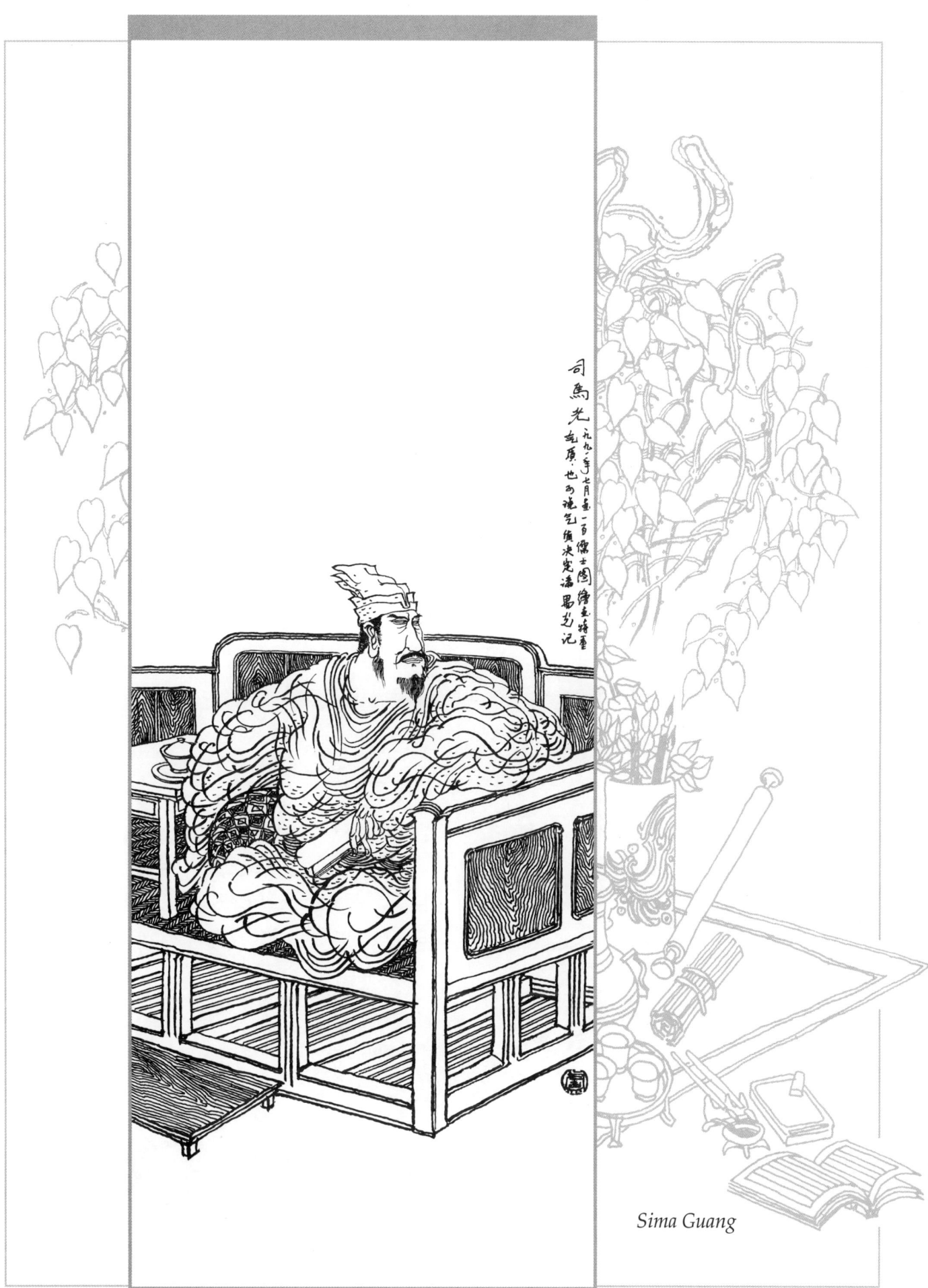

司馬光（一〇一九～一〇八六）字君實，陝州夏縣（今屬山西）涑水鄉人，世稱涑水先生記

Sima Guang

152

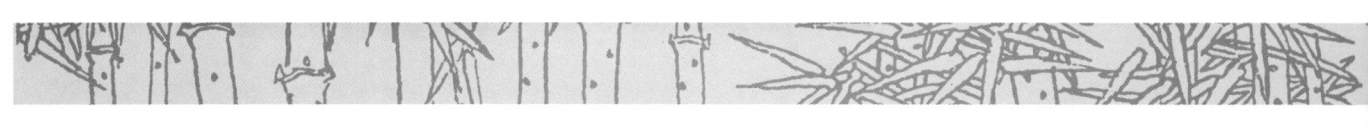

Wang Anshi

王安石

During the reign of Emperor Yingzong of the Northern Song Dynasty, a rumour was going among the officials and people in the capital Bianjing that "cuckoos flying northward foretold unrest in the country", which caused popular anxiety in the capital. It was said that the year saw many cuckoos twittering in the trees when the birds had never appeared in the place before. Some said that birds from the south were an ill omen for an official from the south taking charge of the cabinet and bringing endless unrest to the country and misery and hardships to the people. It turned out that the rumour had been spread by a conservative official Shao Bowen, and the "official from the south" he alluded to was Wang Anshi (1021–1086) who was later to carry out a reform in the country.

With the courtesy name Jiefu and literary name Banshan, Wang Anshi was also known as Wang Jinggong as his title, Duke of Jinggong, granted by the emperor. He was from Linchuan of Fuzhou (present Fuzhou city of Jiangxi), but was born in the official mansion of his father, Wang Yi, who was then Assistant Director of Linjiang Military District.

As a child, he was conversant with all the Confucian classics, which produced a profound influence on his ideology. With great ambition in mind, he was determined to make spectacular achievement. He had followed his father to Shaozhou south of the Nanling Range where he spent three years. During this period he broadened his view and gained considerable knowledge of the local conditions and customs. In 1042, he emerged fourth in the Jinshi degree national examination held in the capital, and was appointed assistant magistrate of Yangzhou.

In 1047, Wang Anshi was appointed Magistrate of Yinxian County, and in the three years at this post, he did very well in undertaking irrigation projects, and developing farming and sericulture. As a result, he was twice recommended by important ministers in the court for official posts in the capital. However, he politely declined the recommendations, as he intended to achieve considerable successes first in carrying out his reforms in the localities. Thus he served for 18 years as a local official before taking a post in the imperial institute of documents in the capital. The next year he was transferred to the post of Director of National Revenue as he was good at financial management. By this time, Wang Anshi had gained rich political and social experience after more than 20 years in his official career.

During the second year of the Xining period (1069) under the reign of Emperor Shenzong, he was appointed Deputy Premier in charge of the important task of the reform. This was the beginning of the well-known "Xining Reform" of the Northern Song Dynasty. In this year, measures were promulgated in relation to contribution balancing, young crops, and water conservancy. When he became the premier in the following year, measures of Bao-Jia household administration, and exemption of corvee were issued. Later, the imperial examination system, market transaction system, and Bao-Jia horse-raising system were also put into practice. These measures accumulated revenue for the state, restrained the privileges of officials, big landlords, and wealthy and powerful merchants, and made the country rich and the army strong.

However, the reform was also taken by corrupt officials as a means to seek private gains. That, coupled with the repeated demand by conservative officials headed by Sima Guang for termination of the reform, forced Wang Anshi to resign the position as premier to take the post of prefect of Jiangning in the capacity of scholar of Guanwen Palace. By the time he became premier again a year later, things had changed a lot with officials of the reforming group engaged in internal strife, and the conservatives intensifying their efforts to control the central power. And Wang Anshi had to retire to Jiangning from the post of premier in 1076.

Keeping in mind Wang's meritorious service in carrying out the reform for the purpose of making the country rich and the army strong, Emperor Shenzong granted him the title of Duke of Jinggong in 1080. Before the emperor's death in 1085, he again granted Wang the title of Sikong. Wang Anshi died a year later at the age of 66.

Wang was also a literary giant, being one of "the eight prose masters of the Tang and Song dynasties". His prose works were powerful and his poems vigorous. His extant writings were *Collected Works of Wang Jinggong* and the remnant part of *New Meanings of the Rites of Zhou*.

王安石 一九九二年五月 [印]

Wang Anshi

Cheng Hao & Cheng Yi

程顥 · 程頤

It was said that the Northern Song philosopher Zhou Dunyi happened to get the "diagram of boundless ultimate" of the Taoist priest Chen Tuan, and was suddenly enlightened after pondering over this wonderful diagram.

Introducing Taoism into Confucianism, Zhou made concise, straight and systematic description of the construction of the whole universe: The boundless ultimate gave rise to the supreme ultimate which through its motion and rest produced yin, yang, and all the things living and changing endlessly. And nurtured by the excellence of the supreme ultimate, human beings became the most intelligent. In imitation of the "supreme ultimate", the sage established the "human ultimate" which was "sincerity", the root of the five constant virtues and the source of all actions (from *On the Diagram of Supreme Ultimate by Zhou Dunyi*).

This philosopher had two advanced disciples who developed his theory to perfection. They were two brothers, Cheng Hao (1031–1085) and Cheng Yi (1033–1107), known to later generations as "the Cheng Brothers".

Cheng Hao was from Henan (in present Henan Province) with the courtesy name Bochun. He and his younger brother, Cheng Yi, were both disciples of Zhou Dunyi. The two brothers were very diligent and after earnest studies of the theory created by their master, both became his best disciples and excelled in learning.

In the Jiayou period of the reign of Emperor Renzong of the Northern Song Dynasty, Cheng Hao passed the Jinshi degree national examination, and served at such local posts as chief secretary of Exian County and Shangyuan County, and magistrate of Jincheng. In 1068, the first year of the Xining period of Emperor Shenzong, he was recommended as aide to the crown prince and supervising censor.

Since he was against Wang Anshi's reform, he retired to Luoyang in 1069 when Wang became the premier, and was engaged in teaching for over 10 years. His lectures were so vivid that his disciples said they had the feeling of bathing in spring wind. He put forward the idea that "the heaven" was "the reason" as well as "the mind" and that the origin of knowledge and truth was in the mind. The emphasis of learning should be on knowing "benevolence", and safeguarding the feudal order of three cardinal guides (sovereign guides subject, father guides son, and husband guides wife) and five constant virtues (benevolence, righteousness, propriety, wisdom, and loyalty). Cheng Hao died in 1085 at the age of 54, leaving behind his writing *On Human Nature*, and *On the Knowledge of Benevolence,* both of which were included in *Complete Works of the Cheng Brothers*.

His younger brother Cheng Yi had the courtesy name Zhengshu. At first he was only engaged in scholarship. Not until the death of his brother in the first year of the Yuanyou period of Emperor Zhezong, did he take up the post of editing official in the imperial secretariat at the recommendation of Sima Guang and Lu Gongzhu. Later he was promoted to be Imperial Lecturer of Chongzheng Palace. He was against the reform initiated by Wang Anshi, and was thus removed from office as a member of "The Old Party" after Emperor Zhezong took over the rein of government. Not until Emperor Huizong succeeded to the throne in 1101 was he allowed to return to Luoyang from his hometown. He lived to the age of 75.

His philosophical ideas were quite similar to those of his elder brother. He lectured for over 30 years, and was of the opinion that all things in the world, in the final analysis, were one "reason", and the reason of one thing was the reason of all things. He was sure that things were in a state of flux and was of the opinion that the "contradictions" within a thing was the source of its motion. But he did not think the two sides of the contradiction could be transformed into each other. An advocate of elimination of human desire and the safeguarding of heavenly reason, he was against widows remarrying, and preached that "to die of hunger was nothing serious, but to lose the chastity was all that mattered."

Among his writings were *On the Book of Changes*, and *On the Type of Favourite Learning of Master Yan* both included in *Complete Works of the Cheng Brothers*. The theory of the Cheng Brothers was inherited and developed by Zhu Xi into what was known as Cheng-Zhu school of learning.

一九九二年
五月五日
畫于我
秀山麓
三元古
宮野珠
齋圖

程顥
程頤

Cheng Hao &
Cheng Yi

Shen Kuo

沈括

With his talent, a Confucian scholar, Shen Kuo (1030–1095), of the Northern Song Dynasty achieved quite a few "number ones" for China in the field of science and technology. He created a new calendar of "12 solar terms" several hundred years before the introduction of similar calendars in foreign countries. He was the first to discover the geomagnetic deflection, more than 400 years before Christopher Columbus made the same discovery in 1492. He initiated the method for topographic survey, and the "24-point mapping method". He also expounded the origin of the special scene of the grotesque rocks of the Yandang Mountain in Wenzhou, the formation of the plains, and the changes between sea and land. All these were done several centuries earlier than in foreign countries.

Shen Kuo was from Qiantang (present Hangzhou of Zhejiang) with the courtesy name Cunzhong. His father, Shen Zhou, was a magistrate, and according to the official system of the Northern Song Dynasty, he was made Chief Secretary of Shuyang at the age of 20 in recognition of the services of his father. He read widely from early childhood, not only in Confucian classics, but also in other schools of learning, as well as medicine, divination, mathematics, science etc., laying a solid foundation for his future development.

Though he became an official on the strength of his father's service, Shen Kuo was free of the bad ways of the sons of rich families. As a young man of true ability and learning, he made spectacular achievements at his post in gaining 46,000 hectares of land after dredging the Shushui River. When he was promoted to be magistrate of Ningguo County, he again built the Wanchun embankment for the benefit of the locality.

In the eighth year of the Jiayou period of the reign of Emperor Renzong (1063), Shen Kuo was appointed Imperial Collator after passing the Jinshi degree examination. And after he was made Director of Astronomy in the first year of the reign of Emperor Shenzong, he improved such instruments as the celestial globe, etc. and compiled the "Fengyuan calendar", making contributions to the development of astronomy in ancient China.

When Wang Anshi became the premier in the second year of the Xining period of the reign of Emperor Shenzong, Shen Kuo participated in his reform. He made an inspection tour to Liangzhe and Hebeixilu, carrying out the "young crops policy" and starting irrigation projects. In the eighth year of the Xining period (1075), he was sent as an envoy to the kingdom of Liao, where he rebuffed Liao's unreasonable demand for the seizure of Huangwei area. He also wrote *Illustrated Records of the Mission to Qidan* which provided favourable conditions for the military operations of the Song army in later years. After that, he was promoted Member of the Imperial Academy and Acting Director of National Revenue. In 1080, he took the post of governor of Fuyanlu, but two years later he was demoted and exiled to Suizhou and Xiuzhou as a result of the military defeat of his subordinate official, Xu Xi, which led to the fall of Yongle into the hands of Liao. Not until 1090 did he regain freedom and settle down in Mengxi Garden in Runzhou where he wrote *Notes at Mengxi* and other works. He lived to the age of 65.

His most important work, *Notes at Mengxi*, was in 30 volumes. It was not only a general record of the data of science and technology, but also a valuable historical record in which there were over 120 items on history and archaeology. It was also a work of literature of strong appeal with natural and smooth language. And there were even three volumes on music showing the writer's literary accomplishment and artistic talent. In philosophy, Shen Kuo was versed in the *Book of Changes*, and the theory of Yin and Yang and the Five Elements, on the basis of which he developed his own simple materialist world outlook, theory of knowledge, and dialectics.

Shen Kuo was a prolific author. Records show that he had 37 types of works, most of which are lost. Besides *Notes at Mengxi*, passed down to the present were 22 volumes *Collection of Changxing* (originally 41 volumes) which were of a comprehensive nature, and *Selected Prescriptions*.

沈括
一九九二年五月吉

Shen Kuo

Su Shi

In the period of Jiayou under the reign of Emperor Renzong of the Northern Song Dynasty, a 21-year-old young man passed the Jinshi degree national examination with excellent grades, attracting wide attention with the first display of his ability. This young man excelled later in poetry, ci (a new form of poem), prose, calligraphy, and painting. In poems and ci, he blazed a trail in founding the powerful and free school; in prose writing, he was among the "eight prose masters of the Tang and Song dynasties"; in calligraphy, he was the number one of the "four great calligraphers of the Song Dynasty", the other three being Cai Xiang, Huang Tingjian, and Mi Pei; in painting, he was a great master in depicting bamboo, withered trees, and grotesque rocks. This young Jinshi scholar was Su Shi (1037–1101) who was admired as another great star following Qu Yuan, Li Bai, and Du Fu.

Su Shi was from Meishan of Jiazhou (in present Sichuan) with Zizhan as his courtesy name and Dongpo as his literary name. He was born in a family of scholars. Excelling in prose writing, his father Su Xun was one of the "eight prose masters of the Tang and Song dynasties", and his mother Madame Cheng was a woman of great literary attainments. After passing the Jinshi degree examination, he began serving the government. Su Shi had a chequered career and his last post was at Hainan island, then known as the "remote corner of the world".

After leaving Hainan, Su Shi first went to Yongzhou. Then on the way back to the north, he died in Changzhou in 1101. Of the 66 years of life of this literary giant, more than 30 years were spent in demotion from one place to another. He was buried in the Small Emei Mountain in Jiaxian County of Henan and was granted the posthumous title of Wenzhong, meaning literary and loyal.

As the leader of the literary circle of his time, Su Shi had profound influence on the art and literature of later generations. Among his poems, passed down to the present day are over 4,000 vivid and original pieces full of figures of speech and in a free and unrestrained style. The Chinese idiom "Marks of goose claws on the snow", which refers to traces of past events, had its origin in the following poem of his:

To what shall I compare traces of life?
A goose on a land of snow it may be like.

Marks of claws it leaves from time to time.
Little does it care the way it has flown.
And the lines of the following two famous poems have been on the lips of the Chinese people generation after generation:

Rain after Shine on the West Lake
Sparkling in the sun the ripples offer a grand scene.
Misty hills in the rain also presents a special sight.
The West Lake is just as beautiful as the West Lady
Who's equally charming in plain dress or in bright.

Writing on the Xilin Cliff
A range is seen in the front, but a peak
from the side.
Different views appear at varying distance
and height.
I can't tell the true face of the Lushan Mount,
Simply because I myself am within its bound.

Passed down to the present are several thousand pieces of his prose works, most of which are smooth and eloquent. In prose writing Su Shi was placed in parallel with the great writer Ouyang Xiu and together they were referred to as "Ou-Su". He and his father Su Xun and his brother Su Zhe were all among the "eight prose masters of the Tang and Song dynasties".

Su Shi also composed over 300 pieces of ci, which were forceful, open and magnanimous, breaking through the "flowery style" tradition of this new form of poem, and initiating the powerful and free style. They are so bold and forceful that people said that they should be sung by strong and big men in the company of instruments made of bronze and steel. In his ci, there are scenes of ancient battlefield; grand picturesque sight; heroes; scholars; patriots; and country girls. His ci covered such a wide range of subjects, making the reader feel new and fresh. However, the writings of his later years revealed Taoist ideas from time to time, which had a lot to do with the perilous circumstances and the frustrations in his official career.

His works have been widely printed since his time including 40 volumes of *Collected Works of Dongpo*, 20 volumes of *Sequel to Collected Works of Dongpo*, 15 volumes of *Memorials Presented to the Emperors*, and 13 volumes of *Imperial Edicts Drafted by Dongpo* etc.

Su Shi

Lu You

陸游

Nothing will I worry about after my death,
But for the country's unification I do crave.
When our troops recover the lost land in the north,
Forget not to let me know when you visit my grave.

The above poem entitled *To My Sons* was written by the great Southern Song Dynasty poet Lu You (1125–1210) at the end of his life. With strong appeal and patriotic passion, it has been on the lips of the Chinese people for hundreds of years.

Lu You was from Shanyin of Yuezhou (present Shaoxing of Zhejiang) with Wuguan as his courtesy name, and Fangwong as his literary name. He was born in a small boat on the Huaihe River in 1125 when his father, Lu Zai, a deputy financial inspector, was on his way to the capital together with his wife. He loved reading early in his childhood, as was shown in his lines:

Indulged in books as early as I began to prattle,
I dimmed my eyes reading so many volumes.

A staunch patriot, his father and his friends cried bitterly over the tragic death of the patriotic General Yue Fei and condemned the treacherous Prime Minister Qin Hui for his merciless persecution of loyal officials and for the harm he did to the country.

In 1153, the 29-year-old Lu You came out first in the national examination, which was the decision of the upright chief examiner Chen Yuanmao against the order of the treacherous premier Qin Hui. In the palace examination the next year, however, Qin Hui deleted Lu You's name from the list and put in his grandson's name Qin Xun instead, even threatening to punish Chen Yuanmao who had failed to carry out his order.

Lu You served in various official posts but suffered setbacks in his career. Unable to realize his ambition as the court was only after temporary peace, the gloomy and worrying poet took refuge in liquor, styling himself Fangwong (meaning unrestrained old man). It was just in this period that he perfected his proficiency in poetic composition, becoming a great poet of a unique school. He went on expressing his ambition to recover the lost land in his poems as was shown by the lines:

Most of the poems express the joy of fighting,
A true hero is Fangwong from time immemorial.

In 1178, Emperor Xiaozong put Lu You in charge of tea and salt administration in Fujian, and later transferred him to Jiangxi for the same post. But before long he was back at home without any official post until five years later when he was appointed Director of Yanzhou Military District, Deputy Superintendent of Military Supplies, Department Director of the Board of Rites, etc. When Emperor Guangzong succeeded to the throne in 1190, Lu You presented a proposal that earnest efforts be made to make the country strong and prosperous. His honest advice, however, offended the rulers and cost him his official post. Living among the peasants in the subsequent dozen years, he wrote a lot of poems reflecting the ruthless reality of the countryside or describing the rural scenery in a placid style.

In 1202, Han Tuozhou, an advocate of war against the Jin, recommended Lu You for the post of history compiler. Lu You accepted the appointment without hesitation and took part in the compilation of *Records of Two Reigns*, and *History of Three Reigns* at the advanced age of 78. He resigned his post after finishing the compilation. With Han Tuozhou put to death in 1206, the advocates of peace dominated the power of the court, and Lu You was deprived in 1208 of the half salary he had enjoyed as a retired imperial drafter of documents. Though already 84, he remained a devoted patriot till death. With the regret of his failure to see the unification of the country, he wrote the poem *To My Sons* before his death at the age of 86.

Lu You was a well-known great patriotic poet in Chinese history and was admired as "Li Bai the junior" for the romantic sentiment in his poems. Among the tens of thousands of poems written by him, more than 9,000 have been handed down to the present time. Impassioned and unconstrained, and full of power and grandeur, most of his poems were on the recovery of the lost land and the unification of the country against capitulationism, and some reflected the sufferings of the people and voiced his criticism of the political situation of the time. His works were compiled in *Collection of Weinan*, *Jiannan Poems*, and *Notes of Laoxue'an*.

Lu You

Zhu Xi

In the second year of the Chunxi period under the reign of Emperor Xiaozong of the southern Song Dynasty (1175), a famous philosophy debate was held at Ehu Temple in Xingzhou between two groups of well-known Confucian scholars. On one side was the Rationalist School (Cheng-Zhu School) represented by Zhu Xi (1130–1200), and on the other was the "Mind Learning School" headed by Lu Jiuyuan. It was indeed a heated debate with the protagonists of both sides citing quotations from classics and composing poems ridiculing each other. The heated exchange of the Ehu Temple Meeting disturbed its organizer, Lu Zuqian, who had intended to invite Zhu and Lu for a direct discussion so as to reconcile their ideas only to find the "peaceful discussion" he had expected turning into a face to face polemic.

Zhu Xi's courtesy name was Yuanhui or Zhonghui and his literary name was Hui'an or Ziyang. He was from Wuyuan of Huizhou (in present Jiangxi Province) but was born in Fujian when his father, Zhu Song, was an official there. His father died when he was 14 years old, and four years later he passed the Jinshi national examination. In 1153, he was appointed Chief Secretary of Tong'an County where he served for three years before returning home to study under Li Dong, a third-generation disciple of Cheng Yi. So Zhu Xi was the fourth-generation disciple of the "Cheng brothers".

After Emperor Xiaozong succeeded to the throne in 1162, an imperial edict was issued for frank comments on state affairs. Zhu Xi presented a memorial in favour of resistance against the Jin invaders. He suggested that Emperor Xiaozong study the honest and proper "imperial learning" through careful observation that would rectify ethics and establish institution and order in the court. He pleaded with the emperor to fight against the invaders for the sake of "heavenly reason". The next year he was appointed Instructor of the Military Academy, and he went to the capital, Lin'an, to take office in 1165. However, he resigned the post after a short period due to disagreement with the premier who was in favour of peace with the invaders. After that he declined quite a few appointments by the court until 1178 when he took charge of the Nankang Military District. At this post, he repaired the Bailudong Academy at Lushan Mountain where he gave lectures, which promoted education in the locality.

After Emperor Ningzong succeeded to the throne, Zhu Xi became imperial lecturer and drafter of imperial edicts, thanks to the recommendation of the premier Zhao Ruyu. However, he was removed from office for making advice to the emperor to guard against Han Tuozhou who was monopolizing power. Han forced the premier out of the court and dismissed Zhu Xi and many other officials. Rationalism was banned as pseudo-learning and Zhu Xi's disciples were accused as members of "pseudo-learning party", "traitorous party", and "die-hard party". And there were even people who advised the emperor to put Zhu Xi to death. Zhu Xi died of illness at the age of 71.

Zhu Xi was well read and made annotations to a lot of classics, contributing in varying degrees to Confucian classics, history, literature, music and natural science. In philosophy, he developed the theory of the "Cheng brothers" on the relation of reason and qi into a comprehensive rationalist system of objective idealism. He put forward the theory that things were complementary to each other and everything was always capable of being divided into two infinitely. While holding that reason and qi were interdependent and could not be separated, he asserted that "reason existed before qi". Zhu stressed the method of elicitation and inspiration in the 50 years when he was engaged in education. In natural science, he proved geological changes from sea to mountain based on his study of spiral shells found in the mountains.

After his death, Emperor Ningzong granted him the posthumous title of Wen (learning) and Medium Minister. The next emperor, Lizong, awarded him the title of Grand Master and Duke of Hui, and later he was given the honour of enjoying worship in company of Confucius. Starting from the Yuan Dynasty, Zhu Xi's rationalism became the official philosophy of the country, and his *Annotations to the Four Classics* were used in the imperial examinations.

Zhu Xi's style of study, reading widely and making careful analyses, had positive influence on scholars of later generations. Among his many extant works were *Annotations to the Four Classics*, *Comments on the Book of Songs*, *Annotations to the Songs of the South*, *Outlines of History as a Mirror*, *The Original Meanings of the Book of Changes* etc. People of later generations compiled his works into *Quotations from Master Zhu*, *Collected Works of Hui'an*, *Posthumous Works of Master Zhu*" etc.

朱熹

Zhu Xi

Lu Jiuyuan

After the beginning of the Qiandao period under the reign of Emperor Xiaozong of the Southern Song Dynasty, three branch schools of Confucianism emerged: The first represented by Zhu Xi advocating "gaining knowledge through studying the objects"; the second represented by the Lu brothers advocating "clarifying the mind"; the third represented by Lu Zuqian on absorbing the merits of the first two branches.

The second branch was created by three brothers, Lu Jiushao, Lu Jiuling, and Lu Jiuyuan (1139–1193). It was already quite rare for three brothers to be interested in philosophy at the same time, and even more precious and rarer for them to make achievements in the same philosophical field. Among the three brothers, the youngest, Lu Jiuyuan, was the most distinguished in achievement and fame.

Lu Jiuyuan's courtesy name was Zijing. He styled himself Old Man Cunzhai Xiangshan, while other scholars called him Mr Xiangshan. He was from Jinxi of Fuzhou (in present Jiangxi). He passed the Jinshi national examination in the Qiandao period during the reign of Emperor Xiaozong and was appointed Chief Secretary of Jin'an County before transferred to the post of Chief Secretary of Chong'an County. Later, he served as Director of the Imperial College, and Supervisor in charge of construction of palaces, imperial ancestral temples and tombs. In 1191, during the reign of Emperor Guangzong, he was imperial aide, and concurrently in charge of the Jingmen military region. He died in that post in 1193.

Together with his two elder brothers, Lu Jiuyuan established the "Lu Branch School of Learning". The eldest brother, Lu Jiushao, opposed Zhu Xi's theory that there was something called "Wuji" above "Taiji" or the "Supreme Ultimate", thinking that "Explanations to the Taiji Chart" was not the work of Zhou Dunyi. The second brother, Lu Jiuling, passed the Jinshi degree examination in the Qiandao period and once served as Instructor of Xingguo military region. He stressed the importance of practising feudal ethics.

Combining the Meditation (Zen) Sect of Buddhism with the subjective idealist thinking of the Zisi-Mencius branch of Confucianism, Lu Jiuyuan created the ideological system of "mind learning". This held that "mind was the reason" asserting that heavenly reason, human reason, and object reason all existed in the mind which was the only true reality. He was of the opinion that the "mind" and the "reason" would never change. Lu carried on a long running debate with Zhu Xi. His theory was inherited and developed by Wang Shouren of the Ming Dynasty into the Lu-Wang Branch of Learning.

Lu Jiuyuan's writings were collected in *Complete Works of Mr Xiangshan*, Lu Jiushao's in *Suoshan Diary* and *Collected Works of Suoshan*, and Lu Jiuling's in *Collected Works of Fuzhai*.

陸九淵

陆九渊

一九九一年七月三十日画于鹏峰山麓三元古宫

Lu Jiuyuan

168

Xin Qiji

辛棄疾

One day in the 31st year of the Shaoxing period of the reign of Emperor Gaozong of the Southern Song Dynasty (1161), two horses were galloping on the road from Yunzhou to the camp of the Jin army. The rider in the front was a monk named Yirui carrying the seal of Geng Jing, leader of the anti-Jin volunteer army, which he had stolen to present to the Jin army for reward. Chasing behind was Xin Qiji (1140–1207), the secretary of the volunteer army, who wanted to get back the seal from the traitor. When the two horses were getting nearer, Yirui begged his former friend for mercy. Without paying any heed to the monk, Xin Qiji killed him and seized back the seal. Thus the 22-year-old Xin Qiji won high prestige among the volunteers for his courage and martial arts.

Xin Qiji was from Licheng of Qizhou (present Jinan of Shandong) with the courtesy name Yiu'an and literary name Jiaxuan. He was born in Licheng under the rule of the Jin invaders and witnessed their cruel oppression of the people. With strong national hatred, he made earnest efforts in reading and practising martial arts. When the ruler of Jin, Wanyan Liang, led an army of 400,000 soldiers to invade the Song Dynasty, heroes in central China arose to resist them. Xin Qiji joined the volunteer troops of Gengjing in Yunzhou with more than 2,000 soldiers and was appointed secretary. He then persuaded the monk Yirui to join the anti-Jin forces with his 1,000 soldiers. Contrary to his expectation, Yirui later stole the seal of the commander hoping to get reward from the Jin invaders.

In 1162, the generals of the invading Jin army staged a coup d'etat and killed Wanyan Liang before leading their troops back to the north. Regarding this as a good opportunity for all the anti-Jin troops in the north and the south to join forces for the recovery of the lost land, Xin Qiji suggested that Geng Jing get in touch with the court of the Southern Song. Geng then sent Xin as an envoy to Lin'an, where Emperor Gaozong granted him an audience and appointed Geng Jing governor of Tianping, and Xin Qiji secretary of the governor. But another traitor of the volunteers, Zhang Anguo, murdered Geng Jing and took the post of prefect of Jizhou of the Jin regime. After getting back to the north, Xin Qiji led 50 mounted soldiers to break into the Jin camp of 50,000 men with the suddenness and swiftness of a thunderbolt, and captured Zhang Anguo alive, calling on 10,000

soldiers to come over from the enemy's side. The Jin troops were surprised by their heroic move and by the time they realized what had happened and organized a chase, Xin had already led the soldiers across the Huaihe River.

Xin Qiji served at quite a few senior local posts. With the belief that "the people are the foundation of the country", he would undertake irrigation projects, restrain powerful local gentry, and start schools wherever he served his post.

When he was out of office for 20 years, he wrote a lot of impassioned ci poems. After the "Ehu Meeting" with another ci poet Chen Liang in 1188, Xin turned out one excellent piece after another. A good example was the ci written to the tune of Pozhenzi for Chen Liang:

Drunk, I made the lamp brighter to see my sword better;
Awoke, I heard horns resounding throughout the camp.
Beef grilled was granted to my warriors gallant,
Amidst majestic martial music from countless instruments.
What a magnificent scene of autumn manoeuvre!
On gallant steeds galloping at full speed,
The valiant fighters shot with bows twanging.
My ambition it has been to recover land lost
For the sovereign, and to win fame everlasting.
What a pity, white hair is growing.

It can be seen that he never forgot to recover the lost land even in banishment.

In 1207, Xin Qiji was appointed to a senior position in the court in charge of imperial edicts but he declined the post due to old age and illness. On the 10th of the ninth month of the year, Xin Qiji died at the age of 68.

Xin Qiji remained a resolute advocate of resistance against Jin invasion throughout his life. Most of the extant 600 ci poems of his expressed his strong wish to recover the lost land for the unification of the country. Those pieces admiring the beauty of the landscape were fresh and elegant. Following the free and unrestrained style of Su Dongpo, he broadened the scope and enriched the contents of ci. They enjoyed parallel popularity and were known as "Su-Xin". However, his style was freer, breaking through the restrictions of rhyming and temperament and forming a distinct style of his own. His writings were passed down in *Collected Ci Poems by Jiaxuan*.

Xin Qiji

Zhao Bingwen

Ten years after the founding of the Jin Dynasty by Emperor Taizu, it wiped out the Liao kingdom in 1125 under the leadership of Emperor Taizong. The next year, it took Bianjing, the capital of the Northern Song Dynasty, and captured Emperor Huizong and Emperor Qinzong, putting an end to the Northern Song Dynasty. Since then, the Jin Dynasty became stronger and stronger. Reforming the old customs and adopting the Han system, Emperor Taizong of Jin established his rule over central China.

By the time Emperor Shizong of Jin came to throne in 1161, the Jin and the Southern Song had been at a stalemate. In order to get the support of the nobility of various nationalities, Emperor Shizong made efforts to develop the culture of the Han nationality. The Rationalist scholar of the Jin Dynasty, Zhao Bingwen (1158–1232), lived during this period. The atmosphere of the Han culture in central China produced a profound influence on him and enabled him to lay the foundation in his study of Confucianism and his literary creation.

His courtesy name was Zhouchen and his literary name Xianxian Old Man. He was from Fuyang of Cizhou (present Cixian County, Hebei Province). He passed the Jinshi national examination in his early twenties in the Dading period of the reign of Emperor Shizong and was appointed Department Director in the Ministry of Revenue. He was fond of Tang Dynasty poetry especially the prose and poetry of the great Tang poet Han Yu from which he got the influence of Han's Confucian ideology. In philosophy, he followed the rationalist ideology of Cheng Hao and his brother Cheng Yi. The combination of Han Yu's ideology and the rationalism of the Cheng brothers gave rise to Zhao Bingwen's unique academic ideology.

He was promoted in his official career to the position of Deputy Drafter of Imperial Edicts and later in the Taihe period of the reign of Emperor Zhangzong to Compiler of the Imperial Academy. After Emperor Xuanzong succeeded to the throne, Zhao Bingwen, with his qualifications as master of rationalism and a minister having served three emperors, was made Minister of Rites and Imperial Reading Companion. Later he was further promoted to Senior Minister and Guardian of the Army. He took as his own task the advocating of humanity, justice, virtue, and human nature, holding that the Tao was the universe itself and the root of all things. To get the truth of the heavenly principle, it was necessary to have a clear understanding of reason. He also raised the idea that the "medium" was "human nature itself", and virtue or evil was derived from the "medium". His achievement in the study of rationalism was the best in the Jin Dynasty though he was behind Zhu Xi of the Southern Song in this respect.

Zhao Bingwen died at the age of 75. Among his works were *On the Book of Changes*, *On the Doctrine of the Mean* etc. He was also a literary writer. Most of his poems were on natural scenery which were collected in *Fushui River Collection of Xianxian Old Man*.

趙秉文

Zhao Bingwen

Yelü Chucai

In 1218, a descendant of the Khitan royal family went from the Middle Capital of Jin (present Beijing) to the north beyond the desert. At the grand sight of troops, horses, chariots, and tents all over the place, he could not help getting excited as Genghis Khan was going to grant him an audience.

Yelü Chucai's (1190–1244) courtesy name was Jinqing and he was born in a family of Khitan nationality in the Middle Capital of the Jin Dynasty. His ancestors were royal family members of the Liao Dynasty, but his grand uncle began to serve Jin just before Jin overthrew Liao. His father, Yelü Lu, had been Jin's premier. His family declined, however, after the death of his father when he was only a year old. Thus he was brought up by his mother, Madame Yang. He studied hard and read widely in astronomy, geography, law, history, mathematics, medicine, Buddhism, Taoism, divination, and Confucian classics. He was quick-witted in writing, and the articles written by him seldom needed any corrections.

At 17, Yelü Chucai acquitted himself well in an audience granted by Emperor Zhangzong of the Jin Dynasty, and was made a subordinate official. Six or seven years later he was promoted to the position of deputy magistrate of Kaizhou. He remained in the Middle Capital as an official without much to do after Jin moved the capital to the southern Capital (present Kaifeng) in 1214 under the threat of the Mongols fighting southward. The next year, the Middle Capital was captured by the Mongol army and Yelü Chucai turned to study Zen Buddhism under the direction of Old Man Wansong. Three years later he became a famous Buddhist in the city of Yanjing. At the time he was waiting for a chance "to cultivate his morality with Buddhism, and to administer the country with Confucianism".

The chance came in the 13th year of the reign of Emperor Taizu, Genghis Khan (1218), who was then enlisting the royal family members of the conquered Liao Dynasty. Hearing that Yelü Chucai was learned and talented, the Great Khan sent for him and granted him an audience north of the desert. Pleased with his handsome beard, tall stature, and resounding voice as well as his erudition, Genghis Khan kept him by his side, calling him "Long Beard Man" The next year, he followed the Khan in his westward expedition to Khwarezm serving as a secretary in charge of documents, calendar, and divination. He did quite well in organizing immigrants for cultivating wasteland, and in establishing a new calendar. He served for 10 years in the westward expedition till the death of Genghis Khan in 1227. In the winter of that year, Yelü Chucai returned to Yanjing and participated in the scheme for the inheritance of the crown. In 1229, Ogodai took over as Great Khan.

In opposition to the suggestion of the Mongol nobles that the farmland should be turned into pasture, Yelü Chucai advocated maintaining agriculture and handicraft production in central China so as to levy tax for military supply. After trial practice, his policy turned out to be very successful, and he was then appointed premier. Yelü paid great attention to maintaining the population. The Mongol troops had intended to massacre the inhabitants of Bianjing after they captured the city at the beginning of 1233. It was only after his repeated persuasion that Ogodai decided to punish only the royal family members of the Jin Dynasty; thus 1,470,000 people escaped death. He also persuaded the Khan to release prisoners of war and to lift the ban on helping refugees, saving a large number of refugees from death. He formulated a relatively lenient taxation system, enabling the people in central China to recuperate. He took measures to enlarge census registration, and weaken the privilege of the nomadic Mongol nobles in central China.

The fundamental measures of his "administering the country with Confucianism" were: Choosing Confucian scholars to take charge of taxation in 10 regions, employing large numbers of civil officials; recommending Confucianism to Ogodai, and presenting a memorial for making the 51st generation descendant of Confucius, Kong Yuancuo, the Duke of Sage Descendant when Bianjing was captured; enlisting Confucian scholars and establishing the imperial college; setting up the house of Confucian classics and the compilation house for compiling and printing Confucian classics; and inviting famous scholars to lecture on Confucian classics.

Yelü Chucai was estranged by the Empress Dowager who came into power after the death of Ogodai in 1241 since she was in favour of another minister. Seeing evil officials in power and the state affairs deteriorating day by day, Yelü Chucai died in depression and anxiety at the age of 55. His writings were compiled in *Collected Works of the Lay Buddhist Zhanran*.

耶律楚材

Yelü Chucai

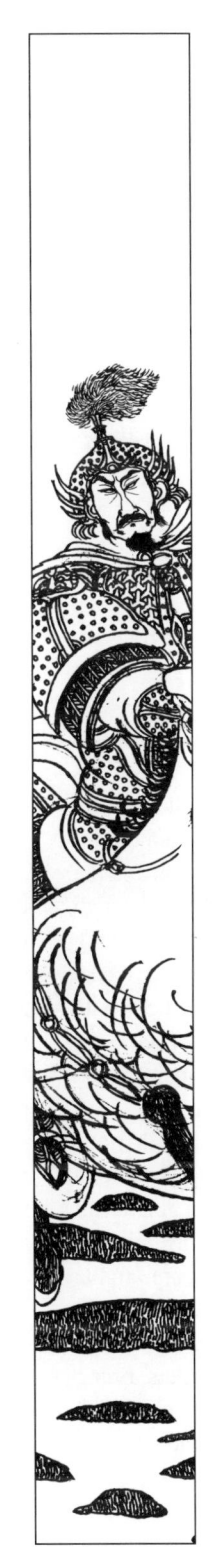

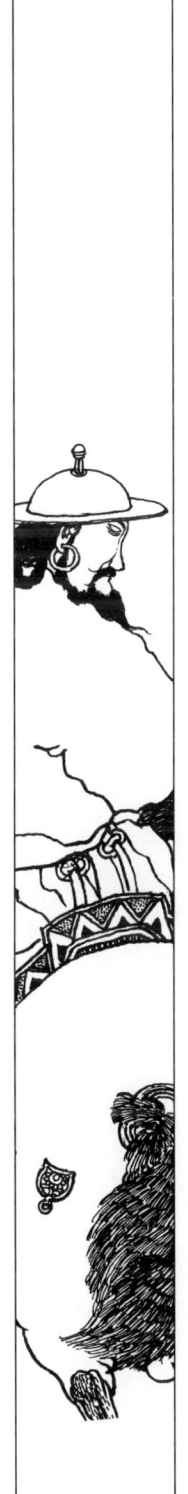

Guan Hanqing

關漢卿

In 1958, the great Yuan Dynasty dramatist Guan Hanqing (c. 1220–c. 1300) was listed as a "cultural celebrity of the world" to commemorate his important contribution to the culture of mankind. Many countries staged his drama, *The Injustice Suffered by Dou'e*, and carried out research on his life and works.

In the Chinese film with Guan Hanqing as the title-role, he was admired for what he wrote in a non-drama song as a "bronze bean" which "is solid and resounding and cannot be damaged through steaming, boiling, hammering, or frying". He, "the bronze bean", was against the oppressive rule of the Mongol aristocrats, and through his dramas exposed and castigated the feudal forces and expressed his sympathy and admiration for the common people by pouring out his grievances and indignation.

Of the 60-odd dramas written by him, 18 have been passed down to the present. With very high artistic value, his works enriched the treasury of classic Chinese literature and are gems in the world history of the arts.

His original name is not known to us. Hanqing was his courtesy name and Yizhai his literary name. He was from Dadu (present Beijing), and spent his childhood in the period when the Jin and Song dynasties perished in succession and the Yuan Dynasty unified China. Having gone through the upheaval of wars, he had a deep understanding of the cruel rule of the Mongols. Disdaining to take any official post in the Yuan Dynasty, he would rather associate himself with actors and actresses and other labourers at the bottom of society, and devote his energy and talent to drama.

With the development of Chinese literature, there developed in the Song Dynasty a new form of poetry ci written to certain tunes with lines of uneven length. And with the formation of the stratum of city residents, there appeared in the Yuan Dynasty a new literary form of "drama" with plots and characters and non-drama songs accompanied on strings, flutes, and clappers. Being the political, economic, and cultural centre of North China, the Yuan capital Dadu attracted many talented people who formed societies of writers of dramas and songs. Thus dramas originated and prospered in Dadu.

Witty and humorous, and learned and versed in writing, Guan Hanqing joined the "Yujing Society of Drama and Song Writers", and became the most talented dramatist of the organization. Some of his good friends were also writers of dramas and songs or actors and actresses. The famous song writer, Wang Heqing, and drama writer, Yang Xianzhi, both had close relations with Guan Hanqing, who was also in close touch with singing girls who performed roles in dramas. He had a particularly profound friendship with the famous actress Zhu Lianxiu who was unique in her artistic performance. Gifted and refined, Guan was good at singing, dancing and playing strings and flutes, in addition to being a master of prose and poetry. He was universally admired at the time as the leader of the theatre and the best writer of dramas. These artistic practices in turn facilitated his drama creation.

Among his dramas were *Zhao Pan'er Saving the Deceived Girl*, *Magistrate Bao Conducting Inquest on the Butterfly Dream*, *The Injustice Suffered by Dou'er*, *The Repining Girl and the Moon-Worshipping Pavilion*, *Lord Guan Going to the Enemy's Banquet with a Single Sword*, *Magistrate Bao Executing Lu Zhailang by Strategy*, etc. These dramas were true to life, covering a wide range of subjects drawn from materials either in daily life or historical legends.

Guan denounced wars that brought disaster to the people and condemned the feudal rulers who savagely oppressed the people. He advocated resistance to oppression, and supported killing corrupt officials to rid the people of the source of evil. Repudiated in his works were the feudal official system, privileges system, patriarchal system, marriage system, prostitution system, and ruthless oppression and exploitation. In depicting brave, resourceful, and kind-hearted women, he expressed deep sympathy for women who were most cruelly oppressed, and made them fulfil their wish by ingeniously combining realism and romanticism.

His representative works were the tragedy *The Injustice Suffered by Dou'er*, the comedy *Saving the Deceived Girl*, and the historical drama *Going to the Enemy's Banquet with a Single Sword*. He also wrote many songs of which 57 short songs, 13 sequences of songs, and two incomplete sequences of songs were still extant. His excellent contribution made him founder of the tradition of realistic drama.

Guan Hanqing

Wang Shifu

王實甫

Since the Tang Dynasty poet Yuan Zhen wrote *The Story of the Girl Yingying*, the complicated love story of the young scholar, Zhang, and the girl, Cui Yingying, had moved generations of readers. It was a pity that the heroine in his story was deserted in the end and the romance became a tragedy. So a popular story-teller of the Jin Dynasty named Dong changed it into a tragicomedy.

It was the Yuan Dynasty dramatist, Wang Shifu, who made the love story popular throughout the country. Vivid and colourful, his poetic drama, *The Story of the West Chamber*, far exceeded the original story in theme and artistic value. Later generations commented that *Romance of the Western Chamber* is the best among all the dramas and stories".

The name of the dramatist was Dexin, and Shifu was his courtesy name. He was from Dadu (present-day Beijing) and was engaged in drama writing roughly from the closing years of the 13th century to the beginning of the 14th century, a little later than Guan Hanqing, who was active in drama writing roughly from 1260s to the first few years of the 14th century.

Wang Shifu was also born in the Jin Dynasty and lived into the Yuan Dynasty, but he died many years after the death of Guan Hanqing. He had been a county magistrate in the Yuan Dynasty and was later promoted to be inspector of Shaanxi before resigning his official post. It was only after his resignation that he was completely engaged in drama writing. He wrote a non-drama song in his late years describing the ease and leisure of his life of retirement in scenic places with musical instruments, chess, poems, and wine for company. So, quite different from Guan Hanqing who lived and wrote among the lower strata of the society, he wrote dramas in ease and leisure among the scholar-official stratum.

In all, Wang Shifu wrote 14 dramas, of which *Romance of the Western Chamber*, *Four Ministers Singing and Dancing in the Lichun Chamber*, *The Story of Lu Mengzheng in a Shabby Kiln in Wind and Snow* have been kept to the present time. *The Story of Su Xiaoqing Selling Tea in a Boat on a Moon-lit Night* and *The Story of Han Caiyun Playing Music at Furong Pavilion* can still be seen with some pages missing. The second

of the above dramas had Yue Shan as the hero who lived a life of drinking, singing, and dancing but at the same time weighed down by worries and grievances after setbacks and demotion in officialdom. People have opined that the drama was most probably a reflection of the writer's own life. Therefore it has its own special value though its artistic achievement leaves much to be desired. In a broad sense, the drama reflected one aspect of the social and political life in the transition from the Jin to the Yuan Dynasty. Just like Guan Hanqing's *Moon-Worshipping Pavilion*, the drama is valuable for people who want to know the social life at the beginning of the Yuan Dynasty.

Wang's representative drama was *Romance of the Western Chamber* with 21 acts which broke the tradition of Yuan dramas that generally had only four acts. Instead of assigning all the sung parts to the protagonist as had been the tradition, some songs were shared by two or three characters. The writer made great efforts in depicting the vivid images of the Old Lady (symbol of feudal ethics), Yingying (personification of betrayal of feudal ethics), the Red Maid, the Young Scholar Zhang, and Monk Huiming. The most successfully depicted image was the Red Maid who helped to bring about the happy union of Yingying and the Young Scholar. Brave, upright, clever, and resourceful, she had a justified, beneficial, and moderate struggle against the Old Lady, cleverly protecting herself as well as the love between Yingying and Zhang. The acts "First Meeting", "Pining for Love", "The Tryst", "Interrogating the Red Maid", and "Parting" all had memorable lines. The "Interrupted Dream at the Thatched Bridge" was the climax of the drama in which the words of the songs were most plaintively touching.

All these showed the profound craftsmanship of this great master of the Grace School Dramatists of the Yuan Dynasty. His wording was elegant and enchanting, and his narration and description were elaborate and touching. The Grace School represented by Wang Shifu and the Natural School (characterized with simple natural language) represented by Guan Hanqing enhanced each other's beauty, forming the rich and colourful artistic style of the Yuan dramas and promoting the development of this literary form.

王实甫

Wang Shifu

Wen Tianxiang

During the reign of Emperor Lizong of the Southern Song Dynasty, a child who had just begun schooling pledged to follow the examples of the past sages when he saw the portraits of Ouyang Xiu and Hu Quan in the county school. This child was Wen Tianxiang (1236–1283), who did come out first in the Jinshi examination after a dozen years and later became a great patriotic hero of the Chinese nation.

His courtesy name was Songrui and he was born into a family of scholars in Luling of Jizhou (modern Ji'an of Jingxi Province). As a child, he was fond of reading, quick to learn and active in thinking. In 1256, he went to the capital Lin'an, and in the imperial examination he advocated reforms in view of the corruption of the officials. Emperor Lizong praised him a lot after reading his paper and made him first among the Jinshi scholars. Later he was appointed Director of Ninghai Military District.

The year 1259 saw the Mongol army invading southward on a large scale and Ezhou was exposed to imminent danger. When a eunuch, Dong Songchen, proposed moving the capital to Siming, no one dared to make any objection. At this juncture, Wen Tianxiang came out boldly and presented a memorial in which he demanded putting the eunuch to death to strengthen the fighting will of the army and the people against the enemies. But his memorial was shelved and did not reach the emperor. In indignation he resigned and left the capital. Before long, he was called out to take command of the defence of Ruizhou before being transferred to the capital to be a department director, supervisor of military supplies, and temporary director of the imperial academy. However, he was removed from office for satirizing the treacherous Premier Jia Sidao. He then lived a quiet reading life for over a decade by the Wenshan Hill in his hometown Luling.

In 1271, Kublai Khan founded the Yuan Dynasty and launched a massive attack on the Southern Song Empire.

In 1276, the Yuan troops under the command of Boyan stationed themselves at Gaoting Hill only 15 kilometres from the city of Lin'an. In view of the dangerous situation, many officials of the Southern Song headed by the premier, Liu Mengyan, fled the capital one after another. It was only then that the court appointed Wen Tianxiang as Right Premier and sent him to the Yuan army for negotiation. Wen demanded that Boyan withdraw his troops before negotiation, whereas the Yuan general demanded that Wen surrender to him. Wen Tianxiang replied sternly, "Being the Number One scholar and premier of the great Song, I am ready to die for my country. I live when Song exists, and will die if Song is no more. What is there to be feared even if you put swords before me and a boiling cauldron behind?" With the help of a boatman, Wen managed to escape at Jingkou on the way to the north under escort in the spring of that year.

In 1278 Wen won a great victory in Yundu, recovering 10 counties of Ganzhou and four counties of Jizhou from Mongol occupation. That boosted the morale of the troops and the people of the Southern Song, and the volunteer anti-Yuan troops in Hunan and Jiangxi joined Wen's army one after another.

The Yuan Court sent crack troops under the command of Marshal Li Heng to launch fierce attacks against Wen's forces. At Kongkeng, Wen suffered heavy losses under the surprise attack of the Yuan troops, and his wife and children were taken prisoner. He, however, collected the remnant troops after breaking through the enemy and led them to eastern Guangdong. In autumn that year, the Southern Song Court in exile conferred the title of "the Duke of Faith" on Wen and ordered him to defend Chaoyang. Unfortunately he was taken prisoner in the sneak attack of the light cavalry troops under the command of the Yuan general, Zhang Hongfan. In the Yuan camp, Wen Tianxiang resolutely refused to pay obeisance to the Yuan general. In reply to Zhang's request to write a letter to General Zhang Shijie inducing him to capitulate, Wen wrote a poem *Passing the Lingdingyang Sea*

Who can live forever without dying?
I'd rather keep my loyalty ever shining.

In 1282, Kublai Khan decided to put Wen Tianxiang to death as the Yuan Left Premier was assassinated by anti-Yuan patriots and there were rumours that the anti-Yuan volunteer troops in Hebei were trying to rescue Wen. Before execution, the Yuan emperor personally tried to induce Wen to surrender. Wen replied, "I have been the Number One scholar and premier of Song. Now that Song is no more, I would rather die than live." Thus Wen Tianxiang sacrificed his life heroically at the age of only 47.

Wen Tianxiang's writings were collected in the *Complete Works of Mr Wenshan*. His poems *Passing the Lingdingyang Sea*, and *The Song to the Noble Spirit* were full of power and magnitude.

文天祥

Wen Tianxiang

Shi Nai'an & Luo Guanzhong

施耐庵 • 羅貫中

When Zhu Yuanzhang's uprising army fought to Jinling at the end of the Yuan Dynasty, a famous scholar of eastern Zhejiang, Liu Bowen, came to the service of Zhu at his invitation. Overjoyed, Zhu said to him, "I have invited you for the sake of the country, but I am indeed sorry to make you go through all the ordeals with me." To his pleasant surprise, Liu replied that his good friend Shi Nai'an (1296–1370) was much more capable than himself. Zhu then sent Liu on a trip to invite the capable man to his service. Shi Nai'an, however, hid himself at the news as he preferred living a quiet life writing his novel to taking any official post. Indeed, his *Water Margin* turned out to be one of the four great novels of China.

His name was Shi Yanduan and his courtesy name was Zi'an. According to the "Sequel to the Annals of Xinghua County", his original name was Shi Er. His family had moved from Gusu (modern Suzhou) to Xinghua (in present-day Jiangsu Province). Though from a poor family of a boatman, Shi Nai'an was clever and eager to learn in his childhood. He went to study in Hushuguan at 13 and was always one of the best students. He was fairly successful with his degrees, passing the Xiucai degree county examination at 19, the Juren degree provincial examination at 29, and the Jinshi degree national examination at 35. He was, nevertheless, not a pedantic scholar but a superb talent conversant with both the past and the present, being erudite not only in Confucian classics, but also in other schools of learning, prose and poetry, astronomy and geography, medicine, divination, astrology, and martial arts.

He was appointed magistrate of Qiantang County after passing the Jinshi examination, but was on the post for only two years as he disliked the ways of the officials and dignitaries. He went back home and devoted himself to collecting old stories and writings. On the basis of the stories about the uprising of Song Jiang and other Liangshan heroes recorded in such books as *Stories of the Xuanhe Period of the Song Dynasty*, *Records of Events of the Eastern Capital*, *Outlines of the Ten Reigns of the Northern Song Dynasty* etc., he began to write *Stories of the Rebel Heroes* (the original title of *Water Margin*).

In 1356, to get away from interference, Shi Nai'an immediately moved from Gusu to Zhutang Town of Jiangyin where he did teaching while writing the *Water Margin* until 1365. During this period he even refused to see his good friend, Liu Bowen, who came to invite him on behalf of Zhu Yuanzhang. When writing his novel, he would ask his disciples to make improvements after finishing each chapter. Luo Guanzhong (1330–1400) was the one who helped him the most.

In 1366, Shi moved to Xinghua and then to Huai'an. He died in 1370 at the age of 75.

Shi Nai'an's competent assistant, Luo Guanzhong, was named Luo Ben with Guanzhong as his courtesy name, and Huhai Sanren his literary name. His ancestral home was in Taiyuan of Shanxi, and they moved to Qiantang (present-day Hangzhou of Zhejiang Province) in the chaotic days towards the end of the Yuan Dynasty. It was said he had the ambition to found a new dynasty himself in place of the Yuan Dynasty, and had some relations with the uprising leader Zhang Shicheng. He was in close touch with the common people, and collected and collated a lot of stories popular among them. While helping Shi Nai'an to write the *Water Margin*, he learned the way of novel writing.

Luo Guanzhong was an unsociable person, but the folk songs written by him were lucid and refreshing. Following Shi Nai'an's way, Luo Guanzhong completed the 24-volume novel the *Romance of Three Kingdoms* of 700,000 words in 240 sections (becoming 120 chapters towards the end of the Ming Dynasty) through recreation based on the *History of the Three Kingdoms* by Chen Shou of the Jin Dynasty and the notes to the book made by Pei Songzhi of Song of the Southern Dynasties, as well as stories about the three kingdoms told among the people and in a book by a Yuan Dynasty dramatist Zhong Sicheng. The *Romance of Three Kingdoms* became a novel of epic nature which produced an important influence on classic novel creation as well as peasant uprisings and the development of military strategy.

In addition to the *Romance of Three Kingdoms*, there is another novel written by him *The Suppression of Rebelling Devils* that has practically kept its original features.

Luo Guanzhong lived in Fujian in his last years until his death at the age of 70.

The *Water Margin* and the *Romance of Three Kingdoms* have become the gems among the world cultural and artistic works.

施耐庵
羅貫中 一九九二年 八月二十七日畫于羊城 兼省山麓野味齋 愚弟 陳鳳畫一百儒士圖

Shi Nai'an &
Luo Guanzhong

184

Liu Ji

劉基

In 1327 during the Yuan Dynasty, a young man came into a bookstore in Qingtian County. Taking a book from a shelf, he glanced through it from cover to cover before putting it back and leaving the store. The shop assistant came over and saw that it was a very difficult book on astronomy. Early next morning, the same lad came again. Intending to baffle him, the assistant asked him to retell the contents of the book, only to be dumbstruck as the latter recited everything in the book without any mistake. This genius with a photographic memory was Liu Ji (1311–1375).

Styled Bowen, Liu Ji was born in a family of scholars in Wuyang Village of Qingtian County, Chuzhou Prefecture, Zhejiang Province. His father, Liu Yue, was an honest and intelligent county teacher and had taught patriots against the Yuan Dynasty. The uprightness, frankness, and patriotism of his father produced profound influence on his growth.

By the time he was 17, Liu had a good mastery of the Rationalist learning of Confucianism and had read extensively books of various schools of thought. He was especially good at astronomy, geography, military tactics, and mathematics. Three years after he passed the Jinshi national examination at the age of 23, Liu was appointed magistrate of Gao'an County, Jiangxi Province, and did well in his post. A corrupt Mongol noble was removed from office as a result of Liu's thorough investigation of the evil he did. However, because he was upright and outspoken, he could not get along with the corrupt officials; and he resigned from his office.

Still harbouring some illusion about the rulers of the Yuan Dynasty, Liu gave counsel to the court in the suppression of the military rebellion of Fang Guozhen in 1351, and was as a result promoted as an official in the province. However, he suffered a blow later when the court decided to offer amnesty to Fang and put Liu into custody in Shaoxing. When he saw the surging of the Red Turban Uprising across the country, he realized that the Yuan Dynasty was rotten to the core.

By that time, the Red Turban Army led by Zhu Yuanzhang had captured Chuzhou and was enlisting qualified people. Knowing that the uprising army had been getting stronger in the six years of victorious fighting in Anhui and Zhejiang since Zhu rose in revolt in Haozhou in 1352, Liu Ji accepted Zhu's offer after the latter invited him twice with valuable gifts. In 1360 Liu went to Jinling and offered 18 strategies to Zhu Yuanzhang for wiping out the Mongols and unifying the country. Zhu was overjoyed and kept him for devising important military actions. Greatly moved, Liu Ji did everything possible in offering counsel to Zhu.

Despite Liu's suggestion to give up the "Junior King of Ming" Han Lin'er, the nominal head of the Red Turbans, Zhu Yuanzhang led an army to Han's rescue, which only gave a chance for a sneak attack on his base area by Chen Youliang, leader of another peasant uprising army, who almost succeeded in his raid. Then, against all odds, Liu Ji resolutely advocated attacking Chen Youliang who was the strongest among the rebelling forces. Following his advice, Zhu Yuanzhang won a complete victory with Chen shot dead by an arrow when he and his troops tried to break out of an encirclement at Boyang Lake.

In 1368 Zhu sent people to have the "Junior King of Ming" Han Lin'er drowned according to the advice of Liu Ji. That year, Zhu Yuanzhang came to the throne in Yingtian and founded the Ming Dynasty. Liu Ji was made Inspector General and Grand Historian and Grand Councilor of the Crown Prince.

A wise and resourceful man of wide knowledge and experience, Liu well knew that he had offended some important officials as a result of his frank and straightforward advice to the emperor. Therefore, he was bent on retiring at the height of his official career, and presented many memorials to the emperor for that purpose. In 1370, he was granted more important titles such as Grand Scholar of Hongwen Academy, the Earl of Faith etc. The next year he was allowed to retire after presenting another memorial.

In 1374, the premier Hu Weiyong brought a false charge alleging that Liu was engaged in conspiracy to occupy the land that betokened imperial position. The suspicious emperor issued an imperial edict depriving him of his salary. Liu had to go to the capital to plead guilty and ask for punishment. He fell ill and died at the age of 65 after returning to his hometown. Four years later, Hu Weiyong was put to death for abusing power and Liu's unjust case was reversed. Recalling his advice in respect to the three premiers, the emperor Zhu Yuanzhang was full of remorse, and issued an edict for Liu's descendants to inherit the title of the Earl of Faith generation after generation. The writings of Liu Ji were compiled into *Collected Works of the Earl of Faith*.

Liu Ji

王守仁

Wang Shouren

In 1491 during the reign of Emperor Hongzhi of the Ming Dynasty, a 19-year-old man was meditating in front of the bamboo bush of the royal academy. While people thought he was being stupid, he was actually trying hard to find out the "heavenly law" in the bamboo following the Rationalist approach of "attaining knowledge through investigating things". However, he fell ill instead of gaining any knowledge after investigating the bamboo for seven days. This young man was Wang Shouren (1472–1529) who later became a great philosopher and educator of the Ming Dynasty.

With the courtesy name Bo'an and literary name Yangming, Wang Shouren was from Yuyao (in present Zhejiang Province). He followed his father to the capital Beijing in 1481 and went to Hongdu of Jiangxi to get married at the age of 17. At that time he had tried to learn the way of nourishing life from a Taoist priest. On his way back to Yuyao, he called on the famous Rationalist scholar, Lou Liang, and developed a strong interest in the Rationalist theory of "attaining knowledge through investigating things".

After his failure with the bamboo, however, he turned to poetry and prose and eight-legged essays so as to get degrees through examinations. He earned the Jinshi degree at the age of 28, and was made a junior official in the Ministry of Construction. He returned to Shaoxing at the age of 31 because of illness, and had a house built for recuperation by the Yangming Cave in the Weiwuan Mountain, 10 kilometres southeast of the city, hence he was also referred to as Mr Yangming.

He began to teach disciples at the age of 34, and created a new branch of learning called "Mind Learning" following Lu Jiuyuan's theory that "the mind is the law", and "the universe is my mind and my mind is the universe". He was jailed and beaten the next year for opposing the powerful eunuch Liu Jin. In the following three years after he was demoted as Longchang Posthouse official in Guizhou, he often sat meditating before finally realizing the "way of the sage". He then wrote *Suppositions on the Five Classics* and had the Longgang Academy built. He took up the post of chief lecturer of Guiyang Academy in 1509 where he put forward the theory of "the unification of knowledge and practice".

He was promoted as magistrate of Luling County in 1510 and further promoted as assistant inspector general in 1516 when he was sent on an inspection tour in Gannan, Tingzhou, and Zhangzhou. For his meritorious service in suppressing the rebellions of Dayuling and other places, he rose to the position of deputy inspector-general. And in Ganzhou, he established the Lianxi Academy in open opposition to Zhu Xi's "rationalism".

In 1519, Wang Shouren put down the rebellion of Prince Ning with his distinguished military ability. The next year he took Wang Yin as his disciple, teaching him "attaining knowledge though investigating things". In his lecture he put forward the theory of "manifesting innate morality" for distinguishing right and wrong which was influenced by Zen.

He was promoted to be Minister of War of Nanjing in 1521. However, he went on with his lecturing in the academy instead of going to the post. He established the Jishan Academy at Yuecheng in 1524 where he lectured to more than 300 disciples. The following year he reestablished the Yangming Academy, teaching his major disciples Wang Ji and Qian Dehong the essence of "mind learning": "Having no virtue or evil is the state of the mind; virtue and evil are the effect of the will; knowing the virtue and the evil is the innate morality; and practising virtue while removing evil is to investigate things".

In 1527, the court appointed Wang Shouren Left Inspector General in charge of military affairs in Guangdong, Guangxi, Jiangxi, and Huguang against the uprisings of the Yao and the Zhuang nationalities in Guangxi and the armed revolt of the national minority headmen in Hetian Prefecture. Wang succeeded in putting down the uprisings with the dual tactics of mollification and conciliation and ruthless suppression. Being seriously ill, he went back to the north the next year and died in a boat on the way, at the age of 58. He was awarded the posthumous title of Wencheng meaning achievements in learning.

As a subjective idealist philosopher, Wang Shouren developed the theory of "mind learning" by Lu Jiuyuan. He developed Confucianism with both Buddhist and Taoist characteristics and produced a wide influence as far as to Japan. He left behind him 38 volumes of *Complete Works of Wang Wencheng*.

Wang Shouren

188

Wu Cheng'en

The Monkey King in the *Pilgrimage to the West* written by the famous novelist Wu Cheng'en (c. 1504–c. 1582) in the Ming Dynasty has been a much-loved household name. Some say Wu created the image of the Monkey King on the basis of the character "Wuzhiqi" in the story *Litang* written by Li Gongzuo in the Tang Dynasty. Others say the image was based on the "Monkey Monk" in the *Story of the Tang Monk Acquiring the Buddhist Scriptures*. Still others say the writer was under the influence of the supernatural monkey in the Indian epic *The Story of Rama*. Whatever the case, one thing is sure: Wu Cheng'en had to be a well-read learned scholar to be able to write such a great novel which deserves to be called a gem in world literature.

With the courtesy name Ruzhong and literary name Sheyang Shanren, Wu Cheng'en was from Shanyang (present-day Huai'an of Jiangsu Province). His family had a scholarly background but was later reduced to being small businessmen. Selling coloured threads and laces for a living, his father Wu Rui was nevertheless very fond of reading. Under the influence of his father, Wu Cheng'en read extensively from the six classics and books of various schools of learning, to popular books about deities, demons, and ghosts. He was also fond of legends and other strange stories.

Being able to write good articles in his childhood, he was widely known in his hometown as the "child scholar". He won favourable comments for his elegant poems and prose works when studying at the Longxi Academy of Huai'an at the age of 26. The notes and stories he wrote in his spare time were lively and humorous and had a strong appeal. However, he failed repeatedly in examinations. In his poem *Song of Erlang Searching the Mountain* written at 36, he revealed the sufferings of the people caused by Emperor Jiajing in his southern tour and by the corrupt officials and generals, sighing over his inability to remove the evils, and expressing his indignation at the feudal rulers and his depression over the impossibility of bringing his learning into play.

At 39, he began to write the mythological novel *Pilgrimage to the West* based on the story about the eminent monk, Xuan Zhuang, of the Tang Dynasty who went to India for Buddhist scriptures. At that time *The Story of the Pilgrimage by Sanzang Monk for Buddhist Scriptures* written in the Song Dynasty and *The Story of the Westward Pilgrimage* in the Yuan Dynasty were already fairly popular among the people. In the former the main characters were the Monkey and the Sand God in addition to Xuan Zhuang, while in the latter the images of Xuan Zhuang and his three disciples the Monkey, the Pig and the Sand Monk all appeared. These provided good artistic prototypes for Wu's novel *Pilgrimage to the West*.

Not until he was 41 was he made a candidate for the imperial college. Poor as he was, he was reluctant to take up an official post. It was only under the persuasion of a famous local figure Li Chunfang that he went to Beijing to wait for an official appointment. He stayed in the capital for three years before he was granted a junior post of assistant magistrate of Changxing County, Zhejiang Province. However, he left the post in indignation after only a year for being at odds with his superiors. Beginning from 1562, he served in the office of Prince Jing in Hubei until 1566 when he went to Hangzhou and made Xuanmiao Temple his home, living on writing.

Wu returned to his hometown in his late years. *Pilgrimage to the West* was probably completed at this time. With rich imagination and romantic approach, Wu Cheng'en created in his mythological novel the image of the rebellious hero Monkey King Sun Wukong who dared to resist and dared to fight. He feared nothing, be it heaven, earth, gods or devils. Other impressive images were the simple, straightforward and lovable Pig who was a bit selfish but had the courage to correct his own mistakes, and the Tang Monk who was indomitable in his determination for acquiring the Buddhist scriptures in spite of all the setbacks.

Living in poverty on writing, Wu Cheng'en created a rich variety of works in his lifetime. A master of calligraphy and verse and prose, he did most of the writings of the inscriptions on bronze and stone tablets of his time. Wu lived the last 10 years of his life in his hometown. It was a great pity that most of his poems and articles were lost after his death since he was poor and childless.

The block-printed edition of the *Pilgrimage to the West* was published in 1592 by the Shidetang Printing House in Nanjing. The rest of his works were collected and printed by Qiu Du, a grandson of his cousin, into a compilation entitled *Works of Mr Sheyang*.

吳承恩

Wu Cheng'en

Zhang Juzheng

張居正

In 1567 under the reign of Emperor Muzong of the Ming Dynasty, the famous general in resisting Japanese pirates, Qi Jiguang, and three other distinguished generals, Li Chengliang, Wang Chonggu, and Fang Fengshi, were in combat readiness along the northern border under the command of Zhang Juzheng (1515–1582), Minister of Rites and Grand Academician of the Wuying Palace.

His courtesy name was Shuda and his literary name Taiyue, and his remote ancestor was from Dingyuan of Fengyang (in present-day Anhui Province) who followed the first emperor of the Ming Dynasty, Zhu Yuanzhang, in his uprising and later settled down in Jiangling (present-day Shashi of Hubei Province). As a child prodigy, he was widely admired in Jingzhou as a "child scholar". In 1547, Zhang Juzheng passed the national examination for Jinshi degree, and two years later he became a member of the imperial academy.

Zhang served at his official post for eight years in the capital before asking for leave on grounds of ill health, as he knew that it was very difficult to realize his political ambition under the fatuous Emperor Shizong and the conspiring premier Yan Song who was preoccupied with framing loyal and upright officials. He spent three years in his hometown studying hard and making a lot of efforts in understanding the circumstances and feelings of the people.

When he returned to Beijing in 1557, the struggle between his master Xu Jie and Yan Song had intensified. Xu Jie was promoted to be Minister of the Civil Official Administration in 1559 and was further promoted as Grand Master of the Crown Prince the next year.

Regarding Zhang Juzheng as a pillar of the country, Xu Jie promoted Zhang and another capable and upright official, Gao Gong, to important posts, and gradually the power of the state came under the control of the three of them.

With the fall of Yan Song in 1562, Xu Jie took up the post of Premier. Four years later, Emperor Muzong succeeded the throne after the death of Emperor Shizong. Following the instruction of the former emperor, Xu Jie and Zhang Juzheng carried on reforms to get rid of malpractices and reverse unjust verdicts, which won wide support from the officials and the people. In 1567, Zhang Juzheng became a member of the Cabinet after being promoted Vice-Minister of Civil Official Administration and Grand Academician. When Xu Jie was forced to retire the following year as a result of taking some inappropriate measures, Gao Gong presided over the Cabinet and was concurrently in charge of the Ministry of Civil Official Administration. Though he attached importance to promoting qualified people, he too failed to improve the situation. When the 10-year-old Emperor Shenzong came to the throne after the death of Emperor Muzong in 1572, Zhang Juzheng became the head of the Cabinet, assisting the child emperor in governing the country, and remained in power for 10 years.

Zhang Juzheng learned a lesson from the failures of Xu Jie and Gao Gong. Capable as they were, they had only taken some minor measures to maintain the status quo without streamlining the economy and adjusting social relations. As early as in 1568, during the reign of Emperor Muzong, Zhang had already put forward his administrative programme in his "Memorial of Six Policies": making comments sparingly, strengthening law and discipline, stressing the authority of imperial edicts, examining and verifying name and reality, consolidating the foundation of the country, and improving the army and armament.

First he created a new approach for administration under the slogan to follow "the established ways of the ancestors". The six ministries of civil official administration, revenue, rites, war, and construction were required to carry out "examination of the work of local officials within the prescribed time". Those who completed the work ahead of schedule were rewarded, while those who went beyond the time limit were punished. Thus the efficiency in administration was greatly improved, rapidly changing such cases as procrastination or even default in paying tax grains. In addition to the six ministries, there were six sections in the Ming Dynasty in charge of supervision in various fields. Zhang Juzheng put the six sections under his direct control so that the orders of the Cabinet could be passed on directly to different localities through the six ministries, guaranteeing the execution of orders and prohibitions.

Zhang Juzheng was indeed the most distinguished reformer and statesman of the Ming Dynasty. When he died at the age of 58, Emperor Shenzong issued an edict for the court to go into mourning for several days, and granted him the distinguished posthumous title of Wenzhong. Among his major works were 46 volumes of *Complete Works of Lord Zhang Wenzhong* with one volume of *Practice of Lord Zhang Wenzhong* appended to it.

張居正

Zhang Juzheng

Li Zhi

During the reign of Emperor Shenzong of the Ming Dynasty, a department director of the Ministry of Punishment in Nanjing, though nearly 50 years old, got down on his knees to a philosopher, Wang Bi, in public. It turned out that this official, Li Zhi (1527–1602), was going through the ceremony required of a disciple to his new master. With a keen mind, he was constantly developing his philosophical ideas by absorbing new things. Later, he surpassed the contemporary thinkers, and the Ming rulers regarded this old man as a serious threat and would be content with nothing less than his destruction.

With the original name Lin Zaizhi, Li Zhi had three courtesy names of Zhuowu, Hongfu, and Wenling Jushi. He was from Jinjiang of Quanzhou (in present Fujian Province), and both his grandfather and father were followers of Islam in which he also believed in his childhood. In 1552 during the reign of Emperor Shizong, he passed the provincial examination, and was appointed Instructor of Gongcheng four years later and Academician of the Nanjing Imperial College after another four years. At the age of 40, he began to have access to Wang Yangming's school of learning with the introduction of a friend. He highly appreciated Wang's theory that "everyone has innate morality".

Li Zhi took up the post of Department Director in the Ministry of Punishment of Nanjing. He was fond of having academic exchanges among friends, and got to know the scholars of the Taizhou school of learning such as Wang Ji, Luo Rufang, and Geng Dingli. Later, he developed such a strong interest in the learning of Wang Yangming that he took as his master Wang Bi, the son of Wang Yangming's advanced student, Wang Yin. As the founder of the Taizhou school of learning, Wang Yin advocated friendship and love of others as well as of oneself based on the idea that the people were the fundamental element. Among his disciples were woodsmen, farmers, and potters.

Beginning from 1577 during the reign of Emperor Shenzong, Li Zhi served in the post of prefect of Yao'an in Yunnan Province for three years before retiring to the Jizu Mountain in Dali to study Tibetan Buddhist scriptures. He combined his ideology against inequality and feudal ethics with Wang Yangming's doctrine of innate morality, and the Buddhist idea of all living things being equal and capable of becoming Buddha. At 55, he went to Huang'an and lived in seclusion in the home of Geng Dingli. After Geng's death in 1584, disputes broke out between his brother Geng Dingxiang and Li Zhi. The next year, Li had to get his family back to his hometown while he himself went to Macheng of Hubei where he shut himself in the Zhifo Yard reading scriptures. Under the influence of capitalism which was already in the budding in the southeast coastal regions, Li Zhi publicly advocated "private ownership", "seeking profit", and laying emphasis on utility and material gain. During this time, he wrote some important works such as *The Book to be Burned*, *The Book to be Stored*, and *Collection of Early Thoughts*.

At the age of 73, he printed *The Book to be Stored* which was against metaphysics and against taking the remarks of Confucius as the only criterion to judge right and wrong. With extraordinary dialectical approach towards history, the book became the cause of his persecution by the feudal rulers, as it denounced the six classics, criticized the pedantic Rationalists as "vulgar scholars", and openly denied that Confucian classics were "the best theory of all ages", all of which were beyond the tolerance of the feudal ruling class.

When Li Zhi went back to Macheng of Hubei Province in 1600, Geng Dingxiang dismantled his Zhifo Yard in collaboration with the local officials. Li Zhi had to run away to Tongzhou of Hebei where he completed the book *Causes of Changes of the Nine Administrative Divisions*. In 1602, the Imperial Court issued an order to arrest him on the alleged charge of "initiating rebellious ideas among the people". Li Zhi committed suicide in prison at the age of 76.

Among his other works were *A Continuation to the Book to be Burned*, and *Collected Works of Li Wenling*, *Books to be Stored* etc. He also made comments on the Chinese literary classics *Water Margin*, and *Romance of the Western Chamber*, regarding these books as "the best writings of all ages". In philosophy, Li Zhi was of the opinion that "all things under heaven originated from two sources instead of one", adhering to the idea that "nothing exists beyond the mind". Inheriting and revising Wang Yangming's theory of "innate morality", he put forward the theory of "child-like innocence" which, in his opinion, should be preserved.

李贽

李贽
一九九三年
五月八日

Li Zhi

Huang Zongxi

黃宗羲

In the first year of the reign of Emperor Chongzhen of the Ming Dynasty, a 19-year-old lad went all the way alone from Zhejiang to Beijing with a memorial and an iron hammer to bring an accusation to the emperor against the eunuch clique. This young man was Huang Zongxi (1610–1695), son of a famous Donglin scholar and former inspector of Shandong, Huang Zunsu, who had been framed and tortured to death for the struggle he and the other Donglin scholars had waged against the arch eunuch Wei Zhongxian and his lackeys.

In his memorial, Huang Zongxi enumerated the crimes of Wei Zhongxian and his eunuch clique who had brought disaster to the country and the people. When he arrived in Beijing, however, Wei had committed suicide to escape punishment. So he could only beat up a eunuch clique remnant, Xu Xianchun, with his iron hammer in the tribunal, and pull off the beard of another eunuch clique lackey, Cui Yingyuan, at the prison gate, before going back to his hometown to offer sacrifices at his father's grave. Huang Zongxi thus became well-known, and people admired him for what he did against the eunuch clique, calling him respectfully "filial son Huang".

His courtesy name was Taichong, and his literary name Lizhou. He was also referred to by later generations as Mr Nanlei as he had built a study in Nanlei Lane in Yuyao. He was from Huangzhupu of Yuyao (in present Zhejiang Province). After being registered as a student of the county school, he followed his father to the capital where he gained a good understanding of the political situation at the court under the influence of the Donglin scholars who were in close touch with his father. After the death of his father, he followed his instruction and took a contemporary scholar, Liu Zongzhou, as his master under whose guidance he studied diligently all the different schools of learning. By reading one book a day, he covered within two years the history of 21 dynasties as well as the records of the preceding reigns of the Ming Dynasty, and became a well-known learned scholar.

At the age of 21, Huang Zongxi joined the Fushe Society in Nanjing, and played a leading role in the struggle against eunuchs and dignitaries. They put up a "Notice Against Intrigues in Nanjing" revealing the conspiracy of the eunuch Ruan Dacheng and his gang which forced Ruan to restrain himself in his underhand activities. When the Qing army fought their way into China, the eunuch clique headed by Ma Shiying and Ruan Dacheng took the lead in putting Prince Fu on the throne, establishing the Hongguang Court in the South. They put all the 140 people who signed on the "Notice Against Intrigues in Nanjing" on the blacklist, and Huang Zongxi was thus put into prison. He was released from prison when the Hongguang Court collapsed under the attack of the Qing army.

After getting back to Zhejiang he recruited several hundred men to form a "Loyal Battalion" in service of the regime under Prince Lu of the Southern Ming forces. He was appointed Imperial Supervisor in charge of the defence of the Qiantang River together with other anti-Qing forces. After the defence line was broken through, his troops continued resistance in the Siming Mountain until heavy casualties made it impossible to go on fighting. He then went to Zhoushan secretly to join Prince Lu who made him Deputy Inspector-General. With a view to borrowing troops, he crossed the sea to Japan but did not succeed in his efforts. Not long after his return, Prince Lu's regime collapsed, and so did the other regimes of the Ming. Seeing no hope to restore the Ming Dynasty, Huang Zongxi was forced to give up armed struggle.

He then went back to his hometown devoting himself to writing and teaching, declining three times the offer of official posts by the Qing government. Learned and versatile, he made many lectures to eager participants in Ningbo, Shaoxing, Haining, and Chongde, and was admired as one of the three great Confucian scholars of the time (the other two being Sun Qifeng and Li Yong). He had a good command of astronomy, mathematics, music, history, Confucian classics, Buddhism, and Taoism, with his greatest achievement made in the field of history. His two important works *Anthology of Academic Works of the Song and Yuan Dynasties* and *Anthology of Academic Works of the Ming Dynasty* heralded the historical studies in eastern Zhejiang Province.

His democratic political and economic ideas were contained in his book *Notes on Reform of Political System*.

In the field of literature, he emphasized the necessity for prose and verse to reflect reality and express true feelings.

Huang Zongxi died at the age of 86. In addition to the above works, he also had *Writings of Nanlei* which was included in *The Collected Works by Huang Lizhou* compiled by later generations.

Huang Zongxi

Gu Yanwu

顧炎武

*E*ven an ordinary man is responsible for the rise and fall of the country. This famous remark put forward by Gu Yanwu (1613–1682), a distinguished thinker at the end of the Ming Dynasty, has encouraged Chinese patriots for several hundred years. Gu pointed out that there was a difference between "the downfall of the dynasty and the downfall of the country". The former was only the change of the royal family and the title of the dynasty involving only the sovereign and the officials, having little to do with the common people, while the latter was the fall of the nation and its culture involving the destiny of the whole nation. Therefore he held that "a person was responsible for safeguarding the nation no matter how humble he was".

His original name was Gu Jiang with Ningren as his courtesy name, and he sometimes signed his name as Jiang Shanyong. People also referred to him as Mr Tinglin. He was from a retired official's family in Kunshan (in present Jiangsu Province). When he was six years old, Madam Wang, who had adopted him as son, taught him to read the *Great Learning* and told him stories about loyal officials and righteous people. His grandfather instructed him to study practical subjects such as astronomy, geography, art of war, agriculture, water conservancy, and the institutions and systems of various dynasties. At 10, he had read the *Art of War by Sunzi*, the *History Book by Zuo Qiuming*, the *Strategies of the Warring States*, the *Records of the Historian*, and *History as a Mirror*. He entered school at 14, and together with his good friend Gui Zhuang joined the Fushe Society which attempted to make reforms.

After Nanjing was captured by the Qing army in 1645, the 23-year-old Gu Yanwu joined the anti-Qing uprising in Suzhou which was put down not long after. He then went back to his hometown and started another uprising, killing the local Qing magistrate. They put up resistance against the Qing for 21 days before the city was captured and his two brothers killed, his sister-in-law committed suicide, and the right arm of his own mother cut off by the Qing troops. Before long the city of Changshou was also lost and his foster mother committed suicide by way of fasting, leaving behind an instruction that Gu Yanwu "should never take any official post in the invading Qing regime". The downfall of the nation and the tragedy of his family only made Gu more resolute in his struggle against the Qing Dynasty. He went to various places in Jiangsu and Zhejiang provinces to unite the anti-Qing forces in the coastal areas, and wrote a series of patriotic poems.

Intending to seize the 50 hectares of fertile land of the Gu family and to deal a heavy blow to the anti-Qing forces, Ye Fangyuan, a lackey of the Qing Dynasty, instigated someone to inform against Gu Yanwu. Ye kidnapped and tortured him, forcing Gu to leave his hometown for Shandong in 1657. Thus Gu Yanwu stayed in northern China for 10 years going from one place to another for anti-Qing activities. Meanwhile he wrote two important geographical works *The Advantages and Shortcomings of the Provinces*, and *Zhaocheng Records of Geography*.

By 1665, the Qing Dynasty had entered into prosperity under the reign of Emperor Kangxi while most of the anti-Qing forces in various parts of the country had been defeated. Gu Yanwu had to return to Shandong Province and lived in seclusion by the Changbai Mountain in Zhangqiu County, where he continued his most important academic work, *Rizhilu*. In his works, he advocated practical learning against empty talk of "mind, reason, character, and life". In philosophy, he was for the theory of the philosopher Zhang Zai about the unity of the Great Void, the qi, and all the things of creation, holding that the qi was the substance of the universe. He raised the demand that the sovereign should reign with the power divided to him and put forward the famous slogan that "even an ordinary man is responsible for the rise and fall of the country". He had always upheld patriotism. His determination was well expressed in his poem the *Jingwei Bird*:

> *My will it is to fill the East Sea.*
> *It'll ne'er change even I'm drowned.*
> *My heart will never cease*
> *Before the sea is filled to be ground.*

In his late years, Gu Yanwu devoted himself to the study of Confucian classics with emphasis on textual research which had considerable influence on the later Jiangsu school and Anhui school of textual research. In phonology, he wrote the *Five Books on Phonology*, and *Supplement and Correction to Rimes*.

Gu Yanwu died at the age of 70. In addition to the above, another important work of his was *A Collection of Verse and Prose Writings by Tinglin*.

顧炎武
九二年五月
十二日匡子
野味之齋

Gu Yanwu

Wang Fuzhi

王夫之

In the 31st year of the reign of Emperor Kangxi of the Qing Dynasty (1692), an adherent of the former Ming Dynasty was reading aloud in the forest by the Shi Chuanshan Hill. It turned out to be Wang Fuzhi (1619–1692) reading the inscriptions he had written himself on the tablet to be erected at his own grave. His life-long career and pursuits were all embodied in the inscription.

His courtesy name was Ernong and literary name Jiangzhai. Following Prince Yan of the Ming Dynasty in his southern expedition, his early ancestor was awarded a hereditary military post in Hengzhou for his meritorious deeds in battles, and the family thus moved from Gaoyou (in present Jiangsu Province) to Hengyang (in present Hunan Province). Wang Fuzhi was also respectfully referred to as Mr Chuanshan, as he led a hermit's life at the Shi Chuanshan Hill in his late years.

He passed the Juren degree provincial examination at the age of 24 amidst the chaos of wars in the closing years of the Ming Dynasty. After his failure to get to the capital for the national examination the following year, he returned to the south and had a thatched house built at the foot of the Lianhua Peak where he concentrated on learning and research.

After the downfall of the Ming Dynasty, Wang Fuzhi organized an army against the Qing troops at Hengshan Mountain in October 1647. He went to Zhaoqing after his military defeat where he was appointed an official in the southern Ming court of Emperor Yongli through the recommendation by Qu Shilu. Despite the serious threat of strong enemies at the border, the officials of the southern Ming were still engaged in internal strife. Wang Fuzhi presented three memorials to the emperor revealing the crime of a senior official, Wang Huadeng, pleading with Emperor Yongli that he should not disappoint the people by bringing new disgrace to the country. Later, however, Wang Fuzhi had to resign his official post and go back to Hengzhou, since Wang Huadeng and his clique plotted to kill him. After the downfall of the southern Ming, he lived in seclusion in places in Hunan such as Wuxi, Chenzhou, Leiyang, Jinyang, and Lianjun. In 1675, he moved to Shi Chuanshan Hill to write, declining both the invitation by General Wu Sangui and the calls by Qing Dynasty officials. He persisted in writing till his death at the age of 74 though he had been "so poor that he could hardly afford books and paper and ink".

In his 40 years of learning and writing, Wang Fuzhi researched astronomy, calendar, mathematics, and geography, and made distinguished achievements in Confucian classics, history, and literature. He held that "things are opposite to each other and against each other", and "they are repellent to each other and transgress each other". Therefore, "nothing can remain the same without changing." He put forward the idea of approaching history "by seeing the inevitable trend" so as to know the law of historical development. He raised the point that "the way was getting newer", confirming that history was constantly progressing. Thus he promoted materialism and dialectics to a new height. Wang Fuzhi, Huang Zongxi, and Gu Yanwu were referred to as the three masters of the early Qing Dynasty.

Wang Fuzhi was a prolific writer. Among his important works were *Notes on the Book of Changes*, *The Extended Meaning of the Book of History*, *On Reading the Four Books*, *Notes on the Book Zhengmeng by Master Zhang*, *Records of Thinking and Questioning*, *The Yellow Book*, *The Nightmare*, *On Reading History as a Mirror*, *On the Song Dynasty*, etc. *The Collections of Wang Chuanshan* compiled by later generations comprised more than 300 volumes of his works.

王夫之 一九九二年四月二十四日畫于野味齋

Wang Fuzhi

202

Cao Xueqin

The greatest realistic novel in the history of Chinese literature, the *Dream of the Red Chamber*, is such a wonderful book that after Zhi Yanzhai first commented on it early in the 16th year of the reign of Emperor Qianlong (1751), countless scholars have made comments on it and carried out research into the book for more than 200 years, forming a new branch of learning called "Redology" which has gone far beyond the boundary of China and gained considerable development in the United States, Canada, France, Japan, the former Soviet Union, Australia, Singapore, Thailand etc. Scholars of Redology not only study the novel itself but also its author, Cao Xueqin (c. 1715–c. 1764).

His name was Cao Zhan and the name registered in his family tree was Cao Tianyou. Xueqin was his courtesy name and Qinpu was his other courtesy name. His literary name was Qinxi which was changed to Mengruan in his late years. His family was from Liaoyang, belonging to the White Banner of the Han Army. He was born in about 1715 (the 54th year of the reign of Emperor Kangxi), and it was said that General Cao Bin, who made great contribution to the founding of the Northern Song Dynasty, was his ancestor. His great grandmother was the wet nurse of Emperor Kangxi, and his aunt was married to Prince Ping. His great grandfather Cao Xi, grandfather Cao Yin, father Cao Yong and uncle Cao Fu had one after another held the hereditary post of Jiangning Administrator of textiles for 58 years during the reign of Emperor Kangxi. Cao Yin played the host in four of the Emperor's six tours to southern China, with his official mansion serving as the temporary imperial palace.

A gifted child, Cao Xueqin already knew 3,000 characters at the age of three, and at five, he had read all the major Confucian classics. However, he suffered a severe blow at the age of 14 when his uncle was removed from office for his failure to meet the deficit of public money and the Cao family home was searched with their property confiscated. After that, the whole family went to the capital to plead guilty, and thus Cao Xueqin moved from Jinling (present-day Nanjing)

to Beijing where he went to study in an official school. At around 18, he was admitted into the Board of Royal Family Affairs, and three years later he was promoted a department director. Meanwhile the imperial court exempted his uncle from paying the balance of the deficit, and the Cao family showed signs of recovery.

During the sixth year of the reign of Emperor Qianlong (1741), Cao Xueqin, who was about 27 years old at the time, began to write the *Dream of the Red Chamber*. Shortly after he passed the provincial examination in the ninth year of the reign of Emperor Qianlong, the Cao's home was searched for a second time, and the big family that had enjoyed power and wealth for almost a century finally went bankrupt. Cao Xueqin became poor and led a very hard life. Nevertheless, he never slackened his efforts in writing, and finally completed his novel in 1751 after proof-reading 10 times and making additions and deletions five times. He composed a title poem to the novel:

> Absurd ideas throughout the book,
> In hot and bitter tears it is written.
> People all say the author is crazy.
> Who knows what he really means?

The following five titles were recorded in the first chapter: The Story of the Stone, The Love Story of A Romantic Monk, The Dream of the Red Chamber, The Treasured Mirror of Romance, and The Twelve Ladies of Jinling. These were probably titles used for five different proof-readings. With the tragedy of love between the hero Jia Baoyu and the heroine Lin Daiyu as the main threads, the novel described the prosperity and decline of four big families of Jia, Wang, Shi, and Xue.

Research showed that Cao wrote 110 chapters of the *Dream of the Red Chamber*, of which only the first 80 chapters remained, and the last 30 chapters were already lost in the late years of his life. (The last 40 chapters of the present 120-chapter version were written by Gao He.) Cao Xueqin suffered a heavy blow with the death of his 12-year-old son in the smallpox epidemic in Beijing. The great realistic writer of ancient China died in poverty at the premature age of about 48.

曹雪芹

Cao Xueqin

Dai Zhen

During the reign of Emperor Qianlong of the Qing Dynasty, the largest collection of books, the *Complete Library in Four Divisions*, was compiled, classified into four divisions of classical works, historical works, philosophical works, and belles-lettres, comprising 3,457 categories, 36,000 volumes, and 79,070 fascicles. The 160 compilers headed by Ji Xiaolan were all learned scholars with the Jinshi degree after passing the national examination, and quite a number of them were senior officials. The only exception was Dai Zhen (1723–1777) who had been a mere village private teacher. Though he only had the intermediate Juren degree earned after passing the provincial examination, he was known throughout the country as the master of phonology and the authority on Confucian classics. No wonder the emperor and the chief compiler invited him to join the compilation work.

He had three courtesy names, Dongyuan, Shenxiu, and Gaoxi, and his hometown was in Xiuning (a place in present-day Anhui Province). Though from a peddler's family, he was diligent and eager to learn in his childhood and studied the ancient-script classics under the guidance of Jiang Shui, a famous scholar of Confucian classics and phonology.

After passing the provincial Juren degree examination during the reign of Emperor Qianlong, Dai Zhen never passed national examinations again and had to make a living as a teacher in a private school in the countryside. Despite his setbacks, he never gave up his efforts in learning, and made profound studies in Confucian classics, astronomy, calendar, geography, phonology, exegetics etc. and developed some original ideas.

With a good memory and an extensive knowledge, he was well-versed in ancient pronunciation, and established examples of rime shifts between different tones and in the same tone. On the basis of analyzing the rime book Guangyun, he created the theory of classifying ancient Chinese pronunciation into nine categories, 25 sections, and of the mutual shift between the level high tone, the rising tone and the entering tone. In Confucian classics and linguistics, he also made important

discoveries. He made marked achievements in exploring the meaning of ancient books by means of exegetics. As a result, he was respected as the master of textual research of the Anhui School in the Qianlong-Jiaqing period. In the study of Confucian classics, he put emphasis on the meaning of the classics against following the way of the scholars of the Han Dynasty.

In philosophy he also achieved a lot, holding that the world is the process of the change of "qi" which comprised yin and yang and the five elements, being the substance of Tao or reason. He pointed out that Tao or reason above the entity was the qi before the formation of shape, while the qi below the entity was the matter that had taken a particular shape. In this way he refuted the theory of the Rationalists of the Song Dynasty that "reason was above matter". He emphasized the necessity of understanding the law or reason of things by means of observation, and advocated that human nature was originally virtuous. Holding that "the reason of heaven" was in unity with "human desire", he was against the rationalist idea of "rejecting human desire to preserve the reason of heaven".

Thanks to Dai Zhen's distinguished attainments in philosophy, phonology, and Confucian classics, his disciples Duan Yucai and Wang Niansun made considerable achievements under his guidance. It was only natural that in 1773 when Emperor Qianlong organized the compiling committee for the *Complete Library in Four Divisions*, Dai was appointed a compiler, granted the Jinshi degree, and admitted into the Imperial Academy. Though he did not live to see the completion of the Library in 1782, his efforts and contribution were not forgotten.

Dai Zhen died at the age of 55, leaving behind him a large number of works including *The Original Virtue*, *The Original Resemblance*, *The Study of the Meaning of the Mencius*, *On Pronunciation and Riming*, *The Classification of Pronunciation and Riming*, *The Study of Dialects*, etc. Scholars of later generation compiled *Collection of Works by Dai Zhen*.

Dai Zhen

焦循

Jiao Xun

During the reign of Emperor Kangxi, there was a child who had a strong interest in the profound and difficult classic, the *Book of Changes*, and was able to speak eloquently when discussing it with others.

This child was Jiao Xun (1763–1820), styled Litang. He was from a family in Ganquan (present-day Yangchou of Jiangsu Province) that had been engaged in the study of the *Book of Changes* for generations, and his comprehension of the book as a child won admiration from many people. What was more, this child prodigy also had a strong interest in mathematics which seemed so boring to many, and enjoyed sitting for hours making calculations.

After passing the Juren degree provincial examination during the reign of Emperor Jiaqing, Jiao Xun gave up his efforts to become an official and devoted himself to the study of the *Book of Changes* and mathematics. A good friend of his, Yuan Yuan, was also a scholar of Confucian classics. Though one year younger than Jiao, Yuan was quite successful in examinations and official career. Yuan passed the Jinshi degree national examination early during the reign of Emperor Qianlong and became a member of the imperial academy. After being appointed Education Commissioner of Shandong, he invited Jiao Xun to join his staff and the two of them often discussed Confusion classics. In 1798, Yuan was promoted to Governor of Zhejiang Province and Jiao again served as a member of his staff. The splendid achievements of the governor in building sea-walls and fighting the pirates revived Jiao's intention to become an official. After failing in the national examination organized by the Ministry of Rites,

however, he went back to his hometown on the excuse of disease in his feet and had a Diaogu House built in which he devoted all his time studying the classics and mathematics.

After concentrated efforts for more than 10 years, he made spectacular achievements in his studies, succeeding in blazing a new trail in the study of the *Book of Changes* on the basis of the principles of mathematics, and phonology and exegetics. He was so delighted with his success that he went on explaining the other Confucian classics in the same way. On the basis of the *Book of Changes* and mathematics, he developed his own philosophical system, holding that the changes of all things were based on "one reason" and "governed by numbers", and "reason" and "number" had long been in existence and were the root of the universe. Jiao Xun's creative efforts in studying the *Book of Changes* and philosophy by means of mathematics won admiration from later generations. Also interested in local operas, he studied, accumulated, and recorded some opera scripts which would have been lost if not for him.

Jiao Xun died at the age of 58. Among his many works on Confucian classics were *On the Study of the Book of Changes*, *The Correct Comprehension of the Mencius*, *Notes on the Analects of Confucius*. Based on more than 100 types of records, he wrote *On Operas*, leaving behind a lot of material for study by later generations. Among his mathematical works were *On the Arc*, *On the Circle*, and *On addition, Subtraction, Multiplication, and Division*. *On Flower Cultivation* and *A Collection of Poems and Essays Written in the Diaogu House* were his other important works.

Jiao Xun

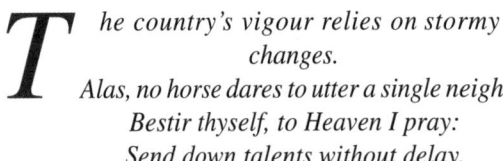

Gong Zizhen

The country's vigour relies on stormy changes.
Alas, no horse dares to utter a single neigh.
Bestir thyself, to Heaven I pray:
Send down talents without delay.

This is a very popular poem by the Qing Dynasty poet Gong Zizhen (1792–1841). It means that China has to undergo great social changes to regain vitality, yet the miserable reality is a state of dead silence. So the poet prays to Heaven for talents of all kinds to revitalize the country. Criticizing the state of society and expressing the poet's pursuit of ideal, his poems are easy, lucid, and elegant in style. Popular lines are fairly common in his poems, of which here is another good example expressing his determination to sacrifice himself for his ideal:

The falling flowers are heartless by no means;
Turning into Spring soil they'll nourish the plant.

Also named Gongzuo, he had Ceren for courtesy name and Dingan for literary name. He was from Renhe (present day Hangzhou), and his father had been in charge of Susong Military Affairs, and acting intendant of Jiangsu Province. His maternal grandfather Duan Yucai was a famous Confucian scholar of the Qianjia school of learning. Gong studied under his guidance and learned the essence of Confucian classics, epigraphy, and exegetics.

In the 23rd year of the reign of Emperor Jiaqing (1818), Gong Zizhen passed the Juren degree provincial examination and moved to Beijing the next year. He served as a secretary of the Cabinet from 1820 and remained at the post without any promotion for 15 years. During this period, he studied *Spring and Autumn by Gongyang*, and together with another Confucian scholar Wei Yuan, advocated *Modern-Script Confucian Classics*, and emphasized the importance of applying the classics in practice through thorough understanding. He also studied Buddhism, contemporary laws and institutions, as well as geography, languages, customs, and history of the national minorities in the border regions. Being a great scholar, he also wrote *On the Establishment of a Province in the Western Regions*.

He passed the Jinshi degree national examination in 1829, but failed many times in the imperial examination since his handwriting was not in conformity with the requirement. As a result, he was never admitted into the imperial academy, and thus lost the chance to be promoted to high posts. Not until 1835 was he transferred to the post of an official in charge of matters related to the royal family members. In 1837, he was transferred to the Ministry of Rites.

Being an official in the capital for many years, Gong knew very well the corruption of the Qing Dynasty. Out of discontent, he pointed out that the society then was declining with a severe shortage of qualified people, a wide gap between the rich and the poor, and acute problems. Predicting that "trouble would soon occur", he proposed strengthening coastal defence, combat readiness, and consolidating the northwest border by way of transmigration to the area. He emphasized the necessity of carrying out reforms, made the suggestion to divide land by family units, and appealed for "getting qualified people of all kinds without any prejudice".

In philosophy, he was against "interaction between Heaven and Man" and "catastrophism of the five elements", emphasizing the replacement of "Tao" (natural law) and "Taiji" (the grand origin of the universe) with "ego", holding that man's subjective spirit was the dominator of everything in the universe. He saw that all things existed in contradiction to each other and were in the process of flux. He held that "human nature was neither virtuous nor evil" against the theory of "virtuous human nature" by Mencius and that of "evil human nature" by Xunzi.

In the winter of 1838, Emperor Daoguang appointed Lin Zexu Imperial Commissioner to Guangdong to ban opium. Gong Zizhen was overjoyed at the news for he had long been worrying about the harm of opium to China. He wrote an article specially for the occasion of Lin's departure, bidding him to put opium under a strict ban and be prepared at all times with strong troops and efficient firearms against possible armed intervention of foreign aggressors. Gong Zizhen resigned his official post in 1838, and on the way back to his home in the south he wrote a poem expressing his admiration and support for the meritorious deeds of his old friend Lin Zexu in eliminating opium.

In 1841, Gong Zizhen was invited to be a tutor of Yunyang Institute in Danyang, Jiangsu Province. However, he died of a sudden disease at the age of 50 shortly after arrival. His works were collected in *Complete Works by Gong Zizhen*.

龔自珍
一九九二年七月二日畫

Gong Zizhen

Wei Yuan

魏源

In 1854, Wei Yuan's book, *Countries of the World*, found its way to Japan which was then under the rule of the Tokugawa Shogunate. The fleets of the United States, Britain, and Russia had invaded Japan one after another and forced it to open its ports to trade. Worried about the fate of their country, the Japanese patriots highly appreciated Wei's idea of "resisting the foreigners with the strong points learned from them". *Countries of the World* played an enlightening role among the Japanese people and laid the ideological basis for the Meiji Restoration.

Wei Yuan (1794–1857) was styled Moshen and was from Shaoyang County, Hunan Province. He was made a county student at 15, and followed his father to Beijing at 22, where he studied *Spring and Autumn by Gongyang* under the direction of Liu Fenglu, a distinguished scholar of Modern-Script Confucian classics. At the time, Gong Zizhen was also in the capital, and the two of them became good friends from the first time they met, and were often found together studying Confucian classics, composing poems and writing essays.

In the second year of the reign of Emperor Daoguang (1822), Wei Yuan passed the Juren degree provincial examination. At the invitation of He Changling, chief administrator of Jiangsu Province, Wei served in his staff, participating in the compilation of *A Collection of Important Works of the Qing Dynasty*. This enabled him to have a comprehensive knowledge of the history of the dynasty and from then on, he began to study the causes of the weakness of the country. At 33, he went to Hangzhou to study Buddhism, trying to incorporate Buddhism into Confucianism. The next year, he served as secretary of the Cabinet, which gave him access to its rich collection of books. In 1834, Wei helped Tao Shu, Governor-General of Jiangsu, Jiangxi, and Anhui, with the reform of salt administration of Huaibei. His distinguished ability made the reform a success, and he was therefore admired as "a specialist of salt administration".

In the second year after the outbreak of the Opium War in 1840, Wei Yuan went to the east of Zhejiang Province and served as a staff member of the patriotic Governor-General Yu Qian. At his post Yu Qian made active efforts to prepare against the war of foreign aggression, and Wei followed him and took part in the battle against the British invaders at Zhenhai in 1841. However, the cowardly general in command, Yu Buyun, deserted Baoshan without making any resistance. Thus after Jinjiling, another strategic point of Zhenjiang, was captured by the British, the Governor-General committed suicide and the resistance against the British in the province ended in failure.

After the battle, Wei Yuan racked his brains over the cause of the bitter defeat. In 1842, he wrote the book *Meritorious Deeds* on the history of the founding of the Qing Dynasty and the unification and expansion of the country as well as the foreign affairs of the dynasty. Wei Yuan laid emphasis on the last part of the book, hoping that the Qing government would learn a lesson from the defeat and make earnest efforts in cultivating qualified people, and consolidating domestic administration so as to save the country from declining.

Wei Yuan held Lin Zexu in high esteem. Based on Lin's successful experience against British aggression in Guangdong, and Lin's book *The Four Continents* as well as his own reflection on China's defeat in the Opium War, Wei wrote the book *Countries of the World* in 1844 which covered the geography, religion, and history of many countries, and dwelt on the domestic and foreign affairs of China. He raised the point of eliminating undesirable ways and practices, putting emphasis on practicality, and basing national defence on preparedness. Strategies and tactics were also raised in the book. He held that the Western countries had three strong points: warships, firearms, and the ways of raising and training the troops, and that China should invite Western engineers and other specialists, and try to "subdue the foreigners with the strong points learnt from them". Suggestions were made for China to start ship-building and firearm factories so that the country could turn the strong points of Western nations to the country's advantage. These ideas of Wei Yuan were quite progressive at that time.

Wei Yuan died at the age of 65 while visiting the beautiful West Lake. Among his other important works were *A New History of the Yuan Dynasty*, *The Old Meaning of the Book of History*, *The Old Meaning of the Book of Songs*, *The Old Meaning of Spring and Autumn by Gongyang*, and *The Original Meaning of Laozi*.

Wei Yuan

Zeng Guofan

曾國藩

Zeng Guofan's father was a village teacher who did not pass the Xiucai degree county examination until 43 years old. He composed a couplet as family motto to the effect that children of the family should be resigned to farming and reading and had Zeng Guofan (1811–1872) copy it on the wall. But Zeng Guofan betrayed the teaching of his father. He not only took official posts, but organized a strong "Hunan Army" to suppress the uprising of the Taiping Heavenly Kingdom, and became a famous official in the "Resurgence of the Qing Dynasty" in the latter part of the 19th century. He was also an advocate of the Rationalist school of thought, holding that the purpose of learning was to restore the sense of morality. He initiated the Westernization Movement with a view to making the country strong against foreign aggression.

Styled Bohan with Disheng as his literary name, Zeng Guofan was from Xiangxiang County, Hunan Province. He entered his family school at six, and began to read the five Confucian classics at eight under the guidance of his father. At 14, his name was top on the list among the children who passed the examination in Changsha. After that he went on reading such books as *The Rites of Zhou*, *The Rites of Ceremony*, and *Records of the Historian*. He passed the Xiucai degree county examination at 22, the Juren degree provincial examination at 24, and the Jinshi degree national examination at 28. Two years later he was admitted into the Imperial Academy, and at 37 he was promoted to the position of Cabinet Scholar and concurrently Vice-Minister of Rites. During the reign of Emperor Daoguang, he had a successful official career at the posts of Vice-Minister of Military Affairs, Vice-Minister of Construction, and Vice-Minister of Civial Official Administration. He was determined to "cultivate personal morality, regulate the family and run the country".

In 1853, the Taiping Heavenly Kingdom made Nanjing their capital. Seeing the weakness and corruption of the Eight Banners of Manchu troops, Emperor Xianfeng ordered that the officials and gentry along the Yangtze River organize local troops. With local peasants as soldiers, his friends and local scholars as officers, and loyalty to the emperor and adherence to the traditional moral principle as the theory for education, Zeng Guofan organized and trained a Hunan Army with strict discipline that obeyed only his orders.

However, his troops were routed by the Taiping Army at Yuezhou in the first major battle in 1856. Ashamed and indignant, Zeng tried to drown himself but was rescued. He rallied his forces for further battles only to find his water-borne troops annihilated by General Shi Dakai of the Taiping Army. Again he tried to commit suicide in a lake but was saved. Taking advantage of the internal strife among the Taiping leaders in 1856, Zeng's Hunan army captured Wuhan before fighting down the Yangtze River and seizing the Taiping capital of Nanjing in 1864. In the course of military actions against the Taiping rebellion, Zeng was promoted again and again until he was made governor in command of the military affairs of the four provinces in the lower reaches of the Yangtze River and Grand Scholar (equal to the position of premier). Thus Zeng Guofan became the leader of the most powerful group of the Qing Court.

In 1870, Zeng Guofan was sent to Tianjin to settle a missionary case. He went so far as to apologize and pay reparations to the French, and kill the Chinese citizens involved in the case. From then on, the Qing Court followed his policy "to suppress domestic riots before making resistance against foreign aggression". Zeng Guofan put forward the policy of ruling the country with benevolence in peace and prosperity, and with force and severe punishment in times of disorder.

In learning, Zeng Guofan held in esteem the Cheng-Zhu Rationalist school of Confucianism. He held that "heaven and earth have rationale and qi". Rationale was a moral concept whereas qi was a material concept, and it was necessary to restore the rationale of the Three Cardinal Guides (monarch guides subject, father guides son, and husband guides wife) and the Five Constant Virtues (benevolence, righteousness, propriety, wisdom, and loyalty). Politically and economically, he emphasized utility, making efforts to equip the troops with modern Western weapons. He was in favour of buying foreign equipment for production in China, and started the Anqing Weapon Factory. He was actually father of the thought of the late Qing Dynasty to take "Chinese learning as the fundamental structure and Western learning for practical use". Among the *Complete Works of Zeng Guofan*, many were diaries examining himself and letters inculcating his family juniors. Zeng Guofan died at the age of 62.

曾國藩
一九九二年六月十四日

Zeng Guofan

Kang Youwei

康有為

During the reign of Emperor Guangxu of the Qing Dynasty, there was a hardworking young man in Nanhai County, Guangdong Province. A disciple of a distinguished Confucian scholar of the county, Zhu Ciqi, he at first believed that Rationalism was capable of making the country strong. However, after studying the history of past dynasties, he found that he was wrong and began to read the works of modern learning. This young man was Kang Youwei (1858–1927).

His original name was Kang Zuyi with Guangxia as his courtesy name and Changsu as his literary name. He was born into a family of generations of officials and began to read the classics at six. At 11 he studied under the direct guidance of his grandfather, Kang Zanxiu, who was a Rationalist scholar, and at 19 he became a disciple of Zhu Ciqi. After his failure in an examination in Beijing at the age of 25, he went back to Guangdong by way of Shanghai and bought some Chinese-translated Western books. A profound study of western learning enabled him to develop ideas for reform, and he began to write *Truth of the Human World* in 1884.

When he was again in Beijing for examination in 1888, China was becoming weaker with the threat from foreign powers becoming even more serious after the Sino-French War. He wrote a memorial to Emperor Guangxu for reform, but the conservatives prevented his memorial from reaching the emperor. After returning home, Kang started a private school in Guangzhou in 1890 and had as his disciples such celebrated young men as Liang Qichao.

After passing the provincial examination in 1893, Kang Youwei again went to Beijing in May 1895 for the national examination. He learned that the Qing Court was about to sign the humiliating Shimonoseki Treaty with Japan. He worked overnight to draft a memorial of 14,000 characters, in which he proposed three strategies for rejecting the treaty, moving the capital, and practising reform. Together with Liang Qichao and 1,300 scholars from 18 provinces, he tried to present the memorial to the emperor, but was rebuffed by the Court. This was the famous "Gongche Memorial" which marked the beginning of the reform movement. The next day the results of the examination was announced. Kang was the eighth on the list and was appointed a department head of the Ministry of Construction. He was, however, reluctant to take up the post and went on making proposals to the emperor for making the country rich and strong, improving the life of the people, carrying on education, training the troops, and establishing a parliament.

It was only after Kang presented seven memorials from 1888 to 1898 that Emperor Guangxu issued an imperial edict in June 1898 for carrying out the new policy and reform. Kang was granted an audience by the emperor and was awarded the title of Sixth-Grade Official in the Ministry of Foreign Related Affairs with the special power to present memorials directly to the emperor. Later, Liang Qichao and Tan Sitong were also admitted into the core of reformists, and a series of imperial edicts were issued for new policies. However, it was barely 100 days after the beginning of the reform before Empress Dowager Cixi imprisoned the emperor and put to death six leading reformists, among whom was Tan Sitong. Notified by the secret edict of the emperor, Kang Youwei and Liang Qichao fled the capital to Japan via Hongkong.

When he toured America and Southeast Asia in 1899, Kang Youwei organized a Royalist Society in Canada. In 1900, he instructed Tang Caichang to organize an army, intending to take advantage of the Boxers' Uprising to free Emperor Guangxu. The scheme failed, and Tang was put to death. In 1901 and 1902, Kang Youwei was in India revising his *Peace and Harmony of the World* into a book of 170,000 words divided into 10 parts. This was Kang's most important political work, in which he propagated peace and harmony of society, the theory of human nature, and Gongyang's theory of three stages of social development.

After the 1911 Revolution, Kang still insisted on the system of monarchy in the name of "an official of the former dynasty". He went to Shanghai in 1913 and started a magazine for restoration of the monarchy. When Zhang Xun put the last emperor of the Qing Dynasty Pu Yi back to the throne through a coup, Kang drafted the restoration edict for the emperor and was made an important official. The restoration was defeated in 12 days and Kang had to flee to the US Embassy where he stayed for almost half a year. On the birthday of the last emperor in January 1927, Kang made a special trip to Tianjin to pay tribute to the dethroned sovereign despite his own illness. He died shortly after that at the age of 70.

His other important works were *Notes to Liyun, Notes to the Doctrine of the Mean* and *A Collection of Poems by Mr Kang Nanhai*.

康有为
一九○三年七月十五日

Kang Youwei

Liang Qichao

There were two imperial restorations in modern Chinese history, one by Yuan Shikai, and the other of the dethroned last emperor of the Qing Dynasty, Pu Yi, supported by Zhang Xun. The person who played a key role in defeating the two restorations was, paradoxically, Liang Qichao (1873–1929), a former royalist like Kang Youwei. In the struggle against the first restoration, Liang instructed his student, General Cai E, to slip back to Yunnan Province to organize an anti-Yuan army. In the struggle against the second restoration, he helped General Duan Qirui in drawing up military strategies for the expedition against Zhang Xun and defeating the restoration farce in 12 days.

Liang Qichao, with Zhuoru as his courtesy name and Rengong and Cangjiang as his literary names, was from Xinhui of Guangdong Province. As a child prodigy, he passed the Xiucai degree county examination at 11, and the Juren degree provincial examination at 16. He went to the capital for the Jinshi degree national examination at 18, but he failed. From the book *Information About the Globe* he learned that there were five continents besides China, and there was western learning too. After returning home, he became a student of Kang Youwei and accepted his theory of reform.

In 1895, he went to the capital again with Kang for the national examination, where they initiated among the scholars of Guangdong and Hunan Provinces a memorial to the imperial court against signing the humiliating Shimonoseki Treaty with Japan. After his failure to pass the examination for advocating reform in his paper, he stayed in Beijing to help Kang in publishing the "Domestic and Foreign Information" and organizing the Society for National Strengthening in which he served as secretary.

During the "100-Day Reform", he was awarded the title of Sixth-Grade Official in charge of universities and publishing houses. He presented quite a few memorials to the emperor for the abolition of the old examination system and encouragement of technology. After the coup d'etat against the reformists he fled to Japan.

After the 1911 Revolution, Liang published *The Construction of New China* in which he proposed "Republicanism with a nominal monarch". He became the leader of the Republican Party in 1913 which was merged with the Democratic Party and Unification Party in the same year into the Progressive Party in opposition to the revolutionary Guomindang. As a council member of the new party, he served as Minister of Justice in Yuan Shikai's government. However, when Yuan showed intention to restore monarchy, he resigned the post and started the magazine *Great China*. After his failure in dissuading Yuan from proclaiming himself emperor, he published an article raising the banner against monarchy restoration, and instructed General Cai E to slip back to Yunnan for the organization of an army against Yuan. He himself went to the south the next year and organized a military council in which he served as Chairman and Commander. After Yuan's death, he disbanded the council and published an open telegram for Duan Qirui to organize a new Cabinet.

During the restoration of the Royalist General Zhang Xun, Liang took up the post of Adviser in the headquarters of the Expedition Army and drafted the proclamation against the Royalist General. After the defeat of Zhang, he was appointed Minister of Finance until the collapse of Duan's government. In December 1918, he went on a visit to Europe.

In the spring of 1920, Liang retired from politics and became tutor of the Research Institute of Qinghua University and concurrently professor of a few other universities such as Nankai. Academically, he was a distinguished scholar of his time. He made an extensive introduction of western learning, ideology, and culture for the enlightenment of the people, and made comprehensive, systematic, and profound studies of ancient Chinese culture. Among his valuable works were *The Learning of Mohism*, *The Philosophy of Laozi*, *The History of Buddhism in China*, *Chinese Academic History of the Recent 300 Years*, *History of Chinese Culture*, *Introduction to the Learning of the Qing Dynasty* etc. In the field of philosophy, he and Zhang Junmai were both representatives of the "Mystical School" of the 1920s. Also an advocate of "revolution of poetry", and "revolution of novels", he was a forerunner of vernacular Chinese. He also put forward "revolution in the field of history" and repudiated the theory that centres on the monarch. But at the same time he propagated the theory that heroes create the world and was of the opinion that reform should be carried out step by step.

Liang Qichao died of illness in Beijing at the age of 57. His works were collected and compiled into 148 volumes.

梁啟超
一九九二年
六月二日

Liang Qichao

INDEX

INDEX

INDEX

INDEX

A BRIEF CHRONOLOGY OF CHINESE HISTORY

五帝 The Five Emperors: Yellow Emperor, Zhuanxu, Diku, Yao and Shun			About 2500-2100 BC
夏 Xia Dynasty			About 2100-1600 BC
商 Shang Dynasty			About 1600-1100 BC
周 Zhou Dynasty	西周 Western Zhou Dynasty		About 1100-771 BC
	東周 Eastern Zhou Dynasty		770-256 BC
	春秋 Spring and Autumn Period		770-476 BC
	戰國 Warring States		475-221 BC
秦 Qin Dynasty			221-207 BC
漢 Han Dynasty	西漢 Western Han		206 BC-AD 24
	東漢 Eastern Han		25-220
三國 Three Kingdoms	魏 Wei		220-265
	蜀漢 Shu Han		221-263
	吳 Wu		222-280
西晉 Western Jin Dynasty			265-316
東晉 Eastern Jin Dynasty			317-420
南北朝 Northern and Southern Dynasties	南朝 Southern Dynasties	宋 Song	420-479
		齊 Qi	479-502
		梁 Liang	502-557
		陳 Chen	557-589
	北朝 Northern Dynasties	北魏 Northern Wei	386-534
		東魏 Eastern Wei	534-550
		北齊 Northern Qi	550-577
		西魏 Western Wei	535-556
		北周 Northern Zhou	557-581
隋 Sui Dynasty			581-618
唐 Tang Dynasty			618-907
五代 Five Dynasties	後梁 Later Liang		907-923
	後唐 Later Tang		923-936
	後晉 Later Jin		936-946
	後漢 Later Han		947-950
	後周 Later Zhou		951-960
宋 Song Dynasty	北宋 Northern Song Dynasty		960-1127
	南宋 Southern Song Dynasty		1127-1279
元 Yuan Dynasty			1271-1368
明 Ming Dynasty			1368-1644
清 Qing Dynasty			1644-1911
中華民國 Republic of China			1912-1949
中華人民共和國 People's Republic of China			1949-

ASIAPAC COLLECTORS' SERIES

Antique Ceramics

Durable and beautiful, antique ceramics have a timeless appeal. As good pieces become harder to find, being able to differentiate the genuine from the fakes becomes crucial to the collectors. Written by well-known art critic Lee Ying Ho, the book gives an understanding of the origins and types of porcelain. Readers will also be advised on how to identify porcelain by motifs, marks and other characteristics to enjoy its beauty as well as make a wise investment.

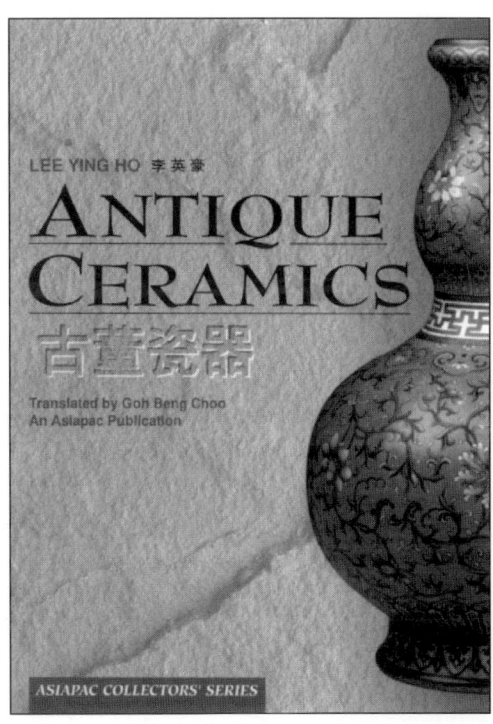

Jadeite

The overwhelming fascination with the gemstone has led to the creation of many beautiful pieces of jadeite jewellery which, with the passage of time, have enjoyed an increase in value and been eagerly traded at auctions.

In this volume, Lee Ying Ho shares with readers the origin, appreciation and worth of jadeite, together with the maintenance of jadeite jewellery, the identification of fakes rampant on the market, and the methods of their production.

100 SERIES ART ALBUM

100 Celebrated Chinese Women

Lu Yanguang captures the spirit of some of China's most influential and famous women, including Queen Mother of the West, Chang'e, Wang Zhaojun Yang Guifei and Hua Mulan. Spanning over 2,000 years of China's history, the characters in this collection reflect the many and varied roles which women have played throughout the ages.

100 Chinese Gods

Lu Yanguang renders his interpretation of Chinese deities with much reverence and ingenuity. A comprehensive range of deities is represented here: from the superior Jade Emperor to the fearsome King Yama of Hell; from the compassionate Midwife Goddess to the ordinary men who through practising Taoism attained immortality and joined the ranks of Heaven.

100 SERIES ART ALBUM

100 Chinese Emperors

Lu Yanguang portrays some of China's most virtuous and notorious emperors, covering a historical span of 5,000 years from Yan Di and Huang Di to the last emperor Puyi. Uniquely synthesized with the historical background as described by the biography, every figure is brought about with life and vitality, revealing the artist's talents.

100 Buddhas in Chinese Buddhism

Lu Yanguang traces the beginnings of Buddhism and how it spread from Central Asia and India to China 2,000 years ago. This collection not only includes those who were revered for their contribution to China's civilization — Sakyamuni, the historical Buddha; Kumarajiva, a pioneer translator of Buddhist scriptures — but also those who spread Buddhism to China, Korea and Japan.

《「一百」藝美系列》

百儒圖

編文：吳伯衡

繪畫：盧延光

翻譯：王學文，隋雲

亞太圖書有限公司出版